Criminal Justice: Local and Global

This book is one of two published by Willan Publishing in association with The Open University:

Criminal Justice: Local and Global (edited by Deborah Drake, John Muncie and Louise Westmarland)

Crime: Local and Global (edited by John Muncie, Deborah Talbot and Reece Walters)

These publications form part of the Open University course *Crime and justice* (DD301).

Details of this and other Open University courses can be obtained from the Student Registration and Enquiry Service, The Open University, PO Box 197, Milton Keynes MK7 6BJ, United Kingdom (tel. +44 (0) 845 300 60 90; email general-enquiries@open.ac.uk).

Alternatively, you can visit the Open University website at www.open.ac.uk where you can learn more about the wide range of courses and packs offered at all levels by The Open University.

To purchase a selection of Open University materials visit www.ouw.co.uk or contact Open University Worldwide, Michael Young Building, Walton Hall, Milton Keynes, MK7 6AA, United Kingdom for a brochure (tel. +44 (0) 1908 858793; fax +44 (0) 1908 858787; email ouw-customer-service@open.ac.uk).

Criminal Justice: Local and Global

Edited by Deborah Drake, John Muncie and Louise Westmarland

The Open University

WILLAN
PUBLISHING

Published by

Willan Publishing
Culmcott House
Mill Street, Uffculme
Cullompton, Devon
EX15 3AT, UK
Tel: +44 (0) 1884 840337
Fax: +44 (0) 1884 840251
email: info@willanpublishing.co.uk
website: www.willanpublishing.co.uk

Published simultaneously in the USA and
Canada by

Willan Publishing
c/o ISBS, 920 NE 58th Ave, Suite 300
Portland, Oregon 97213-3786, USA
Tel: +001 (0) 503 287 3093
Fax: +001 (0) 503 280 8832
email: info@isbs.com
website: www.isbs.com

in association with

The Open University
Walton Hall, Milton Keynes
MK7 6AA, United Kingdom

First published 2010

Edited and designed by The Open University.

Typeset in India by Alden Prepress Services, Chennai.

Printed in the United Kingdom by TJ International Ltd, Padstow.

Library of Congress Cataloguing in Publication data: applied for
British Library Cataloguing in Publication data: applied for

978-1-84392-514-9 (paperback)

978-1-84392-513-2 (hardback)

1.1

The paper used in this publication contains pulp sourced from forests independently certified to the Forest Stewardship Council (FSC) principles and criteria. Chain of custody certification allows the pulp from these forests to be tracked to the end use (see www.fsc-uk.org).

Mixed Sources
Product group from well-managed
forests and other controlled sources
www.fsc.org Cert no. SGS-COC-2482
© 1996 Forest Stewardship Council

Contents

Notes on Contributors

Roy Coleman is a Lecturer in Criminology at the University of Liverpool. He has recently co-authored *Surveillance and Crime* (Sage, 2009) and *State, Power, Crime* (Sage, 2009). His book *Reclaiming the Streets: Surveillance, Social Control and the City* (Willan, 2004) won the Hart Social and Legal Book Prize.

Deborah Drake is a Lecturer in Criminology at The Open University. She has conducted extensive prison research in the areas of resettlement, maximum-security and long-term imprisonment, and in secure settings for children. Her work has primarily focused on the experiences of prisoners, but has also included consideration of staff experiences and working practices.

Ross Fergusson is a Senior Lecturer in Social Policy at The Open University. He is co-editor of *Restorative Justice: Critical Issues* (Sage, 2003) and *Ordering Lives: Family, Work and Welfare* (Routledge, 2000). He publishes and researches in the areas of young people, social exclusion and youth criminal justice.

James Mehigan is a criminal defence barrister and has a PhD in criminology from The Open University. He has worked as a researcher for three human rights organisations. Front Line – The International Foundation for the Protection of Human Rights Defenders; the International Council on Human Rights Policy; and the Ethical Investment Research Service. He is a former member of the Independent Monitoring Board at Pentonville Prison.

John Muncie is a Professor of Criminology and Co-director of the International Centre for Comparative Criminological Research at The Open University. A third edition of his *Youth and Crime* (Sage, 2009) was published recently, and he has co-authored *The Sage Dictionary of Criminology* (Sage, 2006), *Youth Crime and Justice* (Sage, 2006), *Comparative Youth Justice* (Sage, 2006) and *The Student Handbook of Criminal Justice and Criminology* (Cavendish, 2004).

Reece Walters is a Professor of Criminology at The Open University. He has published widely in the areas of environmental crime, crimes of the powerful and the sociology of criminological knowledge. His books include *Eco-Crime and Genetically Modified Food* (Routledge, 2009) and *Deviant Knowledge, Criminology, Politics and Policy* (Willan, 2003). He is an editorial-board member of three international journals including *The British Journal of Criminology*.

Louise Westmarland is a Senior Lecturer in Criminology and Social Policy at The Open University. She has written widely on police and policing, specifically on various aspects of police culture – such as in her book *Gender and Policing: Sex, Power and Police Culture* (Willan, 2001) – and on violence and police culture, ethics and integrity. Most recently, she co-authored *Creating Citizen-Consumers: Changing Publics and Changing Public Services* (Sage, 2007).

Preface

Criminal Justice: Local and Global is the companion textbook to the similarly titled *Crime: Local and Global*. Both are published by Willan Publishing in association with The Open University.

Across the world, crime, disorder and justice are increasingly pressing concerns. Fear of crime and proliferating global threats have contributed to a pervasive sense of insecurity. These books broaden the criminological imagination by *first* exploring the degree to which globalisation has created conditions for 'new' crimes to occur and how far different societies are collaborating to form a common criminal-justice response. *Second*, local concerns – for example, about street crime and violence – are now accompanied by twenty-first century global concerns about 'disorderly' cities, human trafficking, climate change, cyber-crime, terrorism, pollution, and human rights violations. *Third*, these 'threats' to safety and security have clear implications for justice, as the boundaries between crime control and civil liberties are being redrawn. *Finally*, it is increasingly assumed that not only does the threat of crime lie beyond the control of individual nation states, but that societies can freely learn from one another in the formulation of effective crime control policies. These appear as forms of zero tolerance, border controls, surveillance techniques, risk analyses, experiments in restoration and reconciliation, or through recourse to international conventions and declarations of universal human rights.

In these ways, the two books explore the meaning of 'crime' and 'criminal justice' in a globalising world. They do not assume, however, that a focus on 'the global' should replace any other mode of analysis. The idea that the 'global' simply creates homogeneity and convergence is seriously flawed. The books are just as concerned with the ways that (undeniable) international transformations can only fully be made sense of by recognising how they are imagined, reworked or resisted in local contexts. Developing a deeper understanding of how local and global initiatives intersect *and* collide – both in how crime is conceived and how it is responded to – is one of the major challenges facing contemporary criminological inquiry.

Criminal Justice: Local and Global
edited by Deborah Drake, John Muncie and Louise Westmarland.

This book broadens 'everyday' conceptions of criminal justice by exploring the different ways in which 'criminal justice' manifests itself in cultures of control, experiments in restoration and conflict resolution, risk technologies, private security, techniques of surveillance, transnational policing and in conceptions of universal human rights. It is in these broad strategies of crime control and social ordering that the particular role of criminal justice systems is analysed and assessed. Looking beyond the borders of 'criminal justice' (as practised through the police, courts and prisons of individual nation states) forces reconsideration of the viability of viewing criminal justice systems as self-contained sovereign entities. Historically, law making and law enforcement have been the prerogative of the state. That sovereignty is now being challenged by international courts, human rights instruments, multinational private-security enterprises, and possibilities for global surveillance. It is no longer clear what the scope of criminal justice is and who exactly constitutes the subject of its gaze. This uncertainty creates a series of conundrums for the student of 'criminal justice'. 'Criminal justice' is being increasingly challenged not simply by the production of its own 'internal injustices', but also through disjuncture between domestic and international priorities and requirements. What role can individual states perform, on their own, in a world of global threats and insecurities? What meaning remains for state-specific concepts of criminal law and criminal justice?

Crime: Local and Global
edited by John Muncie, Deborah Talbot and Reece Walters.

This companion text broadens 'everyday' conceptions of crime by exploring the different ways in which 'crime' manifests itself in the diverse sites of the city, cyberspace, the body, the corporation, the environment, and the state. It is in these sites that this book begins to unravel how and why certain 'undesirable' behaviours, people, places and events are identified as deserving the criminal label (and thereby criminal sanction), while others are not. The book explores a number of examples – such as 'urban disorders', transgression in cyberspace, human trafficking, corporate violence, environmental pollution, genocide and state-sponsored torture – to consider how far 'the global' is challenging traditional criminological conceptions of the meaning and parameters of crime. Looking beyond the borders of 'crime' (as defined through the criminal law statutes of individual nation states) forces exploration of areas traditionally neglected by criminology. It requires a level of analysis that places 'crime' alongside alternative concepts such as 'harm', 'transgression', 'violence' and 'power'. It compels recognition of a wide range of troubling issues which remain hidden (and thereby unacknowledged) by traditional state-centred criminological perspectives. But what are the implications of this for criminological studies? Should we be seeking a 'global criminology'? And if so, how exactly might this be defined?

Each book is a fully illustrated interactive teaching and learning resource. The chapters should be read sequentially, as each builds on preceding discussions and debates. A number of activities are built into each chapter in order to encourage active engagement and to develop a critical reflective analysis. Each activity is followed by a comments section where the authors offer their response to the questions posed and against which you can compare your own.

The production of these two books has been a long and complex process which has drawn on the expertise of many people. First and foremost, we are indebted to Kate Smith who, as course manager, has ensured that we never veered too far from our production schedules. The work of the central academic course team has been immeasurably enhanced by the advice of a panel of tutors made up of Elaine Ellis, Colin Rogers and Mari Woolfson. We are also grateful for the invaluable contributions made by all of our internal and external authors and for the crucial role played by the external assessor, Suzanne Karstedt.

Responsibility for the high quality of both books also rests with a wide range of production staff, including Donna Collins (secretarial support), Fiona Harris and Adam Nightingale (editing), Paul Hillery (graphic design) and Margaret McManus (media assistance).

We thank them all.

Book Editors:

Deborah Drake, John Muncie and Louise Westmarland

Chapter 1
Interrogating criminal justice

Deborah Drake, John Muncie and Louise Westmarland

Contents

1   Introduction

This chapter is designed to help you to think critically about the concept of justice and what it means in different contexts and communities and at different points in history. A key aim is to situate *criminal justice* among a range of strategies that might be (and are) employed when social harms, such as crimes, occur. Political and popular debates around 'justice' tend to be driven by the equitable (or otherwise) nature of adjudication and the processing of individuals through the criminal courts. As a result, they are, in the main, concerned with how to 'hold offenders to account'. The chapter interrogates such common-sense understandings by exploring some of the defining features of criminal justice and uncovering the consequences of criminal justice being given priority in the resolution of disputes. The particular focus of criminal justice, as a set of procedures and regulations specific to individual nation states, is also exposed in consideration of the growing impact of international legal conventions, the emergence of transnational agencies of surveillance and the global flow of particular penal and crime control discourses and policies. Such developments necessitate moving beyond dominant understandings of 'justice' and 'criminal justice'.

Section 2 of the chapter considers various ways in which the concept of 'justice' can be imagined and put into practice. Criminal justice represents a particular, but no means universal, method of responding to harms, conflicts and troubles. Section 3 examines some of the key characteristics and governing rationales for criminal justice – whether expressed as retribution, due process, crime control or rehabilitation – while Section 4 examines some of the 'injustices' that appear to be built into such procedures and rationales. Indeed, arguably we can learn more about the nature of criminal justice by examining its recurrent 'tensions' and 'failures' than by simply recalling its competing rationales. Section 5 further illustrates the shifting debates over what constitutes 'justice' by moving beyond nation state-specific prescriptions and examining how international cooperation and global relationships also impact on understandings of justice and on how (and by whom) justice might be delivered.

The aims of this chapter are to explore:

■ the relationship between crime control and criminal justice

■ the relationship between criminal justice and other means of delivering 'justice'

■ competing rationales for criminal justice based on due process, crime control, deterrence, retribution, incapacitation and rehabilitation

- the degree to which systems of criminal justice may also be major sources of *injustice* and a significant agency in the creation of further conflict, harm and dispute

- the impact that the emergence of supranational legal orders and international standards is likely to have on questions of national sovereignty and the democratic accountability of the nation state.

2 The constitution of 'justice'

The concept of justice defies any straightforward definition. It often appears as abstract and opaque and can mean different things to different people. Yet it is frequently evoked as a social value that nation states strive to demonstrate and individuals demand.

Activity 1.1

Think about how you would define 'justice' in relation to the problems of crime in your local area or in society at large. Is the criminal justice system always the most effective means of responding to these problems?

Comment

When considering a definition of justice in relation to problems of crime, it is tempting to think first about high-profile (violent) or highly visible (vandalism, graffiti) crimes and the difficulties criminal justice systems have in combating and preventing these. Indeed, this is one of the limitations of reacting to crime after it has occurred – it is rarely an effective crime prevention tool. Further, the ability of the criminal justice system to respond and to deliver justice when a crime occurs can be heavily constrained by the procedural and structural form of the justice system itself. The relationship between crime and justice is sometimes tangential at best, as subsequent sections of this chapter will illustrate. How criminal justice is constituted depends on how crime is constituted. What is defined as a 'crime' dictates, to some extent, how justice will be pursued, and vice versa. However, what if justice were to be imagined outside of the limitations of a crime control or a crime prevention model? Can you think of some ways in which justice might be constituted if it were not constrained by formal criminal justice procedures?

The concept of justice can conjure up a multitude of competing images of fairness, equality, human rights, just deserts, deserved punishment, moral worth, personal liberty, social obligation and public protection.

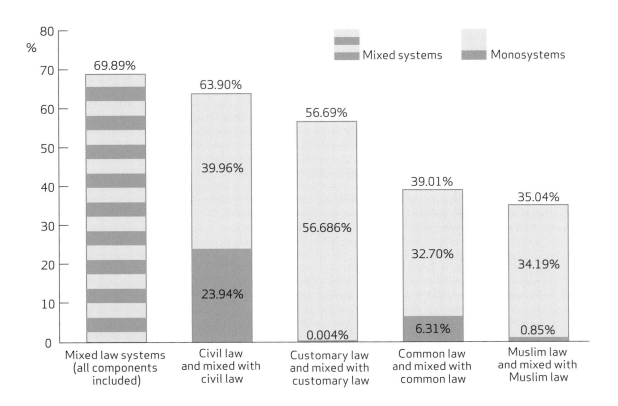

Figure 1.1
Distribution of the
world population (%)
per legal system
(Source: www.juriglobe.
ca/eng/syst-demo/
graph.php)

It has been the subject of continual philosophical debate: is justice universal, derived from fundamental natural or divine principles, or is it invariably tied to specific (and changing) social and political conditions or to particular legal systems?

There is considerable variation between legal systems in the way in which criminal justice is constituted. Figure 1.1 identifies the percentages of the world population that are governed by the different legal systems in use throughout the world.

Mixed legal systems are the most prevalent. They are made up of some combination of civil, common, customary and/or Muslim law.

Very few jurisdictions operate a legal system that is wholly customary. A customary system of law is based on local knowledge, custom and cultural traditions, such as in Jersey and Andorra. The countries that operate customary law systems most often do so within a mixed legal system, combining, for example, customary law and common law principles. However, customary laws may still play a significant role in the adjudication of justice. Similarly, very few countries have legal systems that are influenced wholly by the religious beliefs of the region; the most 'undiluted' religiously based legal systems are those in some Islamic countries where Muslim law systems are guided by Sharia law.

Sharia law is the authority not just on legal matters alone: its rules and regulations also inform many aspects of day-to-day private and public life. But, again, most countries that operate Muslim law systems do so within a mixed system.

Many countries operate legal systems that are wholly civil- or common-law based. For example, most European countries, a large proportion of Asia and most of Central and South America operate civil law systems. Common law systems, by contrast, are found in the UK, the USA, Canada and Oceania. The main distinction to be drawn between common and civil law systems is that common law is principally guided by the courts, which set precedents for the law through rulings on specific cases. In common law procedures responsibility lies with defendants (and their solicitors) and prosecutors to present evidence and to prove their respective cases. The judge holds the responsibility of deciding which case has been presented most convincingly. In a common law system the law can be developed on a case-by-case basis. Civil law systems, by contrast, are inspired by Roman law and operate on codes of law – often established by legal scholars – which then guide judges on how to rule on specific cases. That is, judges in a civil law system have the responsibility of ensuring a just outcome of a case. They act as active investigators during legal proceedings and are thus able to pursue evidentiary lines of questioning with witnesses during the course of a case. Judges are not reliant on solicitors' abilities to prove their respective cases and are often required to guide the proceedings. In addition, the appointment of judges differs between common and civil law systems. In common law systems judges are appointed or elected from the pool of practising solicitors, whereas in civil law systems judges are appointed or elected according to their professional judicial status.

Some countries have a mixed system of law that is nevertheless still heavily based in one system or another. The legal system in Scotland, for example, although a mixed system, retains a high degree of Roman or civil law. The rest of the UK, as mentioned above, and most of the countries that Britain colonised operate a common law legal system.

These differences in legal systems have a direct influence on how justice is constituted and delivered and, arguably, on how it is viewed and defined by the general public. Although this book considers global influences on justice, many of the cases considered in the chapters derive from common law systems. Making this distinction provides a main reference point from which to consider and interrogate various definitions of justice from around the world.

Beliefs about 'what is just' are often contingent on particular circumstances and may shift according to different cultural values and norms. As the following examples suggest, public and political perceptions of justice in the law are susceptible to changing sensibilities in relation to the demands of society, on the one hand, and the rights of individuals, on the other. In addition, the authority of the state can be reinforced or undermined by the public's perception of its ability to uphold and deliver justice effectively.

Figure 1.2
Prometheus cartoon
from 2007

Activity 1.2

First, read Extract 1.1 and consider the following questions as you do so:

■ What might be some of the consequences of repealing laws that protect the rights of accused persons?

■ Are there alternative ways in which justice might have been served for Julie?

■ How can the rights of victims be protected while at the same time ensuring that the rights of the accused are also recognised and carefully guarded?

Extract 1.1

'Justice for Julie' campaign

Julie Hogg, a pizza delivery girl and mother of a three-year-old boy, went missing from her home in Billingham, Stockton-on-Tees, in November 1989, sparking an extensive police hunt.

The body of the 22-year-old was eventually found by Mrs Ming [Julie's mother] during the following February, hidden behind a bath panel, when the keys to her daughter's flat were returned to her.

Billy Dunlop, with whom Julie had previously had a relationship, was charged with her murder but acquitted after a trial. Nine years later he confessed to the crime and was jailed for perjury.

But he was not jailed for her murder because according to the law of double jeopardy as it stood, dating back 800 years to the Middle Ages, Dunlop could not be tried twice for the killing.

It ruled that a person acquitted by a jury could not be tried again on the same charge, not even if new evidence came to light.

Mrs Ming, 61, from Norton, Stockton-on-Tees who worked as a nurse at Middlesbrough General Hospital, fought for more than 15 years to change the law on double jeopardy and launched the Justice for Julie campaign.

Finally, in April 2005, the rule was altered under the 2003 Criminal Justice Act.

Dunlop, who was jailed for life after pleading guilty at the Old Bailey last September, became the first killer to be convicted under the new legislation.

Source: BBC News, 2007

Next, read Extract 1.2 and consider these questions:

■ Can there be any 'universals' of justice: that is, principles or ideas that are internationally agreed, acknowledged and acted on?

■ Is criminal law always the most effective means for resolving disputes and achieving 'justice'? What other means might be employed?

■ Can 'justice' ever be settled? Or is it by its very nature something that will be continually contested, struggled over and disputed?

Extract 1.2

'Justice for Darfur' campaign

Sudan should arrest war crimes suspects now

One year after the International Criminal Court (ICC) issued arrest warrants for two war crimes suspects in Darfur, human rights organisations around the world launched a 'Justice for Darfur' campaign, calling for the two to be arrested.

The organisations behind the campaign, including Amnesty International, Cairo Institute for Human Rights Studies, Coalition for the International Criminal Court, Human Rights First, Human Rights Watch, and Sudan Organization Against Torture, have joined forces to call on the United Nations Security Council, regional organisations and individual governments to press Sudan to cooperate with the ICC.

The ICC has been investigating crimes in the region following a decision three years ago by the UN Security Council to refer to it the situation in Darfur. One year ago – on April 27, 2007 – the ICC issued two arrest warrants against Sudan's former State Minister of the Interior Ahmad Harun and Janjaweed leader Ali Kushayb for 51 counts of war crimes and crimes against humanity. Today the two men – who face charges of persecution, rape, and killing of civilians in four West Darfur villages – remain at large.

...

The Sudanese government has publicly and repeatedly refused to surrender either Ali Kushayb or Ahmad Harun to the Court. Instead, Ahmad Harun has been promoted to State Minister for Humanitarian Affairs, responsible for the welfare of the very victims of his alleged crimes. As well as having considerable power over humanitarian operations, he is responsible for liaison with the international peacekeeping force (UNAMID) tasked with protecting civilians against such crimes. The other suspect, Ali Kushayb, was in custody in Sudan on other charges at the time the ICC warrants were issued, but in October [2007] the government announced he had been released, reportedly due to 'lack of evidence.'

...

[The 'Justice for Darfur' campaign organisers called on states and regional organisations, including] the European Union, a strong supporter of the Court and key player in bringing the Darfur crimes to the ICC Prosecutor, to press Sudan to cooperate with the ICC and comply with the warrants.

Source: Amnesty International Australia, 2008

Comment

The articles in Extracts 1.1 and 1.2 illustrate that individual and collective pursuits of justice can become politicised and sometimes lead to major reforms in the law or to new laws being passed. The case in Extract 1.1 marks an important shift in criminal law in the UK. The law of double jeopardy is of uncertain origin, but versions of it have been part of many formal criminal justice systems for centuries. Although the values that might have brought about this law in the first place cannot be known with certainty, the fact that it was directed towards the protection of accused persons against the power of the state is well documented in many historical and legal writings (Sigler, 1963). Reforms to the law of double jeopardy in the UK and parts of Australia in the early twenty-first century suggest that there was no longer any public or political tolerance for this particular legal protection for the rights of accused persons. A potential consequence of the reform to this law is that it grants the state greater power in prosecuting accused persons and removes some of the safeguarding limits to the power of the state, which previously protected the innocent accused.

In analysing the cases in Extracts 1.1 and 1.2, it should be remembered that considerations of human rights are integral to formulations of justice. Both of the examples rely on the criminal law and criminal courts in order to pursue and achieve 'justice'. They also reflect how the law is not always static but can shift according to national and international pressures. However, advocating law reforms requires critical consideration. For example, reforms that afford rights to victims at the *expense* of offenders or accused persons represent an ideology that suggests that human rights are not universal; that is, they are to be recognised only for those who are deemed to be 'deserving'. Such an ideology leads to a concept of justice that is concerned not with equality or achieving balance in justice matters, but with creating further conflicts, social inequalities and social harms. The questions raised by the extracts include whether the criminal law is the most effective means of achieving justice and whether there might be alternative ways in which justice could have been served in each case. Asking questions such as these creates opportunities for thinking about justice in new and innovative ways. Although definitive answers to these particular questions would be difficult to formulate, these kinds of questions will be asked throughout this book because they encourage critical reflection on how concepts of justice are imagined and materialised, both for individuals and for entire societies.

Justice can be evoked and practised in a wide variety of sites and with multiple purposes. Justice procedures may be formal or informal and several types of justice can be differentiated and considered, such as: criminal justice; civil justice; regulatory justice; informal justice; restorative justice; indigenous justice; populist justice; social justice; global justice; and environmental justice.

Criminal justice is widely assumed to be the major means through which the nation state assumes responsibility for constructing criminal laws and trying, prosecuting and punishing those who offend such laws. *Civil justice* concerns itself with resolving contractual disputes. Typically, a civil action is brought by a *private*, injured party to seek compensation for the harm caused by another, whereas a criminal action is brought by the *state* to punish those transgressing criminal law. Civil remedies usually involve financial reparation, whereas criminal actions give rise to criminal punishments ranging from fines to the death penalty.

Regulatory justice is typically employed to deal with businesses and companies that fail to comply with health and safety legislation, food safety standards, and so on. Non-compliance tends to be responded to through a 'pyramid' of persuasion, warning letters, civil action, enforcement notices and, only in the last instance, criminal prosecution (**Tombs and Whyte, 2010**). In this regard, the use of regulatory (rather than criminal) justice agencies to control business and corporate crime might be considered a form of *informal justice*. Other forms of informal justice generally seek to achieve conflict resolution without recourse to formal state agencies at all. They may be initiated by states themselves or by pressure groups or dissident groups.

Informalism is also one element of *restorative justice*, which seeks to solve problems and address violations of legal and human rights through dialogue and negotiation. Restoration ranges from forms of *indigenous justice*, originating in First Nations cultures, to international peacemaking tribunals, such as the South African Truth and Reconciliation Commission. Rather than privileging the law, professionals and the state, restorative resolutions prioritise exchange between offender, victim and local community in the healing and rebuilding of relationships (discussed further in Chapter 3). In contrast to restorative justice, which seeks to restore or build community relations, *populist justice* can, in some circumstances, take a generally more repressive approach, involving, for example, the vigilante targeting of 'outsiders'.

The notion of *social justice* implies a broad conception of justice associated with social issues such as: personal and social well-being; the prevention of harm; the protection of human rights; and the preservation of relationships of human dignity (explored further in Chapter 7). Here justice is thought of, not as a matter for criminal courts, but as the removal of structural inequalities whereby some sections of the population are systematically and repeatedly disadvantaged relative to others. Some argue that conceiving of social justice in this way is meaningless if limited to individual nation states. That is, in a world of global free market economics and of multinational corporate enterprise, social justice can only be achieved through international collaboration and agreement. It is in this context that the concept of *global justice* becomes a possibility. Global justice is concerned with whether or not there can be globally agreed ethics and institutions that ensure equality, fair treatment and distributive justice the world over. One element of such a global agenda is that of *environmental justice,* which seeks to redress inequitable worldwide distributions of environmental harms (e.g. pollution, famine, drought) and to facilitate universal access to environmental goods (e.g. nutritious food, clean air and water, safe jobs, health care) (**Walters, 2010**).

Such distinctions are important in revealing that *criminal justice* is but one form through which conflicts, disputes and harms might be recognised and addressed. Considering other categories of justice also alerts us to the wide range of agencies, strategies, state powers and tactics that can be employed to address harm. The way in which these tend to be differentially applied to particular social groups can also tell us much about relations of power, how structures of power operate and how social order is maintained (see Section 4).

3   Delivering criminal justice

Criminal justice has multiple meanings (Zedner, 2004). This section examines some of the major theoretical and philosophical justifications for national and international forms of 'delivering criminal justice', particularly in common law systems. A range of mechanisms will be introduced, including: surveillance; crime control; due process; retribution; just deserts; deterrence; incapacitation; corrections; and rehabilitation. Some of the key questions that are addressed in this section include:

■ How is justice delivered?

■ By whom and to whom is justice delivered?

■ How is justice defined and delivered through each of the various mechanisms described in this section?

■ Are unintended harms sometimes caused in the delivery of some forms of justice?

■ Are there other conceptualisations of justice that are not as prevalent within these various approaches – social justice, for instance?

3.1 Surveillance

In 1778, the philosopher Jeremy Bentham coined the phrase 'panopticon' to describe a prison design that allowed for uninterrupted inspection, observation and surveillance of prisoners (Bentham, in McLaughlin et al., 2003). He envisaged the replacement of the old dark and dank prison by a light, architectural form in which inmates would be separated off from each other but placed permanently in full view of

Figure 1.3
Bentham's principle
of 'being able to
continually see without
being seen' at Stateville
Correctional Center,
Illinois, 2002

a central, but unseen, observer. Prisoners would never know when they were being observed but would be forced to behave at all times as if they were.

Being conscious that they were visible at all times would assure the automatic functioning of self-control and self-discipline on the part of prisoners. In this way, Bentham was, first and foremost, championing a new conception of surveillance. He dreamed of entire cities being reorganised along panoptic lines. In other words, the notion of perpetual surveillance could be applied not just to prisons but to workhouses, factories, asylums, hospitals and schools. Many of the emergent urban institutional arrangements of the early nineteenth century (and which continue to the present) were based on the principle that social compliance could be achieved through surveillance (Foucault, 1977).

By the early twenty-first century a range of surveillance techniques, such as CCTV and biometric scanning devices (smart cards, fingerprinting, iris scans, hand geometry scans, voice recognition, DNA testing and digitised facial recognition) were rapidly moving from the realm of science fiction into everyday social reality. The potential for national and international systems of intimate monitoring to identify and classify individuals has been rapidly realised. In the USA the 2001 PATRIOT Act (Uniting and Strengthening America by Providing Appropriate Tools Required to Intercept and Obstruct Terrorism Act), hastily introduced after the attacks of 9/11, provided virtually unaccountable government power – justified in the name of the 'war on terror' – to access individuals' financial records, medical histories, internet usage, book purchases, library usage and travel patterns. Growth in commercial DNA databases raises the prospect of gene tests to underpin surveillance systems in the health insurance industry, excluding those recorded as 'abnormal' or 'high risk'. By 2008, the UK had the highest penetration of CCTV cameras in the world (over 4 million or one for every fourteen people). Pictorial databases of such groups as 'hooligans', political demonstrators, suspected illegal immigrants and environmental campaigners have become commonplace.

All of these developments have widespread consequences for population control, spatial segregation and urban regulation (**Mooney and Talbot, 2010**). Modern forms of social panopticism, it is argued (see, for example, Gandy, 1993), operate in the background, like an 'unseen eye', and apply their logic to entire populations. Oscar Gandy (1993) has referred to this as a 'panoptic sort': a process whereby individuals in their daily lives as citizens, employees and consumers are continually identified, classified and assessed. This information is then used to coordinate and control their access to goods and services. Gandy has argued that this is not just a vision of the future, rather: 'It is standard operating procedure. It is expected. It has its place. Its operation is required by law. And where it is not, people call out for its installation. Its work is never done. Each use generates new uses. Each application justifies another' (Gandy, 1993, p. 15). According to Gandy, surveillance has become a system of power on which rests the survival of global corporate capital. He argues that its reach is pervasive and potentially dangerous because it allocates privilege selectively on the basis of information stored, perpetuating inequality and a mistrust that leads to further surveillance: 'each cycle pushes us further from the democratic ideal' (Gandy, 1993, p. 230). Technologies of surveillance offer protection and reassurance, but their increasingly widespread use also means less private space, the potential for greater state interference and control over citizens, and opportunities for personal information related to the habits and behaviours of individuals to be collected and archived without their consent.

Nevertheless, the sheer volume of new data becoming available might be just as likely to create contradictory simulations of people and places. The meaning of data may become ever less verifiable and forever open to contestation. There are, indeed, subtle distinctions to be made in order to unravel whether the future holds an Orwellian vision of zones of exclusion and zones of safety or whether surveillance can allow us to reimagine the urban as rejuvenated, repopulated and more secure (Chapter 5 discusses this further).

3.2 Crime control and due process

One of the longest-standing disputes in relation to the occurrence of social harms relates to how far justice (and criminal justice in particular) should be geared to, and thereby gain its legitimacy by, prioritising the protection of individual rights, on the one hand, or notions of public safety and of making all individuals responsible for their actions, on the other. One of the first to explore this constant tension was Herbert Packer in an article published in the journal *The University of Pennsylvania Law Review* in 1964. Packer's detailing of two normative models – *crime control values* and *due process values* – is a largely heuristic device to illustrate the competing and shifting demands that are placed on criminal justice at any given time. Crime control emphasises that criminal acts are major threats to the social order and that their repression is the most important function of criminal justice. To achieve this, high rates of apprehension and conviction are required to demonstrate the efficiency, speed and certainty of outcome. The process is geared to the production of maximum convictions. Wrongful conviction and police discretion are tolerated as long as they do not bring the system into disrepute. Packer (1968) referred to this as 'assembly line justice'.

By way of contrast, due process places more emphasis on protecting the individual from unjust acts committed by the state. It does so by foregrounding procedural safeguards such as presumption of innocence, transparency of police and judicial proceedings and effective appeals procedures. The aim is to uphold the moral authority of the criminal process where strict and formal adherence to the law, judicial equality and the protection of individual rights is more significant than punishing offenders. Packer (1968) referred to this as 'obstacle course justice' in which prosecutors have to navigate their way through extensive sets of formal procedure. In a crime control model the primary function of criminal justice is to uphold law and order; in a due process model the primary function is to protect civil liberties.

It is difficult to overstate the impact that Packer's formulation has had on subsequent attempts to make sense of criminal processes, although Peter Kraska (2004) has argued that Packer's analysis should be viewed as primarily a product of the political and social turmoil of the USA in the 1960s. Reflecting the new political agendas opened up by the civil rights movement, Packer's work displays a strong ambivalence towards law enforcement: recognising the essential nature of law in the production of social order, but also stressing how government can over-use and abuse the law for its own ends. Consequently, part of his underlying intent was to regulate the reach of the law by advocating, for example, the decriminalisation of drugs, prostitution and gambling offences.

John Griffiths (1970), however, suggested that to understand criminal justice we need to move beyond the formal goals of 'crime control' and 'due process'. Rather than assuming that criminal justice must always be an endless 'battle', Griffiths proposes an alternative 'family model' driven by the more progressive principles of mutual interest, respect, concern, education and reconciliation. Without such a reimagining, the 'criminal' (typically from among the poor) will be forever viewed as an outcast, and criminal justice will continue to ensure that social relations between the individual and the state are based on hostility (see further discussion of this notion in the context of restorative justice in Chapter 3).

In essence, Packer's models only comment on the regular reproduction of social inequalities and discrimination without criticising them (McBarnet, 1983). This disguises the tendency of the criminal process to protect the interests of the propertied middle classes. Similarly, Walter Miller (1973, p. 142) has argued that 'ideology is the permanent hidden agenda of criminal justice'; it is not an impartial system. Miller differentiates between the 'typical' positions of right- and left-wing politics on matters of law and order. While the right might typically complain about 'excessive leniency', 'erosion of discipline' and 'permissiveness', the left might draw attention to 'excessive criminalisation', 'undue incarceration' and the production of systematic 'racism, sexism, minority oppression and brutality'. Miller's identification of the role of ideology is important because it highlights the vulnerability of the criminal justice system to political power and preference. That is, the way in which the criminal justice system operates and the outcomes it produces (e.g. low or high imprisonment rates, rehabilitative or austere prison conditions, community or zero-tolerance policing strategies) are associated more closely with changing political agendas than with crime rates or, indeed, than with abstract models of justice.

3.3 Punishment: retributive and utilitarian

The pursuit of criminal justice often includes an implicit expectation, first, that someone must be blamed or found guilty and, second, that some form of punishment should be delivered. There would seem to be a near universal belief that society has the right to formally admonish those who transgress its behavioural boundaries. The 'common-sense' response seems to be castigation and punishment. Punishment, however, has no rigid limits. Nicola Lacey (1988, p. 15) warns that 'There is no one neat, polished final justification for punishment: there are only arguments for and against it, which apply differently not only within different political systems but also according to the social and economic conditions holding in different societies in which the institutions exist'. Nevertheless, three essential ideas seem to be present in most modern definitions of punishment:

1   Punishment is deliberately administered by state officials on an individual who is legally defined as being subject to the laws of that state.

2   It requires some normative justification that the pain/deprivation/ suffering is warranted, because punishment involves intentional deprivation and suffering.

3   The usual view of its primary purpose is that it should be instrumental in reducing or containing rates of criminal behaviour.

The dominant philosophical justifications for punishment are typically to be found either in retributive theory, which advocates repayment for harm done, including 'just deserts' (deserved punishment), and/or utilitarian theory, which advocates deterrence, incapacitation and rehabilitation. Whereas the former is most concerned to respond to past offences, the latter is designed to prevent future law breaking.

Retribution underpins notions of 'justice being seen to be done' and 'punishment to fit the crime'. These principles can be found in many world cultures in response to social harms committed. Such ideas are deeply ingrained in many theological texts, such as the *lex talionis* of the Mosaic doctrine expressed in Exodus 21:23–25, which states: 'and if any mischief follows, then thou shalt give life for life, eye for eye, tooth for tooth, hand for hand, foot for foot, burning for burning, wound for wound, stripe for stripe'. In this text, punishing the transgressor is constructed as a positive moral duty. The moral order can be restored and the violation atoned for only by returning a proportionate degree of pain upon the guilty. The development of this school of thought is associated most strongly with the work of Immanuel Kant. Retribution concentrates on harms that have already occurred. It is not concerned with the future conduct of offenders or with crime prevention. Accordingly, it focuses only on punishing individuals who have deliberately violated the law and/or the rights of others. According to retributive theory, the act of punishment restores the moral order that was breached by the wrongdoing. If an individual has been found guilty of a crime, then not only does the guilt make it possible to punish that individual, it makes it necessary to do so. This focus disentangles the meting out of justice from any concern for welfare and social problems. The system is rationalised by concentrating on its core task – identifying and inflicting punishment on those individuals who have failed to comply with the laws and conventions of society.

Figure 1.4
Uma Thurman in
the film *Kill Bill* (dir.
Quentin Tarantino):
a modern-day
representation of a
mythical goddess of
divine justice,
retribution and revenge

Retribution has gone through something of a revival since the 1970s,
particularly in the USA and the UK. Partly in critique of rehabilitation/
correctional strategies (see below), it was argued that any wrongdoing
should be met with a sanction deserved by the severity of the offence.
The consequences of punishment are deemed to be irrelevant. Justice is
served when the guilty are given their 'just deserts'; that is, they are
punished according to the gravity of their offence within a system of
commensurate penalties. The merit of this approach is that, at least in
theory, it removes any expressive, arbitrary and discretional biases from
punishment. The leading proponent of such 'modern retributivism' in
the 1970s was Andrew von Hirsch. In *Doing Justice* (1976) von Hirsch
argued for a reinstatement of retributive principles but tempered by an
acknowledgement of the individual's right to have their case dealt with
'fairly' and 'equitably' through procedures of due process. According to
von Hirsch, in order to reinstate 'justice', the considerable bank of
discretionary powers built up by the state needed to be rolled back. In
theory, the principle of 'just deserts' did offer to set limits to
punishment (whether in custodial or treatment settings) in some
coherent fashion – largely through the principle of proportionality:
that the offender be handed a sentence that is in accordance with what
the act deserves – but the approach has also been subject to critique
from all shades of the political spectrum:

■ There is a recurring difficulty in achieving any consensus on the
   calculation of seriousness and the ranking of offences and therefore it
   would be difficult to determine a proportionate and commensurate
   response.

■ By concentrating on desert, the impact of social and cultural factors on offending patterns is ignored.

■ By denying the social and political contexts in which criminal justice operates, 'just deserts' can readily be appropriated to legitimise punitive penal policies.

■ Punitiveness can be tempered by other means – for example, a commitment to social justice or rights agendas – rather than relying on judicial parsimony (Muncie, 2004).

In contrast to retribution and 'just deserts', *utilitarianism* is more concerned with the outcomes and consequences of punishment beyond those of ensuring that justice has been seen to be done. Utilitarianism is built on the principle of 'the greatest happiness of the greatest number'. Within this school of thought, human behaviour is shaped by pursuit of maximum advantage, pleasure and happiness and the avoidance of pain, unhappiness and costs. Building on these principles, a deterrent model of crime control was formulated by the eighteenth-century classical school of criminology (Beccaria, 1963 [1764]). According to the classical school, crime is rational, self-interested and freely chosen behaviour. Individuals *rationally determine* what is in their own *self-interest* and act accordingly. The primary purpose of criminal law is to protect the well-being of the community, not to punish offenders. The logic of classicism is that the individual who has committed a crime will find the punishment so unpleasant that the offence will not be repeated. In the long run, the individual's punishment serves a general deterrence. As a result, classicism looks to the prevention of *future* crime.

Deterrence is based on the premise of affording rational, self-interested individuals good reasons not to commit crimes. Since the punishment must be one that can be calculated, it must be the same for all individuals, regardless of age, mentality, social status or gender. The theory of deterrence is therefore premised on equal treatment for all. Individual differences stemming from personal experiences or social factors are denied or ignored: in this way, it is the act that is judged, rather than the individual. Clemency, pardons and mitigating circumstances are excluded. To do otherwise would violate the equal rights of all individuals. Thus, it follows that the punishment should fit the crime, not the individual (Roshier, 1989). A deterrent model of punishment argues that:

■ the pain of possible punishment must exceed the potential pleasure of committing an offence

■ if punishment for a given offence is certain, it need not be severe to have a deterrant effect; where it is less certain, it needs to be more severe

- punishment should avoid the evils of over- and under-punishing offences

- punishment should be *public*, *prompt* and *certain* rather than necessarily severe

- punishment should publicly symbolise the offence, so that if a crime is committed the offender can be sure that punishment will follow

- preventing future crime is more significant than punishing past offences

- prevention requires that laws should be clear, simple and universally supported.

Such principles had a considerable impact on the reformation of the criminal justice system across Europe and the USA in the latter half of the eighteenth century and continue to do so in various new expressions of utilitarianism – now associated with neo-conservatism. Neo-conservatism stresses the need for strong government and social authoritarianism in order to create a disciplined and hierarchical society in which individual needs are subordinate to those of the 'nation'. For neo-conservatives, forms of justice that seek to understand the mitigating circumstances behind the commission of a crime act simply to absolve individuals of responsibility for their actions and offer a 'culture of excuses' for criminality. James Q. Wilson (1975, pp. 41–2), for example, argued that criminality can be accounted for by the existence of rationally calculating 'lower class' people who attach little importance to the opinion of others and are 'inclined to uninhibited, expressive conduct'. Wilson's key proposition is that crime rates can be reduced only by increasing the certainty of criminal sanctions.

The utilitarian theory of punishment also includes the notion of *incapacitation*, which assumes that offenders will commit a certain number of crimes over a given period of time if they remain in society and that a substantial reduction in the total crime rate can be achieved through incarceration. During the 1980s and 1990s, incapacitation became the dominant rationale, particularly for the penal system in the USA. Abiding by the principles of utilitarianism, a philosophy of incapacitation maintains that society should be protected for as long as possible from the threat of the 'dangerous criminal'. As a result, the individual (and their rights) may have to be sacrificed for the 'greater good'. However, utilitarian strategies have been subjected to critical challenge on various grounds:

- Increasing the use of prison may reduce, rather than increase, its stigmatising (deterrent) effect (i.e. serving a prison sentence may become commonplace within some communities).

■ Not all crime and offending can be attributable to a rational calculation of risks and benefits. Some may be opportunistic, others impulsive, others committed out of desperation.

■ Expanding prison populations imposes substantial economic costs and, of all interventions, generally returns the highest rates of reoffending.

■ Individual rights are sacrificed for the 'good' of the majority.

■ There is little correlation between rates of crime and levels of imprisonment. Roger Tarling (1993) estimated that a 25 per cent increase in prison populations would achieve only a 1 per cent fall in the crime rate.

■ Punishment is imposed differentially on the least powerful groups in society – hence the over-representation of certain populations in prisons.

■ The 'inevitability' of increasing imprisonment rates should be subjected to continual challenge – there are alternatives to imprisonment (Hudson, 1996).

In spite of considerable evidence that imprisonment is an unreliable means through which to control crime and deliver justice, the use of imprisonment is a proliferating practice throughout the world. Penal mentalities and strategies have become key elements in what has been termed 'the new punitiveness' to be found in the USA and elsewhere, particularly since the 1990s (see Chapter 2). Numerous developments, particularly, but not always, originating in the USA, have led some analysts to consider whether penal policy and practice are now reverting back to those of some 200 years ago. In particular, rising rates of imprisonment, chain gangs, 'supermax' prisons, naming and shaming, public humiliation of offenders, three-strikes laws, mandatory minimum sentencing, austere prison regimes, zero tolerance, the death penalty: all appear as draconian and disproportionate responses to offending (Parenti, 1999). This 'new punitiveness' appears to de-emphasise just deserts, rehabilitation and deterrence and focuses closely on what might be called 'incapacitation-plus'. Incapacitation appears not simply to be based on confinement, but also to be driven by vengeance and cruelty, where the primary objective is largely one of taking satisfaction in the pain of others (Simon, 2001; Goldson, 2005; Pratt et al., 2005). This new punitiveness, which is identifiable in a number of both Western and non-Western countries, calls for a particular form of 'justice' that is neither impartial nor carefully meted out, but is emotionally driven and unrestrained.

3.4 Corrections: penal welfare and rehabilitation

The term 'corrections' is a catch-all to refer to all manner of strategies and programmes designed to treat, reform or rehabilitate offenders in either penal or community settings. In accordance with deterrence theory, it is forward looking and is designed to prevent further offending. In contrast to both retribution and deterrence, however, it does not assume that offending is always and everywhere a result of deliberative rational action. Rather, it takes into account that behaviour is often determined by factors outside of an individual's control. This proposition is central to all forms of positivist criminology. Individual positivism focuses on biological and psychological factors, locating the sources of crime primarily *within* the individual. Such foregrounding of *individual* pathology contends that offending can de dealt with through various individualised methods of treatment. Sociological positivism, on the other hand, maintains that more insights could be gained by studying the social context and social constraints or opportunities external to individuals. The foregrounding of *social* pathology allows broader issues, such as social and economic reform, to enter the crime control agenda. Of key importance is the recognition that once the aberrant condition can be identified, it can then be treated and the problem resolved. Such an approach gradually gathered support through the first half of the twentieth century and reached an apogee in the 1960s. This period is usually viewed as the high point of the *rehabilitative ideal*. By addressing specific needs and problems, it is argued that treatment programmes can prevent people from reoffending. Instead of the punishment fitting the crime, the treatment needs to match the individual offender.

This shift to more individualised forms of penality first occurred in Britain in the late nineteenth century and the early decades of the twentieth century. It is in this period that David Garland (1985) finds the origins of rehabilitation – a penal welfare model of crime control, premised on ideas of individual pathology and treatment. A series of competing discourses and types of professional expertise – psychiatric, medical, social work, legal – came to claim a greater influence in judicial proceedings. This marked a radical departure from ideas of 'criminal justice', 'crime control' and 'full criminal responsibility' and a move towards a focus on welfare and therapeutic treatment to suit each individual. Ronald Clarke and Derek Cornish (1983) have argued that it would be hard to overstate the influence of this medico-psychological model, particularly in the post-Second World War period. A generation of social workers and probation officers were taught that the major determinants of delinquent behaviour were located firmly within the individual and, in particular, within emotional disturbances resulting from unsatisfactory human relationships. However, by the late 1960s, doubts, which had never been totally assuaged throughout the period of rehabilitation's dominance, were voiced by critics on both the right and the left of the political spectrum. Stanley Cohen (1985) drew attention to the abuses that might occur in the development of forms of social control under the guise of 'benevolent treatment'. He argued that a lack of due process and proportionality violated individual rights and that, by appearing to be benign, recourse to formal justice was encouraged. In other words, rehabilitation came to be viewed not as a liberal alternative to punishment but, rather, as an extension of the state's armoury of punitive measures. Such an argument was most forcibly put in an American Friends Service Committee report (1971). The Committee was established to investigate the state of American prisons and prisoner rights in the wake of the 1971 Attica prison riot in New York State. The report was particularly critical of indeterminate sentencing whereby prisoners would not know the dates of their release and were never informed of the relationship between their particular offence and the length of sentence they were given. Rehabilitation was condemned as encouraging excessive intervention and denying offenders their due rights – it encourages any number of professional diagnoses and interventions to locate the cause of the deviant behaviour and then constructs (arguably unwarranted) intensive programmes of treatment in order to cure it.

The most influential critique of rehabilitation, however, came from evaluations of various programmes, which suggested that different types of treatment made little or no difference to subsequent rates of reoffending or reconviction. The most widely quoted study was that of Robert Martinson (1974) who, after analysing 231 studies of particular treatment programmes in the USA, argued that 'with few and isolated exceptions, the rehabilitative efforts that have been reported so far have had no appreciable effect on recidivism' (Martinson, 1974, p. 24). The often cited (although not strictly accurate) conclusion drawn from this study was that 'nothing works'. This devastating assessment prompted a collapse of faith in correctionalism, initially in relation to prison-based 'treatment programmes', but subsequently expanded to include all manner of probation interventions and community corrections. Doubt was cast over the efficacy of many fundamental aspects of criminal justice.

The responses in the UK and the USA to the acceptance of the idea that 'nothing works' were varied. Certainly some practitioners and policy makers attempted to keep alive a modified rehabilitative ideal. Maeve McMahon (1992) argued that community-based correctional programmes should be expanded not simply because they are just as effective as institutional programmes, but also because they are less costly and more humane. Francis Cullen and Karen Gilbert (1982) contended that, at the very least, rehabilitation forces the state to recognise that it has an obligation to care for the offender's welfare and needs.

Other defenders of rehabilitation (e.g. Ross et al., 1988) have argued that, rather than being the defining rationale for the system, treatment efforts should be restricted to specific types of offenders, such as young offenders and sex offenders. Indeed, since the 1980s there has been something of a revival of rehabilitation in the form of risk-management programmes specifically focused on 'high-risk' populations, 'what works' and evidence-based principles, but stressing offender responsibility and accountability (discussed further in Chapter 4).

4   Criminal injustices

Criminal justice and the criminal law that it supports originated, in many countries, in the transition from stateless to state-run societies. Following the historical development of criminal justice is a useful first step in developing a critical approach to understanding the inner workings of contemporary criminal justice. The origins of criminal justice in Europe appear indelibly tied to the systematic generation of social inequalities and the repression of the powerless. In early societies, where property was communally owned, a common morality was maintained through custom rather than through rule of law. Pieter Spierenburg (1984) identifies the twelfth century as witnessing the birth of 'punishment', public penal law and forms of regulation akin to 'criminal justice', and the beginnings of a long process whereby the resolution of disputes through vengeance or voluntary reconciliation was to be transferred from individuals and their families to the state. Here again, however, recourse to 'justice' was often class specific. For example, although duelling was made illegal in most European countries in the early nineteenth century, participants in a fair duel were rarely prosecuted or, if they were, they were not convicted. Only 'gentlemen' were considered to have had sufficient honour to be qualified to duel.

Although it remains important to recognise these long historical roots, most modern, British-led systems of criminal justice began to take on their current centralised, bureaucratic and 'impersonal' form only from the late eighteenth century onwards. Eighteenth-century justice has been characterised as excessively irregular, unpredictable and partial in its application. The law was unsystematic and its enforcement localised. It was deeply intertwined with local structures of wealth, power, property and office (Hay, 1975). It was only by the mid nineteenth century that many of the principles of criminal justice with which we are now familiar were put into practice: including systematic legal

Figure 1.5
The famous
Burr–Hamilton duel
between two
prominent American
politicians, sitting Vice
President Aaron Burr
and the former
Secretary of the
Treasury Alexander
Hamilton, on 11 July
1804

regulations, the aim of punishment to reform the offender as well as to deliver retribution, the establishment of a full-time professional police force and the construction of the penitentiary.

These shifts have, however, been unable to resolve the contradictions of purpose or the inconsistencies in functioning typically to be found in formal systems of delivering justice. A critical socio-legal perspective on the role and function of systems of criminal justice gathered strength in many English-speaking countries in the 1970s. One of its original protagonists, Richard Quinney (1977), argued that it is precisely through law that a powerful, ruling class is able to preserve a particular social order in which their own economic and social interests can be maintained and promoted. In this perspective, due process, crime control, rehabilitation, correction, and so on, are all means through which legal and judicial justification is given to repressive, harmful and coercive social orders. 'Crime control' and evocation of a 'justice ideal' are key means through which any perceived threats to existing relations of power are regulated. The state routinely suppresses the 'dangerous' and the 'subversive' in the name of justice. Quinney viewed these processes as gathering strength in the USA during the 1960s and 1970s with the growth of new repressive crime control programmes, the militarisation of law enforcement and 'a new justice model' prioritising deterrence and punishment. One initial step in resisting such development lies, he argued, in recognising the limitations of recourse to notions of 'justice' to secure a more equitable and cooperative future.

This early theorisation was Marxist in origin and has been critiqued subsequently for its instrumentalism in suggesting that the economically powerful *intentionally* (and successfully) use criminal justice solely for the purposes of oppressing the economically disadvantaged. More contemporary work stresses that there is no simple conspiracy or necessarily deliberative attempt on the part of elites to oppress the disadvantaged. Rather, the particular ways in which 'the crime problem' is articulated and acted on by governmental agencies tend to reproduce structures of class, 'race' and gender discrimination. For example, Jeffrey Reiman's (2007) work, *The Rich Get Richer and the Poor Get Prison*, argues that the aim of criminal justice is not to reduce crime or to achieve justice, but to construct a public image of the perpetual threat of crime from particular sections of society. To do this, a significant and particular population defined as 'criminal' must be maintained and the criminal justice system must be designed to fail to reduce crime. Reiman refers to this 'upside-down' idea of criminal justice as *pyrrhic defeat* theory in which criminal justice serves the powerful, not by its success but by its very failure. The public is continually presented with a partial and distorted image that crime is largely the actions of the poor. More dangerous acts committed by the powerful are ignored or not defined as criminal. The image conveyed is one in which the real danger comes from below rather than from above. Criminal justice must be seen to fight (some) crime, but never enough to reduce or eliminate it. This helps to explain why criminal justice regularly produces the same 'problem populations' and also why it often appears to be in perpetual crisis. The ideological fiction of criminal justice benefits the economically powerful by helping to keep their own crimes hidden while legitimising inequalities in wealth through the criminalisation and control of the powerless. Steven Box (1987) argues that this process tends to make particular groups – the young, the unemployed and those from minority ethnic communities – the most vulnerable to arrest and prosecution, not because they commit more crime but because they coincide with media, public and political images of 'dangerousness'. A self-fulfilling cycle ensues. The meaning of 'crime' and 'justice' becomes tightly circumscribed.

Although Quinney's and Reiman's analyses concentrate in the main on class conflict and class oppression, feminist scholars since the 1970s have drawn attention to how patriarchy and assumptions about gender also form some of the central organising principles of criminal justice. Again, the argument is made that although such concepts as 'fairness' and 'equality before the law' imply a gender-neutral process, in reality the law is deeply imbued with gender- (and 'race'- and class-) specific assumptions about what constitutes 'acceptable behaviour'. In particular, concern has been raised about the ability of criminal justice to take seriously the issue of violence against women, such as rape and domestic abuse; the double jeopardy of being tried for legal infraction and 'inappropriate' gender roles; and the infantilising of women's deviance within a 'mad' or 'sad' dichotomy (Walklate, 2001). As a result, Frances Heidensohn (1986) has considered what an alternative 'female' or 'feminist' conception of justice might look like. Her analysis works through a comparison of two competing models of justice. The first she named Portia. This is based on values of rationality and individualism and stresses rights and due process. The second she named Persephone. This is based on values of care and the personal and stresses informality and reparation. Heidensohn contends that Portia is particularly unresponsive to the needs of women to the extent that it is driven by 'masculine' imperatives. Persephone, by contrast, at least envisages a system where male control of power and resources can begin to be challenged. Heidensohn, of course, recognises the dangers in simply welfarising justice for women and the difficulties of securing any women-centred model within an otherwise patriarchal system. But akin to the work of Griffiths (1970) discussed in Section 3.2 above, and the imagining of a family model of justice, it is indeed quite legitimate to seek recourse to justice through expressions of caring and without invoking criminal justice at all (Masters and Smith, 1998; and see further discussion in Chapter 3).

Further critical work has also exposed the routine differential and discriminatory treatment afforded to minority racial and ethnic groups in criminal justice systems. In particular, African American adult males in the USA constitute over half of all prison admissions, despite comprising under 7 per cent of the country's population. In 2008, one in every nine black men aged 20 to 34 was incarcerated. Loic Wacquant (2001) argues that such manifestly racialised carceral patterning reflects the means by which the penal system has replaced the ghetto as the locus for controlling and punishing black Americans. This is compounded by the ongoing 'war on drugs' that has been distorted in order to legitimise the explicit targeting and criminalisation of black communities. In this way, the ghetto and the prison intersect and mutually reinforce the confinement of a stigmatised population deemed to be socially, economically and politically superfluous. Research in the UK (e.g. Webster, 2007) has found that African Caribbean youth in particular are more likely to be stopped by the police and to be arrested. Once arrested, African Caribbean people are less likely to be cautioned than white people, and more likely to be prosecuted. African Caribbeans are more likely to be charged with indictable-only offences and to be remanded in custody, awaiting trial, rather than released on bail. If found guilty, they are then more likely to be given a custodial sentence and for longer periods than white defendants. Arguably, it is the accumulation of such factors – the 'multiplier effect' – that acts to discriminate against young black people. Certainly, although differential treatment clearly exists, it has not always proved easy to locate exactly where in the criminal justice process overt discrimination and institutionalised racism occurs (Bowling and Phillips, 2002). Yet, as Barbara Hudson (2006, p. 29) argues, it remains abundantly clear that the law in modern Western societies typically reflects the subjectivity of the 'dominant, white, affluent, adult male'. It is white man's law: designed to protect their specific interests by over-penalising those who transgress the 'norm' of white masculinity. The continual construction of racialised narratives of the 'negative other' serves to justify colonial histories and contemporary expressions of white superiority.

Activity 1.3

In what ways have critical criminologists (such as Reiman), critical race theorists (such as Wacquant) and some feminist criminologists (such as Heidensohn) argued that formal criminal justice processes are less a solution and more a part of the problem to be explained?

Comment

The structures and processes of criminal justice have been critiqued in a number of ways, including:

- Criminal justice and criminal law are class, 'race' and gender control strategies that are used to depoliticise political resistance and to control economically and politically marginalised neighbourhoods and groups.

- Moral panics about crime being out of control are used to deflect attention away from material disadvantage and structural inequalities.

- Orthodox crime control strategies are not designed to recognise the crimes of the powerful and state crimes.

- Legal categories that are claimed to be gender and 'race' neutral are riddled with white, male assumptions of what constitutes normal or acceptable behaviour.

- Crime control has now grown into a worldwide industry, controlled by public and private multinational interests. Inevitably, this industry is more committed to developing, than reducing, its core business (Christie, 2000).

5   Beyond the sovereign state

The twin concepts of *globalisation* and *transnationalisation* have gradually permeated criminology, but more in application to transnational crime and policing than in addressing what 'global justice' might look like or, indeed, whether such an ideal is at all achievable. Both concepts also escape easy definition and are often used in a loose and eclectic fashion. While 'globalisation' usually directs our attention to broad structural determinants of policy making, 'transnationalisation' is more concerned with processes of international cooperation. Both concepts also pose some thorny questions for the study of systems of crime control. Policy making in this area has traditionally been studied with regard to national sovereignty and the independence of the nation state. Indeed, at a time when global economic and social pressures appear to be disempowering the nation state, the particular justice systems of different countries remain one of the few means through which the power of sovereign statehood can be (re-)expressed (Muncie, 2005).

5.1 Transnational and global justice

Activity 1.4

What do you understand by the term 'transnational justice'? How do you think this might be realised?

Comment

The concept of transnational justice is relatively new, emerging particularly from philosophy, political science and the study of law. It is concerned primarily with the meaning and application of international law as was first made possible, for example, by the establishment of the United Nations (UN) and the Nuremberg International Military Tribunal in 1945. The United Nations Charter, which came into force in October 1945, sets out basic principles of international relations based on peace, security, respect for human rights and cooperation between nations in addressing international problems. The Universal Declaration of Human Rights (UDHR), adopted by the UN General Assembly in 1948, was the first statutory instrument of universal human rights, but although its principles remain persuasive, they do not carry with them any effective means of enforcement. The Nuremberg Tribunal, however, established new 'international offences' of crimes against peace, war crimes and crimes against humanity (**Green, 2010**).

The conventions and legislations mentioned above notwithstanding, it was not until some forty years later that the idea of 'transnational justice' began to emerge with any force in policy and academic circles. In traditional accounts, the rise in transnational organised crime – involving, for example, money laundering, drug trafficking, child pornography and human trafficking across national borders – prompted the need for consideration of transnational policing and law enforcement (see Chapter 6). In Europe, concern over a lack of coordination between law enforcement agencies eventually led to the creation of Europol, the European Police Office. The completion of the single market, which removed barriers from the movement of goods and people, has also been viewed as a key catalyst in the seeking of greater harmonisation between European Union countries. The collapse of communism between 1989 and 1991 allowed law enforcement agencies in the USA to focus more directly on such issues as the international drug market. As a result, by the early 1990s transnational crime (and subsequently international terrorism) had become a key security issue in both the USA and Europe, leading to demands for a greater convergence in the responses of individual nation states. Equally, the mass murders witnessed in the former Yugoslavia and in Rwanda in the early 1990s led to the establishment of criminal tribunals to deal with these specific war crimes. In 1998, a permanent International Criminal Court was established in The Hague (although not recognised by the USA), directing its attention particularly at crimes against humanity and promising the beginnings of a universal justice (see Chapter 7). Similarly, with the advent of computer crime, a number of countries are now enacting laws with extra-territorial effect. It is in these contexts that the idea of transnational justice has been made possible and is becoming more prevalent (Pakes, 2004; Reichel, 2005).

In some contrast to the reactive and often descriptive accounts of deliberate transnational cooperation, the concept of 'globalisation' sometimes implies (particularly in its 'strong' version) that uncontrollable economic forces have shifted power and authority away from communities and nations and towards 'external' transnational capital. Since the 1970s, sustained assaults on the social logics of the welfare state and public provision, particularly in the UK, the USA, Canada and Australasia, have brought profound shifts in economic, social and political relations associated with the 'free market'. The independence of the modern nation state has been called into question. It has been argued by theorists such as Beck (2000) that neo-liberal unregulated markets, capital mobility and international competitiveness have shifted power away from nation states and narrowed their choice of strategic criminal justice and social policy options. As a result, it is contended that routes to justice are converging (at least, across a so-called 'global North' of Western societies). A combination of macro socio-economic developments, initiatives in international law and accelerations in processes of policy flow and diffusion can be viewed as symptomatic of rapid convergence and homogenisation. Further, the necessity of attracting international capital compels non-Western governments to adopt similar economic, social and criminal justice policies in part aided by geopolitical mobility and subsequent policy transfer, diffusion and learning (Muncie, 2005).

The flow of criminal justice policy around the world has been considered a crucial indicator of the power of globalisation. Indeed, it does appear more and more common for nation states to look worldwide in efforts to discover 'what works' in preventing crime and to reduce reoffending (see further discussion in Chapter 4). This also suggests an emerging global justice. Much of this analysis relies on tracing the export of penal policies from the USA to other advanced industrial economies. Wacquant (1999), in particular, argues that a US-inspired neo-liberal ideology is translated into specific 'justice' projects and then exported to Europe largely through the conduit of the UK. Certainly, many versions of US criminal justice reform, such as zero-tolerance policing, curfews, electronic monitoring, mandatory sentencing and pre-trial detention as a 'short, sharp, shock', have surfaced in many European jurisdictions, either as rhetorical devices or as drivers of policy.

Such an argument is compelling. However, as Richard Sparks (2001, p. 165) has warned, there may be inherent difficulties in this type of comparative analysis because of the 'distracting sway of the American case as a pole of attraction'. Neither should we expect that policy transfer be direct, complete or exact. Rather, it is mediated through national and local cultures, which are themselves changing at the same time (Muncie, 2005). In addition, policy processes operate in ways that are specific to individual countries and the goals of particular policy makers and agendas. Further, policy can operate at various levels, including through its content, instruments, style or goals (Jones and Newburn, 2002). The logic of assuming that we can borrow 'what works' from others is certainly seductive. It implies rational planning and an uncontroversial reliance on a science of crime that is free of any political interference (see Chapter 4).

Economic globalism may speak of the import, largely US inspired, of neo-liberal conceptions of community responsibilisation backed by an authoritarian state. However, legal globalism, largely UN inspired, unveils a contrary vision of universal human rights delivered through social democracies (Muncie, 2005). Globalisation is not one-dimensional. It can simultaneously conjure up images of both the usurpation and the protection of human rights. As a result, the notion

Figure 1.6
Activists protest against
policies of the World
Bank, Washington, DC

of *global justice* remains in a process of development. It is far from clear what justice on a world scale might actually mean, what standards it might adopt and through what agencies (or particular nation states) it might be put into operation. It assumes the existence of some moral universalism that may act to override significant global cultural diversity and disguise histories of colonial oppression and economic under-development. In short, any conception of universal justice and human rights might be particularly Western-inspired and Western-informed notions. Nevertheless, the idea of global justice is becoming more imaginable not only through developments in transnational policing, international policy transfers, international criminal courts, UN conventions and treaties and global networks of policy dissemination, but also through 'anti-globalisation' campaigns and protests. But what future such global forces herald remains unclear. Certainly, they will have to work through the national and local contexts and contingencies which to date have defined systems of criminal justice. Understanding how this hybridity (of the local and the global) might activate multiple lines of invention, contradiction and contestation in how 'justice' is understood and realised is a key issue to be addressed in the following chapters of this book.

6   Conclusion

Interrogating criminal justice is a complex task. In this chapter justice has been discussed in relation to how it is delivered in criminal justice systems, how harm can arise as a result of criminal injustices and how understandings of justice differ in local, global and transnational contexts. The constitution of justice in general, and of criminal justice in particular, often depends on considerations of time and place – what is seen as just or unjust differs across historical and social contexts. It might also depend on differing standpoints of individuals or changing social sensibilities. In spite of attempts by nation states to conceive of the delivery of justice as a zero-sum exercise, the realities of achieving justice are rarely that straightforward. Criminal justice – in particular – needs to be considered within the system in which it is exercised and with full recognition of the power relations that govern that system. Similarly, the strategies that can be used in the pursuit of justice, such as surveillance, crime control, punishment and corrections, must each be considered alongside the power relations, political climates and cultural contexts that surround them.

References

American Friends Service Committee (1971) *Struggle for Justice: A Report on Crime and Punishment in America*, New York, Hill & Wang.

Amnesty International Australia (2008) *Sudan Should Arrest War Crimes Suspects Now*, 28 April [online], www.amnesty.org.au/news/comments/12441/ (Accessed 20 March 2009).

BBC News (2007) 'Mother's battle for daughter's justice', BBC News, 25 October [online], http://news.bbc.co.uk/1/hi/uk/7061929.stm (Accessed 20 March 2009).

Beccaria, C. (1963 [1764]) *On Crimes and Punishments*, New York, Bobbs-Merrill.

Beck, U. (2000) *What is Globalisation?*, Cambridge, Polity.

Bowling, B. and Phillips, C. (2002) *Racism, Crime and Justice*, London, Pearson.

Box, S. (1987) *Recession, Crime and Punishment*, Basingstoke, Macmillan.

Christie, N. (2000) *Crime Control as Industry*, London, Routledge.

Clarke, R.V.G. and Cornish, D.B. (eds) (1983) *Crime Control in Britain: A Review of Policy Research*, Albany, NJ, State University of New York Press.

Cohen, S. (1985) *Visions of Social Control: Crime, Punishment, and Classification*, Cambridge, Polity.

Cullen, F.T. and Gilbert, K.E. (1982) *Reaffirming Rehabilitation*, Cincinnati, OH, Anderson.

Foucault, M. (1977) *Discipline and Punish*, London, Allen Lane.

Gandy, O.H. (1993) *The Panoptic Sort: A Political Economy of Personal Information*, Boulder, CO, Westview.

Garland, D. (1985) *Punishment and Welfare: A History of Penal Strategies*, Aldershot, Gower.

Goldson, B. (2005) 'Taking liberties: policy and the punitive turn' in Hendrick, H. (ed.) *Child Welfare and Social Policy: An Essential Reader*, Bristol, The Policy Press.

Green, P. (2010) 'The state, terrorism and crimes against humanity' in Muncie, J. et al. (eds) (2010).

Griffiths, J. (1970) 'Ideology in criminal procedure or a third model of the criminal process', *Yale Law Journal*, vol. 79, no. 3, pp. 359–91.

Hay, D. (1975) 'Property, authority and criminal law' in Hay, D., Linebaugh, P., Rule, J.G., Thompson, E.P. and Winslow, C. (eds) *Albion's Fatal Tree: Crime and Society in Eighteenth Century England*, London, Allen Lane.

Heidensohn, F. (1986) 'Models of justice: Portia or Persephone? Some thoughts on equality, fairness and gender in the field of criminal justice', *International Journal of the Sociology of Law*, vol. 14, pp. 287–98.

Hudson, B. (1996) *Understanding Justice*, Buckingham, Open University Press.

Hudson, B. (2006) 'Beyond white man's justice: race, gender and justice in late modernity', *Theoretical Criminology*, vol. 10, no. 1, pp. 29–47.

Jones, T. and Newburn, T. (2002) 'Policy convergence and crime control in the USA and the UK', *Criminal Justice*, vol. 2, no. 2, pp. 173–203.

Kraska, P.B. (2004) *Theorizing Criminal Justice: Eight Essential Orientations*, Long Grove, IL, Waveland.

Lacey, N. (1988) *State Punishment: Political Principles and Community Values*, London, Routledge & Kegan Paul.

Martinson, R. (1974) 'What works? – questions and answers about prison reform', *The Public Interest*, no. 35, pp. 22–54.

Masters, G. and Smith, D. (1998) 'Portia and Persephone revisited: thinking about feeling in criminal justice', *Theoretical Criminology*, vol. 2, no. 1, pp. 5–27.

McBarnet, D. (1983) *Conviction: Law, the State and the Construction of Justice*, London, Macmillan.

McLaughlin, E., Muncie, J. and Hughes, G. (eds) (2003) *Criminological Perspectives* (2nd edn), London, Sage.

McMahon, M.W. (1992) *The Persistent Prison? Rethinking Decarceration and Penal Reform*, Toronto, University of Toronto Press.

Miller, W.B. (1973) 'Ideology and criminal justice policy: some current issues', *Journal of Criminal Law and Criminology*, vol. 64, no. 2 pp. 141–54.

Mooney, G. and Talbot, D. (2010) 'Global cities, segregation and transgression' in Muncie, J. et al. (eds) (2010).

Muncie, J. (2004) 'Contemporary criminology, crime and strategies of crime control' in Muncie, J. and Wilson, D. (eds) *The Student Handbook of Criminal Justice and Criminology*, London, Cavendish.

Muncie, J. (2005) 'The globalisation of crime control: the case of youth and juvenile justice', *Theoretical Criminology*, vol. 9, no. 1, pp. 35–64.

Muncie, J., Talbot, D. and Walters, R. (eds) (2010) *Crime: Local and Global*, Cullompton, Willan/Milton Keynes, The Open University.

Packer, H.L. (1964) 'Two models of the criminal process', *The University of Pennsylvania Law Review*, vol. 113, no. 1, pp. 1–23.

Packer, H.L. (1968) *The Limits of the Criminal Sanction*, Stanford, CA, Stanford University Press.

Pakes, F. (2004) *Comparative Criminal Justice*, Cullompton, Willan.

Parenti, C. (1999) *Lockdown America*, London, Verso.

Pratt, J., Brown, D., Brown, M., Hallsworth, S. and Morrison, W. (eds) (2005) *The New Punitiveness*, Cullompton, Willan.

Quinney, R. (1977) *Class, State and Crime: On the Theory and Practice of Criminal Justice*, New York, Longman.

Reichel, P. (ed.) (2005) *Handbook of Transnational Crime and Justice*, Thousand Oaks, CA, Sage.

Reiman, J. (2007) *The Rich Get Richer and the Poor Get Prison* (8th edn), Boston, MA, Pearson/Allyn & Bacon.

Roshier, R. (1989) *Controlling Crime*, Buckingham, Open University Press.

Ross, R., Fabiano, E. and Ewles, C. (1988) 'Reasoning and rehabilitation', *International Journal of Offender Therapy and Comparative Criminology*, vol. 32, no. 1, pp. 29–33.

Sigler, J. (1963) 'A history of double jeopardy', *American Journal of Legal History*, vol. 7, pp. 283–308.

Simon, J. (2001) 'Entitlement to cruelty: neo-liberalism and the punitive mentality in the United States' in Stenson, K. and Sullivan, R. (eds) *Crime, Risk and Justice*, Cullompton, Willan.

Sparks, R. (2001) 'Degrees of estrangement: the cultural theory of risk and comparative penology', *Theoretical Criminology*, vol. 5, no. 2, pp. 159–76.

Spierenburg, P.C. (1984) *The Spectacle of Suffering: Executions and the Evolution of Repression: From a Preindustrial Metropolis to the European Experience*, Cambridge, Cambridge University Press.

Tarling, R. (1993) *Analysing Offending: Data, Models and Interpretations*, London, HMSO.

Tombs, S. and Whyte, D. (2010) 'Crime, harm and corporate power' in Muncie, J. et al. (eds) (2010).

von Hirsch, A. (1976) *Doing Justice: The Choice of Punishments*, New York, Hill & Wang.

Wacquant, L. (1999) 'How penal common sense comes to Europeans: notes on the transatlantic diffusion of the neo-liberal doxa', *European Societies*, vol. 1, no. 3, pp. 319–52.

Wacquant, L. (2001) 'Deadly symbiosis: when ghetto and prison meet and mesh', *Punishment and Society*, vol. 3, no. 1, pp. 95–134.

Walklate, S. (2001) *Gender, Crime and Criminal Justice*, Cullompton, Willan.

Walters, R. (2010) 'Eco crime' in Muncie, J. et al. (eds) (2010).

Webster, C. (2007) *Understanding Race and Crime*, Maidenhead, Open University Press.

Wilson, J.Q. (1975) *Thinking about Crime*, New York, Vintage.

Zedner, L. (2004) *Criminal Justice*, Oxford, Oxford University Press.

Chapter 2
Punitiveness and cultures of control

Deborah Drake

Contents

1   Introduction

This chapter considers approaches to the delivery of justice which suggest that the answer to the problem of crime is to punish offenders with tough penalties. As Chapter 1 has illustrated, the notion of 'justice' and what it is needs to be carefully considered, taking into account, first, what is defined as crime; second, how existing power relations influence the concept of justice; and third, how forms of justice differ between countries and at particular points in history. When questions of justice arise in the contemporary media or in political debate, they often centre on what should be done with those defined as anti-social or 'dangerous', especially in the context of assuring and protecting the rights of victims.

From the mid 1980s in the USA and the mid 1990s in England and Wales and many European countries, there was a discernible trend towards harsher criminal justice policies, especially those that focused on incapacitation (discussed in Chapter 1) as the solution to crime. Examples of some of these policies include:

- increased use of imprisonment, including widening the range of crimes that result in a prison sentence and increasing the lengths of sentences that can be handed down by the courts

- mandatory prison sentences for particular crimes

- zero-tolerance strategies, which impose automatic penalties for first-time offenders

Figure 2.1
Overcrowded prison conditions, California

- three-strikes legislation, which imposes mandatory periods of imprisonment for persons convicted of a third serious or violent offence

- the use of capital punishment in some parts of the USA (the USA, Singapore and Japan are the only developed countries to continue its use).

It is taken for granted that harsh criminal justice policies are resorted to because of increasing levels of public disorder and anti-social behaviour, rising crime rates and a general deterioration of the 'moral framework' of society. However, as this chapter will show, the decision to implement an increasingly harsh approach to justice by many governments across the globe has no clear correspondence either to public demands or to increasing crime rates.

This chapter examines debates that account for the rise of punitiveness in some countries (but not others), in spite of declining crime rates. In Sections 2 and 3 the control of crime through tough policies is considered against the suggestion that a societal adaptation has occurred in response to the uncertainty and increasing insecurity of social life. The chapter questions, however, whether punitiveness and harsh justice approaches are necessary cultural adaptations or whether these trends can be explained in alternative ways when power relations and political decision making are more carefully considered. Section 4 returns to the issues raised throughout regarding punitiveness and crime control, and questions the logic of 'tough-on-crime' policies.

The aims of this chapter are to explore:

- definitions of punitiveness (new and populist)

- the link between crime trends and increasingly punitive measures

- whether the so-called 'punitive turn' is a feature of all Westernised countries

- whether the public are becoming more punitive, demanding harsher policies

- whether 'tough justice' works.

2 Punitiveness defined

The term 'punitive' can be defined, simply, as a concern with or the infliction of punishment. Responses to crime vary across geographical and cultural spaces. Similarly, the use of punishment and the crimes that are defined as punishable change along with cultural attitudes and sensibilities. Punishment within most justice contexts is often justified using four main rationales. First, punishment can be seen to be 'deserved'.

That is, those who contravene the social order (disobey the law) must atone for their actions and some measure of recompense for the harm they have caused must be 'paid back' to society or to the victims of their crime. In general terms, most criminal justice systems in developed countries are based on a retributive model and a variety of sanctions, including fines, community penalties, imprisonment and, in some jurisdictions, capital punishment. A second justification for the use of punishment is an instrumental one, arguing that the threat of punishment for certain crimes will deter future criminality. Wrongdoing is seen here as a rational choice and if the costs of crime outweigh the benefits, criminal conduct will be deterred. In addition, punishment through such means as imprisonment serves the instrumental purpose of incapacitation. That is, once a crime has been committed, further criminal activity can be curtailed if offenders are imprisoned. A third purpose of punishment is its symbolic function as a means of disapproval. Societal denouncement of certain acts can be symbolically communicated to offenders and to society at large through the use of punishment. Finally, perhaps the most controversial aspect of punishment is its rehabilitative potential. Most of the strategies used in criminal justice systems to promote rehabilitation are imposed on offenders, which means that they are compelled to participate in them. The transformative potential of rehabilitation within a punishment context is questionable. Nonetheless, rehabilitation has historically played a major role (at least in principle) in many criminal justice systems and can be seen as an aspect of punishment (as discussed in Chapter 1).

Outlining the justifications for the use of punishment provides a basis for examining trends in criminal justice policy. Justice policies that are more punitive in nature emphasise incapacitation, retribution, deterrence, denouncement and vengeance (Simon and Feeley, 1995; Simon and Jensen, 1996) and de-emphasise rehabilitation or reparation. That is, they identify vindictive punishment as the most appropriate response to crime and put little credence on solving problems of crime by addressing social inequalities or offender and victim needs. Punitive strategies for crime control have been used extensively in the USA and the UK, particularly since the 1980s. From the mid 1990s, punitiveness also appeared to be more prevalent in many countries across the globe. This trend has yielded some controversy because historical analyses have revealed that, until the 1970s, the use of punishment (imprisonment and the death penalty in particular) appeared to be receding, especially in the Western world. Loic Wacquant has noted that penal scholars in the early 1970s argued that the use of incarceration was in decline and saw 'imprisonment not merely as a stagnant institution but as a practice in irreversible if gradual decline, destined to occupy a secondary place in the diversifying arsenal of contemporary instruments of punishment' (Wacquant, 2005, p. 4).

However, the trend of declining imprisonment was abruptly reversed in the latter decades of the twentieth century when many countries began an era of increasing incarceration. Table 2.1 compares the prison populations of selected countries across the world and their rate of increase. Such statistics typically attempt a head count of penal populations at specific times and estimate rates of imprisonment relative to the size of a nation's overall population. Various caveats are usually made of such statistical records; for example, where similar names are given to institutions it should not automatically be assumed that they have the same function. Official descriptions may mask substantial differences in form, culture and purpose (Zedner, 1995). And as the *European Sourcebook of Crime and Criminal Justice Statistics* (Council of Europe, 2006, p. 21) acknowledges, 'the lack of uniform definitions of offences, of common measuring instruments and of common methodology makes comparisons between countries extremely hazardous'. Nevertheless, a remarkable diversity in recourse to imprisonment is a notable feature of any comparative penological research, as indicated in Table 2.1.

Table 2.1 Comparing world prison populations (selected countries)

Country	Total 2005/6	Rate per 100,000 population	Increase/ decrease in rate since 1990s
USA	2,186,230	738	+93
Russia	869,814	611	−74
South Africa	157,402	335	+15
Brazil	361,402	191	+86
England and Wales	79,861	148	+23
Scotland	7131	139	+19
Netherlands	21,013	128	+43
Australia	25,353	126	+31
China	1,548,498	118	+3
Canada	34,096	107	−8
Italy	61,721	104	+19
Germany	78,581	95	+5
France	52,009	85	−5
Northern Ireland	1466	84	−6
Sweden	7450	82	+22
Finland	3954	75	+20
Norway	3048	66	+11
Japan	79,055	62	+22

Source: adapted from Walmsley, 1999, 2006

From Table 2.1 it is evident that out of the eighteen legal jurisdictions represented, only four show a decrease in their rate of prison population since the 1990s and the majority show an increase of 10 per cent or more. Although there are vast variations between countries, there does appear to be something of a global trend towards increasing incarceration.

Activity 2.1

Consider the following questions:

- Is increasing punitiveness inevitable?

- Is punitiveness a response from governments to a public call for the increased use of punishment?

- What sorts of crimes do you think are being targeted when politicians state that they will be 'tough on crime'?

- Do you think the general public is made safer as a result of 'tough-on-crime' policies? Why or why not?

Comment

The questions posed above are meant to encourage critical thinking about punitive measures and the use of imprisonment and to challenge 'common-sense' or reactionary approaches to justice. Later sections of this chapter will present arguments that suggest that the move towards punitiveness is not inevitable. Further, it is important to recognise that harm and violence not only flow from criminal behaviour perpetrated by individuals, but can also be part of the state response to crime. The degrading and inhumane punishment inherent in some 'tough-on-crime' policies delivers harm in a way that might be seen to perpetuate a cycle of state-sanctioned violence. In addition, 'tough-on-crime' policies are directed mostly towards certain forms of crime, such as interpersonal or property crime. The fear of becoming the victim of some form of interpersonal crime is very real for segments of populations across various communities and societies and their circumstances must be taken seriously. However, the response to these types of crimes must also be carefully considered; as should responses to crimes such as corporate crimes or environmental harms, which have more diffuse and ambivalent consequences. While thinking about the use of punishment and punitive measures as you read subsequent sections of this chapter, consider the following quotation, which appeared in an article in *The Observer* newspaper on 18 June 2006:

> Almost 100 years ago, Winston Churchill, then Home Secretary, sought to define a civilised society by the way it treated its prisoners. He said in 1910: 'A calm and dispassionate recognition of the rights

of the accused against the state, and even of convicted criminals against the state ... these are the symbols which, in the treatment of crime and criminals, mark and measure the stored-up strength of a nation and are the sign and the proof of the living virtue in it'.

(Chesshyre, 2006, p. 28)

2.1 The 'new punitiveness'

Due to the increasing use of imprisonment and other criminal justice sanctions in many Westernised countries, some criminologists (e.g. Pratt et al., 2005) have suggested that an era of 'new punitiveness' has begun and that this trend is increasingly global in nature. As suggested above, this has been viewed by some as a leap backwards in the system and philosophy of how justice and punishment should be carried out (Wacquant, 2005).

Figure 2.2
The US leads the world in incarceration rates

John Pratt et al. (2005) provide a clear definition of the new punitiveness and argue that it is not simply reflected in trends towards mass incarceration, but also in the stretching of the former limits of punishment. The new punitiveness includes a breach of 'the principle that punishment should be proportionate to the harm caused' (Pratt et al., 2005, p. xii) and extends beyond the penal realm into civil detention, naming and shaming initiatives and increasingly austere prison regimes. Further, these authors juxtapose the 'new punitiveness' against its referent the 'old punitiveness'. Just as Wacquant (2005) argued in regard to the more recent evolution of punishment in the USA, Pratt et al. suggest that a tempering of punishment was demanded from European societies, beginning in the eighteenth and nineteenth centuries. They argue, using the work of Michel Foucault (1977), that within the penal sphere 'a sovereign form of power characterised by arbitrary, excessive, and destructive force gradually gave way to a form of disciplinary power that was fundamentally more productive in character' (Pratt et al., 2005, p. xii). In essence, Pratt et al. argue that European societies were becoming more restrained, civilised and measured in their use of punishment, but that those trends began to reverse in the latter decades of the twentieth century, hence marking the dawn of a 'new punitiveness'.

2.2 Global punitiveness

It has been suggested by many that the 'punitive turn' is not merely a national trend towards an increased use in more punitive measures, but a trend of global proportions (see, for example, Pratt et al., 2005; Andreas and Nadelmann, 2006). Estella Baker and Julian Roberts (2005) suggest that globalisation (defined here as the creation and proliferation of transnational and global relationships and their processes) is a main contributor to the international 'spread' of punitive policies. They argue that the process of spreading punitive policies occurs in three ways (Baker and Roberts, 2005):

1   through the homogenisation or harmonisation of problems and responses across a diversity of jurisdictions

2   by the acceleration of penal policy transfer across jurisdictions

3   through the promotion of short-term punitive policies at the expense of longer-term evidence-based policies.

They state further that pressures brought on by globalisation result in simplistic penal policies that have considerable mass appeal and great 'portability' from one jurisdiction to another. They argue that 'Globalisation forces work in a number of ways: directly, in terms of political initiatives resulting in statutory reforms; and indirectly, by fostering a climate conducive to the passage of particular policies' (Baker and Roberts, 2005, p. 132).

Transnational policy flows (discussed more fully in Chapters 1 and 3) refer to the importation of political ideas and policies from other countries. In criminal justice, the policy transfer example often cited is the exportation of US crime policies, such as zero-tolerance policing, three-strikes laws or mandatory sentencing, to other countries. Many commentators on crime policy suggest that policy transfer has had a significant influence on the spread of punitive measures in crime control. Trevor Jones and Tim Newburn, however, in their comparison of US and UK measures, suggest a difference in what they call 'hard' and 'soft' policy transfer and argue that 'the study of policy transfer in criminal justice indicates that rhetoric, labels, and nomenclature travel much more easily than the nuts and bolts of policy ... We have mandatory minimum sentences, and the use of "three strikes" labels, but not policies directly modelled on, say, the Californian experience' (Jones and Newburn, 2007, pp. 162–3). This suggests that a language of punitiveness has become more common in criminal justice crime control policy across legal jurisdictions, but that there is much variation in the policies implemented.

2.3 Populist punitiveness

When considering how the new trend of punitiveness emerged, it is important to ask whether it was in response to public pressure for harsher penalties or whether government policy began to dictate a more punitive response to crime control. There is some evidence to suggest that it was both.

The notion of 'populist punitiveness' was first identified by Anthony Bottoms (1995). The term, according to Bottoms (1995, p. 40), 'is intended to convey the notion of politicians tapping into, and using for their purposes, what they believe to be the public's generally punitive stance'. That is, governments hold the perception that the public want a harsh response to crime from the state and so they are simply attempting to meet this demand. Further, Neil Hutton (2003) has argued that politicians may opt for harsher punishments because they think this will reduce crime, build moral consensus and denounce criminal acts and populations; and/or to achieve greater popularity with electoral constituents. Populist punitiveness, then, appears to be firmly grounded in the assumption among politicians that the public are punitive. But what evidence is there for such an assumption? Are people across the world actually becoming more punitive?

The International Crime Victims Survey (ICVS) suggests that punitiveness towards offenders is not a global trend and that British and US cultures are more similar to each other than to many European countries. Michael Tonry has noted that in 1989, when respondents

Figure 2.3

A voracious call for punishment in Monty Python's *The Holy Grail* were asked about their preferred sentence for a young recidivist burglar, the highest percentages of respondents in favour of imprisonment were Americans (52.7 per cent), Northern Irish (45.4 per cent), Scottish (39 per cent), English and Welsh (38.2 per cent) (van Dijk et al. 1990, cited in Tonry, 2004). As Table 2.2 illustrates, eleven years later – in 2000 – these countries were still among the highest ranking in favour of imprisonment.

Table 2.2 Sentence preference for a young recidivist burglar (percentages): 2000 ICVS[1]

Country	Fine (%)	Prison (%)	Community service (%)	Suspended sentence (%)	Other sentence (%)	Don't know (%)	Average length of imprisonment (months)[2] (%)
USA	9	56	20	1	8	6	31
Northern Ireland	8	54	30	4	2	3	21
Scotland	11	52	24	5	4	4	21
Japan	17	51	19		1	13	38
England and Wales	7	51	28	5	4	5	24
Canada	9	45	32	4	7	3	23
Netherlands	11	37	30	10	5	6	19
Australia	8	36	46	3	3	4	27
Sweden	11	31	47	4	3	4	11
Portugal	9	26	54	1	6	4	23
Belgium	11	21	57	5	3	3	17
Poland	10	21	55	6	4	5	31
Denmark	9	20	50	13	4	4	7
Finland	15	19	46	16	2	2	8
France	8	12	69	5	2	5	14
Catalonia (Spain)	15	7	65	1	3	9	23
Average	11	34	41	6	4	5	34

[1] Countries are ranked based on the percentage in favour of 'sending to prison'.

[2] Asked if prison sentence was recommended.

Source: van Kesteren et al., 2000, p. 87, Table 19

Although the survey in Table 2.2 suggests that public attitudes in the UK have been more punitive than in other European countries, other research has suggested that asking different questions of UK respondents yields different results. For example, Mike Hough and Julian Roberts (1998), in their analysis of the British Crime Survey, found that, when the British public are sufficiently informed about the detail and circumstances of particular 'criminal events', they are not as punitive as the media and politicians often suggest. When members of the public are given greater contextual information about individual criminal cases, their opinions on sentencing are not inconsistent with those of the judiciary. Furthermore, the public are not well informed on the harshness of sentences that are actually handed down by British courts. Their perception is that the judiciary is much less harsh than it actually is. Perceptions of punitiveness, then, are difficult to measure accurately.

Moreover, public opinion research has generally found that levels of punitiveness among the general public have remained relatively stable over time (see Bondeson, 2005). However, it is also important to take into account other forms of evidence and other perspectives when considering public demands for harsher penalties and policy decisions on criminal justice. For example, there are a number of victims' movements and victims' rights advocates who have been varyingly vocal and influential in shaping public policy. As Carolyn Hoyle and Lucia Zedner have observed:

> Vocal, determined, or resourceful victims can and have had a profound effect on politics and policy-making ... The victim has been invoked as a potent rhetorical device or symbolic tool to lever up punitiveness ... Similarly the naming of criminal laws and penal measures after individual victims (for example, 'Megan's Law' in America and the (largely unsuccessful) campaign for 'Sarah's Law' in Britain) uses the plight of the victim to legitimate more extensive controls and new punitive measures.
>
> (Hoyle and Zedner, 2007, p. 473)

The difficulty in assessing the impact of victims' movements on crime control policy lies in determining whether more punitive measures are a political response to the plight of victims or whether, as suggested above, victims' rights have been employed as a convenient rationale for increasing state punitiveness towards particular types of offenders. Baker and Roberts (2005, p. 132) note that 'Victims' rights have generally been construed within a punitive rather than a restorative or non-punitive framework'. (Chapter 3 considers restorative approaches and the involvement of victims in criminal justice in greater detail.) The support of victims can be achieved through increasing services provided to them and by creating spaces within criminal justice processes for reparations to be agreed between victims and offenders. However, within a punitive approach to criminal justice, it seems the focus of victim reforms is often directed towards redressing the failure of the criminal justice system to meet victim needs by removing rights from offenders. As Baker and Roberts (2005, p. 132) have stated, 'This tendency results in a punitive zero-sum game in which victims benefit when offenders' procedural rights are curtailed'.

Activity 2.2

Crime is an emotive subject. Victims of crime or vicarious victims of crime (those who have knowledge of others who were victims of crime) respond to their circumstances in different ways, with some favouring harsh penalties and others a less punitive approach. What is common among victims of crime, however, is their desire not to become a victim again and for there to be no further victims. Consider the following questions and then read Extract 2.1:

■ Are there ways in which the needs of victims of crime can be more adequately met?

■ Does recognition of the rights of victims have to be at the expense of the rights of offenders?

Extract 2.1

Victims of crime reject notion of retribution

· Survey shows support for non-custodial sentences
· Majority back face-to-face meetings with offenders

Alan Travis

The notion that victims of crime are strong supporters of jail as the best approach to deterring petty criminals is challenged today with a poll showing that almost two-thirds believe that prison does not stop them reoffending.

...

The survey, commissioned by Victim Support and the think tank Smart Justice, shows that the overwhelming majority of crime victims believe that the best ways to curb non-violent crime are to provide more activities for young people, ensure they are better supervised by their parents, and provide more treatment for drug and mental health problems.

The ICM poll asked crime victims about the best ways of curbing non-violent crimes such as shoplifting, car theft and vandalism. It found that more than half of victims (53%) did not feel the criminal justice system takes account of their needs.

Peter Dunn, Victim Support's head of research, said: 'Victims are often assumed to be vengeful towards offenders and favour harsh punishments.

'This is misleading. Most victims, while feeling angry about what has happened to them, want the offender to stop offending both against them and against other people.'

...

Lucie Russell, of Smart Justice, said the poll was the first of crime victims, and it was clear they did not believe that prison produced law-abiding citizens: 'The survey proves that victims don't want retribution; they want a system that protects the next victim.'

The survey showed that 61% of crime victims did not believe that prison reduced reoffending for non-violent criminals. There was far more support for making offenders work in the community with 54% believing this would be more effective. A majority (51%) also favoured meetings between offenders and victims.

...

... ICM interviewed a random sample of 982 adult victims of crime between December 19 2005 and January 7 2006.

Source: *The Guardian*, 16 January 2006

Comment

In general, there has not been a trend of increasing support from the public for 'tough-on-crime' policies per se. Instead, there is support for crime policies that work to reduce individual reoffending. This, however, is a difficult, lengthy process that depends on a variety of individual, societal, economic and environmental factors. In short, there are no 'quick fixes' for crime or for helping people to move away from a criminal lifestyle.

3   Punitiveness explained?

As already suggested in this chapter, punitiveness has become a core element of party political rhetoric in many countries around the world. To illustrate the way in which this has occurred, consideration of the politics of law and order in the USA and the UK is useful.

The (re-)emergence of 'tough justice' policies began in the USA when Richard Nixon declared a 'war on drugs' in 1971, but they rose most rapidly during the Reagan–Bush administrations (1981–1992). Similarly, law and order politics came to the fore in the UK in the 1979 general election. Although crime rates and crime policy had been part of political agendas in the UK to some extent since the 1960s, prior to then the problem of crime was not seen as directly attributable to specific political policies. As a campaigning tactic leading up to the 1979 general election, the Conservatives argued that the Labour Government had undermined the rule of law and that its 'permissive' policies were the cause of rising crime rates. After Margaret Thatcher's election victory in 1979, the Conservatives implemented a variety of criminal justice policies and began to increase spending on law and order services (including police, courts and prisons) (Downes and Morgan, 2007). In spite of the 'tough-on-crime' rhetoric of the Conservatives, their policies did not deter a temporarily increasing rate of recorded crime, which doubled during the Thatcher administration (although this trend receded in the early 1990s). However, the Conservatives did firmly establish crime as an item for the political agenda and introduce a rhetoric that government policies (and leaders) that (and who) were 'soft on crime' were also without sufficient governmental authority. The move towards 'tough-on-crime' policies marked an important shift in party political sensibilities, priorities and electoral promises. As a result, David Garland (2001) has argued that a new 'culture of control' has emerged. This analysis provides one framework against which the rise in punitiveness might be explained.

3.1 Adapting to crime through a 'culture of control'

According to Garland (2001), crime has come to be viewed as a routine risk that has required a series of political and cultural adaptations. These adaptations have influenced how governments respond to, and how citizens think about, the problem of crime. Garland argues that there are seven conditions that form a 'cultural crime complex' (2001, p. 163) of attitudes, beliefs and assumptions:

1   High crime rates are regarded as a normal social fact.

2   Emotional investment in crime is widespread and intense, encompassing elements of fascination as well as fear, anger and resentment.

3   Crime issues are politicised and regularly represented in emotive terms.

4   Concerns about victims and public safety dominate public policy.

5   Criminal justice is viewed as inadequate or ineffective.

6   Private, defensive routines are widespread and there is a large market in private security.

7   A crime consciousness is institutionalised in the media, popular culture and the built environment.

In this analysis punitive policies are a response to a crisis of confidence in the effectiveness of criminal justice in many Westernised countries. The causes of public disaffection include: the perception that the system has failed to respond adequately to crime; a lack of faith in government; public distrust of 'expert knowledge'; and increased expectations about the performance and accountability of public services. In addition, according to Garland, the political landscape that simultaneously emerged was defined (particularly by Thatcher in the UK and Reagan in the USA) in opposition to the ideals of a welfare/rehabilitation model. It was the combination of such factors that created a climate in which a new punitiveness could emerge. Garland suggests that the notion of 'dangerous populations' is the central focus within cultures of control:

> ... effective crime control came to be viewed as a matter of imposing more controls, increasing disincentive, and if necessary, segregating the dangerous sector of the population. The recurrent image of the offender ceased to be that of the needy delinquent or the feckless misfit and became much more threatening – a matter of career criminals, crackheads, thugs, and predators – and at the same time much more racialised ... In the political reaction against the welfare state and late modernity, crime acted as a lens through which to view the poor – as undeserving, deviant, dangerous, different – and as a barrier to lingering sentiments of fellow feeling and compassion.
>
> (Garland, 2001, p. 102)

The crime complex, in Garland's view, is primarily a response – albeit fuelled by politics and the media – to the realities of a real crime problem. That is, the growing punitiveness and increase in the culture of control in the USA and the UK (and to a lesser degree, according to Garland, in Australia, New Zealand and Canada) are ultimately adaptive responses to increasingly fraught social conditions.

3.2 Punitiveness and responsibilisation

Another influential factor that has been identified as central to the move towards more punitive criminal justice measures is the focus on individual responsibility – an aspect of neo-liberalism. The 'punitive turn', in many nation states, seems to correlate with the de-emphasis on collectivism and welfarism. Neo-liberalism, as a political ideology, as Garland (1996) has noted, suggests that individuals and communities should be aware of social risks (including, for example, health, unemployment and crime) and should manage these with little state intervention (the role of risk in criminal justice is discussed more fully in Chapter 4). This process has been described as one of responsibilisation. The state, then, seeks indirect control by responsibilising individuals to participate in ensuring their own safety, economic security and well-being.

Figure 2.4
Central to neo-liberalism is the focus on individual and corporate competitive drive

Teresa Miller (2002, p. 223) has argued that 'The rhetoric of individuals taking personal responsibility for their own destinies in a land of tremendous opportunity was employed to supplant the notion that societal problems were the appropriate subject of governmental intervention'. Moreover, the interface between an increasing emphasis on personal responsibility for one's social standing, the avoidance of government responsibility for social conditions and the rhetoric that free enterprise provides equal opportunities created a context that increased the 'otherness' of certain populations (e.g. young people, the poor, immigrants, minority ethnic communities, offenders) and encouraged their denouncement.

Activity 2.3

Michael Cavadino and James Dignan (2006) have argued that there is a link between different political economies and specific penal policies. Table 2.3 outlines their typology of 'regime types' and 'socio-economic and penal indices'. Cavadino and Dignan outline a number of socio-economic factors that seem to correlate with indices of punitiveness. Why do you think this might be the case?

Comment

In reflecting on this question, consider the following (Cavadino and Dignan, 2006):

■ There is little, or at least a very weak, relationship between crime rates and rates of imprisonment.

■ Countries with high welfare spending as a proportion of gross domestic product (GDP) tend to have relatively lower imprisonment rates (Downes and Hansen, 2006).

■ The greater the levels of inequality in a society, the higher the overall levels of punishment (Wilkins and Pease, 1987; Beckett and Western, 2001).

In summary, according to the authors of the typology, there is a general association between neo-liberal regimes, income inequality and punishment. This suggests that the problem of crime has far more complex origins than the simple suggestion that some people are more prone than others to cause public disorder or behave anti-socially, or that there has been a general deterioration in the 'moral framework' of society. Indeed, the deterioration that does seem to have occurred in high punishment countries appears to be more in the context of citizen–state relations, especially in regard to universal social and human rights (see further in Chapter 7).

Table 2.3 Typology of political economies and their penal tendencies

Socio-economic and penal indices	Regime types			
	Neo-liberalism	Conservative corporatism	Social democratic corporatism	Oriental corporatism
Economic and social policy organisation	Free market; minimalist or residual welfare state	Status-related, moderately generous welfare state	Universalistic, generous welfare state	Private-sector-based 'welfare corporatism'; bureaucratic, paternalistic
Income differentials	Extreme	Pronounced but not extreme	Relatively limited	Very limited
Status differentials	Formally egalitarian	Moderately hierarchical, based on traditional occupational rankings	Broadly egalitarian; only limited occupational status differentials	Markedly hierarchical, based on traditional patriarchal ranking
Citizen–state relations	Individualised, atomised; limited social rights	Conditional and moderate social rights	Relatively unconditional and generous social rights	Quasi-feudal corporatism; strong sense of duty
Social inclusivity/ exclusivity	Pronounced tendency towards social exclusion, ghetto formation, etc.	Some exclusion in form of limited participation in civil society for some	Very limited tendency towards 'social exclusion'	Alienation of 'outsiders', but otherwise little social exclusion
Political orientation	Right-wing	Centrist	Left-wing	Centre-right
Dominant penal ideology	Law and order	Rehabilitation/ resocialisation	Rights-based	Apology-based restoration and rehabilitation
Mode of punishment	Exclusionary	Mixed	Inclusionary	Inclusionary
Imprisonment rate	High	Medium	Low	Low
Receptiveness to prison privatisation	High	Moderate	Low	Low
Archetypal examples	United States	Germany	Sweden	Japan
Other examples	England and Wales, Australia, New Zealand, South Africa	France, Italy, the Netherlands	Finland	

Source: Cavadino and Dignan, 2006, p. 441, Table 1

The issue of responsibilisation and children, for example, has led to shifting perceptions of young people in many Western societies, with an increasing tendency to view 'disorderly youth' as both troublesome and dangerous (Piper, 2008). This is reflected not only in media stories about young people, but also in policy documents – from various state agencies. In the UK, for example, the *Youth Matters* Green Paper, a purportedly welfare/support-based consultation paper produced by the then Department for Education and Skills (DfES), reflects a language that suggests that children must be held accountable for their actions. The paper states: 'It is wrong that young people who do not respect the opportunities they are given, by committing crimes or behaving anti-socially, should benefit from the same opportunities as the law-abiding majority. So we will put appropriate measures in place to ensure they do not' (DfES, 2005, p. 1).

As Christine Piper argues:

> The 'worthy' child, then, is one who is sufficiently responsible to be seen as worthy of investment, is sufficiently dependent and innocent to garner support and becomes the focus of investment for the future in a risk-based society ... Children can no longer be counted as children unless they behave responsibly like adults!
>
> (Piper, 2008, p. 51)

Likewise, the marginalisation and 'othering' of minority racial groups in the USA reveals a similar story of exclusion and derision. This has been especially apparent since that country's 'wars' on drugs and on crime were declared. In 2008, almost 500,000 people were incarcerated for drugs offences, compared to about 40,000 people in 1980 before the 'war on drugs' was launched. Over half the population in prison for drug-related crimes in the USA is black. Wacquant (2005) has noted that, in 1995, male black prisoners made up a majority of prison entry cohorts (55 per cent), even though black men at that time made up only 7 per cent of the adult population. Similarly, Jonathan Simon (2007, p. 142) has argued that many of the factors that contribute to people being sent to 'prison are targeted at circumstances highly correlated with race'. The examples Simon provides include harsher penalties for those who are in possession of or use crack cocaine (as opposed to the penalties for those who are found with powder cocaine) and federal laws that prevent felons from possessing guns. Simon argues that both of these legal decisions target impoverished populations, higher numbers of whom are African American. Crack cocaine is a less expensive alternative to powder cocaine and gun possession is more likely to be seen as a necessary aspect of self-defence in many deprived African American communities. Wacquant (2005) has called the trend towards increasing numbers of black people and other minority racial groups in prisons 'the colour of punitiveness'. This trend is not peculiar to the USA, although that country is perhaps the starkest example of racialised consequences in criminal justice. An over-representation in prison of black people and people from minority ethnic backgrounds is also found in the UK, while both Australia and Canada also incarcerate disproportionate numbers of their indigenous peoples.

4   Interrogating the rationale behind the 'punitive turn'

This chapter has illustrated that 'tough-on-crime' policies have been implemented in a number of countries despite the fact that the efficacy of such policies is unproven. The most persuasive evidence of their inadequacy is found in consideration of the link between crime rates and imprisonment rates. For example, in the UK the majority of 'tough-on-crime' policies, such as the increased use of imprisonment, were introduced during a time when recorded crime rates were generally declining. Further, there is little evidence to suggest that harsher penalties have any impact on crime rates. The Council of Europe has also long concluded that there is no relation between crime and prison rates: 'High overall crime rates do not necessarily induce high prison rates and vice versa' (Council of Europe, 2003, p. 193). The rationale behind 'tough justice', then, is not as straightforward as it would seem, especially as crime rates have been falling steadily in most Westernised countries since the mid 1990s (Tonry, 2003b).

In order to illustrate the disparities between crime rates and imprisonment rates it is useful to consider an example from two contrasting states – Texas and California – in the USA. Extract 2.2 is from a policy analysis document produced by Mike Males, Christina Stahlkopf and Daniel Macallair (2007) of the Centre on Juvenile and Criminal Justice.

Extract 2.2

Crime rates and youth incarceration in Texas and California compared: public safety or public waste?

Texas and California, the nation's two most populous states, are home to 22% of America's youth. ... From 1995 to 2006, Texas increased the number of youth that were incarcerated under the age of 18 by 48%. This was done through harsh sentencing practices that targeted non-violent, property and drug offenders. In contrast, during the same period, California drastically reduced the total number of juveniles incarcerated in youth prisons by 75% – an unprecedented decline – by imprisoning only the most violent offenders (**Table 1 and Table 2**). As a result, Texas, which has 1.8 million fewer juvenile than California, now imprisons substantially more youth than California. ...

...

The contrasting youth imprisonment practices in Texas and California are striking. ... In 1995, the youth incarceration rate in California was 2.2 times higher than in Texas. However, by 2006, the situation was reversed, and [Texas's] juvenile incarceration rate was 2.6 times higher than in California (**Table 1**).

...

TABLE 1: Youth Incarceration, Texas vs. California (1995–2006).

| | Average Daily Population Incarcerated | | | | | |
| | Rate/100,000 | | Total Imprisoned | | Population [in millions] | |
Year	California	Texas	California	Texas	California	Texas
1995	263.5	118.5	9,674	2,823	3,671.7	2,381.8
1996	261.2	141.4	9,772	3,467	3,741.8	2,452.5
1997	226.1	182.0	8,655	4,561	3,828.3	2,505.8
1998	205.2	206.7	7,991	5,267	3,894.9	2,548.3
1999	190.7	213.9	7,556	5,524	3,962.0	2,582.7
2000	179.7	216.5	7,303	5,646	4,065.0	2,607.9
2001	160.6	207.3	6,727	5,524	4,188.1	2,665.0
2002	138.5	190.8	5,954	5,170	4,299.7	2,710.2
2003	114.3	176.8	5,024	4,825	4,394.2	2,728.6
2004	91.4	178.1	4,067	4,883	4,450.6	2,742.3
2005	74.5	179.1	3,348	4,875	4,493.4	2,721.5
2006	65.7	175.7	2,962	4,800	4,505.8	2,732.5
2005 v 1995	−75%	+48%	−69%	+70%		

...

When evaluating current trends in both states with data from a decade ago, these patterns persist. In Texas today, the profile of incarcerated youth has evolved from violent offenders who were generally male in 1995 to young girls arrested for property or drug offenses (**Table 2**). In comparison, the profile of those juveniles imprisoned in California during the decade studied has changed little, except for the fact that there has been a sharp decline in the number of youths jailed for property and drug offenses.

TABLE 2: Trends in Percentages of Incarcerated Youth Offenders.

Characteristics:	State	1995	2005	Change
Percentage of Youth Incarcerated For:				
Murder	California	5.0%	4.0%	–20%
	Texas	5.0%	1.0%	–80%
Violent crime	California	65.0%	63.8%	–2%
	Texas	32.0%	27.0%	–16%
Property crime	California	23.0%	18.0%	–22%
	Texas	35.0%	39.0%	+11%
Drug offenses	California	6.3%	3.0%	–52%
	Texas	9.0%	11.0%	+22%

...

The starkly different youth incarceration policies of Texas and California offer a rare opportunity to test theoretical assertions that tougher sentencing policies and higher incarceration reduces crime. Texas's youth sentencing policies over the past ten years emphasized increased imprisonment for younger offenders for less serious crimes. In contrast, California increased the overall age of young offenders committed to youth correctional facilities and diverted many juveniles who formerly would have been imprisoned. Under incapacitation theory, the significantly higher rates of youth incarceration in Texas should have produced an accelerated decrease in the crime rate relative to California. However, this study has clearly shown that no such differential effect occurred in the crime rates of the two states. This result suggests that juvenile crime control policies that emphasize incarceration and similar punitive measures need to be reconsidered, and that Texas's current youth incarceration policy is unjustified and unnecessary.

Source: Males et al., 2007

The cases of California and Texas provide a within-country example of how differing sentencing policies have a clear impact on imprisonment rates, but little impact on crime rates. This trend is also observable on a national level. Comparisons of crime rates and imprisonment rates in the USA and the UK over time reveal similar results. In the UK, for example, the number of prisoners was relatively stable during the 1980s and early 1990s, in spite of rising crime rates. The number of sentenced prisoners grew by 77 per cent between 1993 and 2003, just when the crime rate began to drop (Tonry, 2003b). Similarly, the USA overall has experienced a massive increase in its prison population (which has quadrupled since 1980), whereas crime, especially violent and property crime, has declined steadily since the early 1990s. As Tonry (2003b, p. 3) has noted, 'We know that crime rates have been falling in every Western country since the mid-1990s, irrespective of whether imprisonment rates have risen, fallen or held steady'.

4.1 Challenges to cultures of control and public punitiveness

Despite the evidence that there is an apparent increase in punitive crime control measures in several countries across the world, it is important to question the universality of the concepts of 'punitiveness' and 'culture of control'. If the new punitiveness is, in part, a response to the particular insecurities of an increasingly global and insecure society, why are there notable exceptions to the rise in punitiveness in some Westernised countries? In Canada and France, for example, imprisonment rates have been declining, while in several other countries increases have been only moderate. The move towards more punitive measures need not be understood as an inevitable response to the insecurities of social life, nor should it be seen as a sustainable response.

The costs of imprisonment are high and many countries that have chosen a punitive response to crime have begun to face serious economic and social consequences. According to the Centre for Crime and Justice Studies at King's College London, the annual cost per prisoner in the UK in 2008 was £37,500. Further, this research found that when considering the impact on families and wider society, the estimated annual cost of imprisonment for an individual rises by almost a third, to nearly £50,000 (see Solomon, 2008). Similarly, in the USA, state spending on prisons has risen as rapidly as the prison population: to $45 billion a year as of 2008 (Justice Reinvestment, 2008). The high cost of imprisonment means that other social institutions, such as health care and education, are subject to retrenchment and lower levels of government spending. As a result of the economic costs of imprisonment, coupled with the recognition that increasing imprisonment rates do not correlate with decreasing crime rates, many states have once more sought community-based and restorative alternatives to imprisonment, which hold a greater promise of individual rehabilitation and social inclusion (as well as being fiscally attractive) (see Chapter 3).

4.2 Moderated crime control

Increasing punitiveness is not an inevitable response to crime. Part of Garland's thesis suggests that criminal justice policy is a choice, which therefore implies that it could be otherwise (Hudson, 2004).

Anthony Doob and Cheryl Webster (2006) have shown that the Canadian imprisonment rate, which has remained relatively stable, is evidence that increasing punitiveness is not a global phenomenon, nor even a necessary characteristic of Westernised societies. In that country, the ruling political leaders rarely make crime issues a central part of the political platform. That is not to say that Canada has been exempt from 'tough-on-crime' policies or that there has not been any move to enact more stringent legal sanctions. Indeed, Doob and Webster (2006, p. 332) have argued that Canadian punitiveness is characterised by 'talking tough, but acting softly'. They suggest that many of the policies that have been introduced in other countries, which appear to have led to increased levels of imprisonment, have also been passed in Canada. For example, Canada has introduced mandatory minimum sentences, maximum sanctions for some offences and reductions in parole eligibility. However, according to Doob and Webster, enacting a few harsher policies and practices has not led inevitably to an increasingly punitive trend. That is, there have not been any real consequences to Canada's imprisonment rate as a result of policies that sound harsh. The authors further state that:

> While Canada has obviously not been immune to the broader forces that compel other nations toward harsher responses to crime, it has been largely able to restrict or contain their impact. Indeed, the 'Canadian case' – when contrasted with those of the United States and England – appears to suggest that nations are not powerless in the face of these pressures.
>
> (Doob and Webster, 2006, p. 337)

Jeffery Meyer and Pat O'Malley (cited in Doob and Webster, 2006) suggest that the role of government in Canada has been to set a tone of quiet acceptance that a balanced approach to crime is preferable. There is an official culture of moderation in Canada. As illustration, they quote the federal ministry responsible for penitentiaries:

> Most Canadians feel safe in their communities. Conveying these findings to the public is important to counter-balance media portrayals of crime as a pervasive problem. Compared to other issues, the majority of Canadians do not view crime as a priority issue for the government. This information is helpful in ensuring that the government's response to the crime problem is kept in perspective.
>
> (Public Safety and Emergency Preparedness Canada, quoted in Doob and Webster, 2006, p. 341)

The Canadian example represents a more measured approach on the part of politicians and in the practices of the judiciary. The scepticism over the use of imprisonment in Canada reflects cultural views on restraint in the use of punishment and the practice of officials to moderate between emotional responses to crime and a measured approach to justice.

Canada is not the only Westernised country in which a more considered approach to punishment has been evident. James Whitman (2003) has studied the contrasts between American and continental European societies in their approaches to punishment. He focused on the differing political and social histories of the USA, Germany and France. Whitman has argued that at the time of American independence (1776), punishment in continental Europe differed and was based on social status. More restrained forms of punishment were reserved for the elite, whereas lower-status persons were subject to more brutal forms of punishment. Whitman argues that:

> Forms of execution are the most familiar example: nobles were traditionally beheaded; commoners were traditionally hanged [a more degrading form of execution]. There were many other examples, too: low-status offenders were routinely mutilated, branded, flogged, and subjected to forced labour ... High-status offenders were generally spared such treatment. Forms of imprisonment differed by status as well.
>
> (Whitman, 2003, p. 9)

Whitman has suggested that over the last two centuries, in both Germany and France (and many other countries in Europe), high-status punishments have slowly driven out the low-status punishments. Degradation in punishment was eliminated as Europeans gradually came to see historically low-status punishments as unacceptable remnants of the 'inegalitarian status-order of the past'. They have 'levelled up' their treatment of offenders to raise the status of all social members to more measured forms of punishment. However, the history of social status in the USA has been quite different from that of Europe. American society in the nineteenth century strongly opposed a two-tiered system of punishment or any differentiation in treatment of high-status offenders. Instead, the USA has shown a gradual tendency to generalise low-status punishments and in, Whitman's words, to 'level down' its treatment of offenders (Whitman, 2003, p. 11). That is, the tradition of seeing prisoners as deserving low-status punishments never ended in the USA and, according to Whitman, this cultural sensibility continues to drive a system of profound harshness.

A further example of moderation in crime control is illustrated by what John Pratt (2008a, 2008b) has called 'Scandinavian exceptionalism'. Pratt suggests that in countries where there is a commitment to individual over collective interests and where welfare provision is in decline, there is also a decline in trust in government and an increase in punitive attitudes. Conversely, Pratt's study of three Scandinavian countries (Finland, Norway and Sweden) suggests that declines in social solidarity and security coincide with a growing mood of punitiveness. He considers the case of Sweden in contrast to Finland and Norway and notes that cuts made to Sweden's welfare provision in the late 1980s, coupled with recession in the early 1990s, resulted in an important shift in Swedish sensibilities. Pratt is careful, however, not to overstate this shift in Sweden and argues that Sweden still retains its cultural commitment to citizenship and social rights, albeit in a welfare system that has been downsized (Pratt, 2008b). It is notable, however, that a new penal language is evident in Sweden, as in many other European countries, which calls for tougher prisons and harsher sentences. This is in stark contrast to Sweden's previously measured approach to imprisonment and its traditional commitment to humane prison conditions (see Pratt, 2008b). However, Sweden, along with Finland and Norway, continues to have comparatively low imprisonment rates and remarkably humane prison conditions – especially in comparison to many other Westernised countries. According to Pratt, prison administrators in Scandinavian countries recognise that people go to prison as, and not for, punishment. Prison is seen as a loss of liberty only and prison conditions approximate life outside as closely as possible. For example, all prisons are state run (there has been no privatisation); prisoners have direct input into prison governance; core services, such as health care, are provided to prisoners in the community; conjugal visits are encouraged and facilitated; and most prisoners either work or receive full-time education (Pratt, 2008a). The explanation that Pratt provides for Scandinavian exceptionalism is that the presence and combination of four characteristics of Scandinavian society act as protective barriers to punitiveness. These characteristics include:

- strong state bureaucracies that have significant independence from political interference

- a controlled mass media

- high levels of social capital (community cooperation)

- expert power and influence over social matters.

That is not to say that these characteristics are guarantees for preventing a 'punitive turn'. As the examples of Canada and Scandinavia noted above suggest, there can be a number of means by which nation states have been able to avoid the growing trend of punitiveness. Furthermore, it remains to be seen whether moderation in crime control will endure in each of these countries or whether a punitive trend has yet to permeate their borders.

Thus far, this chapter has focused entirely on punitive responses to the 'crimes of everyday life': the crimes that are most visible to individuals and most frequently reported on by the media. However, in questioning the 'spread' of punitiveness, it is also important to consider other types of crimes and other manifestations of social harm.

Activity 2.4

Read Extract 2.3 and consider the following questions as you do so:

■ Do 'tough-on-crime' policies extend to all types of crime or are there crimes that are exempt from punitive responses?

■ Are 'the powerful' differentially treated in criminal justice systems?

■ Why are serious harms, such as corporate crime, environmental crime or genocide, often absent from media or statistical accounts of the crime problem?

Extract 2.3

Corporate crime is 'ignored'

VICTIMS of corporate crime – such as the Maxwell pensions scandal and the BCCI collapse – are largely overlooked by officials because they do not fit Government targets, it was claimed today. The effects of large-scale white-collar crime can often be more devastating than those of robbery or physical assault, but remain "hidden and ignored", said a think-tank report.

The Centre for Crime and Justice Studies (CCJS) suggested there was also little incentive for the Government to document the true scale of corporate fraud because it would lead to an apparent rise in crime rates. "This large area of social injustice therefore remains hidden and is largely bypassed by government," said the report by the University of Birmingham's Dr Basia Spalek. "Financial abuses impact upon victims in multiple ways, producing emotional, psychological, behavioural, physical and financial reactions that can be severe and long-lasting," it said.

Government-backed support for victims of crime is mainly focused on robbery, burglary and some forms of violent crime, the study pointed out. "Individuals experiencing financial crimes and abuses have largely been overlooked," it added.

"The British Crime Survey excludes fraud as well as other types of white-collar deviance, so the extent and impact of white collar offences remains largely undocumented and ignored

by policy-makers. There is little political incentive to document the costs and impacts of white collar crime because this would mean an increase in the overall level of victimisation recorded in the UK."

One victim of the BCCI scandal told the research project, "Street crime can involve you being physically assaulted but with white-collar crime you are physically and mentally assaulted." CCJS director Richard Garside said, "If the real scale of cost and impact of white-collar crime on its victims was properly documented it would raise big questions about the willingness and ability of the state to protect the population from serious harms. As it is, a significant source of social injustice remains hidden and unaddressed by government."

The collapse of Luxembourg-based bank BCCI in 1991 led to thousands losing their savings, while the theft of hundreds of millions of pounds from the Mirror pension funds by Robert Maxwell left 30,000 pensioners with an uncertain financial future. Criminologist Dr Spalek said that the idea that consumers and employees could protect themselves from corporate fraud is misleading. "Policy discussion should be focused on the long-term impact of financial harm and the appropriate regulatory responses, rather than the constant obsession with the slackening of consumer rights and company responsibilities."

Source: *Western Mail*, Aug 20 2007

Comment

Extract 2.3 highlights a common inconsistency within countries that have taken a strong law-and-order stance against crime, namely that 'tough-on-crime' policies do not extend to corporate law breaking. That is not to suggest that punitive strategies would necessarily be a helpful means of overcoming the harms caused by the powerful. However, the inconsistency in criminal justice systems that use the full force of the law when harm is caused by individuals and take a less punitive stance when it is caused (often on a much larger scale with many more victims) by corporations calls into question, as this article suggests, the willingness and the ability of the state to protect the population from the large-scale harms often associated with corporate crime.

The recognition that a lack of punitiveness exists in response to crimes of the powerful calls into question the level of analysis that many criminologists take when considering the problem of crime. Wayne Morrison (2005) argues that criminology needs to think beyond the context of the nation state and to draw a distinction between domestic space, local space and the chaotic space of the international. He suggests that confining criminological thinking to local or civil problems creates a space where people see the measures of social control taken by the powerful as reasonable and necessary responses.

Figure 2.5
The interests of the powerful and wealthy favoured over those of the less powerful and the poor

In terms of the international arena, Morrison draws particularly on the examples of war crimes and genocide to illustrate that punishments in response to these atrocities are sometimes entirely absent or, at the very least, are meted out in moderation or for symbolic purposes. He argues that, in the context of global crimes or those that are of the most significant and damaging proportions, there has been a strikingly non-punitive response. He states that: 'In the twentieth century mass rape, torture, killing on a scale unimaginable in earlier centuries were tolerated and went unpunished' (Morrison, 2005, p. 305).

Morrison's arguments represent a level of analysis that requires a different vantage point from which to consider the problems of crime and criminal justice. How should justice be served when large-scale atrocities are perpetrated during acts of war and are state sanctioned? Why are the same levels of moderation that allow state or war crimes to be seen as 'products of the system' not also extended to many forms of street crime, which can be seen as products of a failing social system (Morrison, 2005)?

5   Conclusion

In spite of the drive in some countries towards more punitive measures and a political culture of control, there is little evidence to suggest that harsh punishments or 'tough-on-crime' policies have the desired effect on crime rates or on criminal behaviour. Other forms of justice (see Chapters 3 and 7) may be more effective and yet punitive measures persist in many countries as the main response to certain types of crime. The costs of punitive responses to crime, however, should be carefully considered. The prison systems in the UK and the USA rose to near bursting point in the early years of the twenty-first century. The economic costs of harsh penalties result in less governmental funding available for other social institutions, such as education (secondary and post-secondary) or health care. In addition, the human costs of harsh penalties are considerable. Prisoners, ex-prisoners and prisoners' families endure the collateral consequences of harsh justice approaches without much apparent benefit. In many cases ex-prisoners return to the same social circumstances from which they came prior to committing their offence and they often experience additional hardships as a result of coming into contact with the criminal justice system, including disenfranchisement (in many US states), a criminal record, unemployment, homelessness and social stigma. The common-sense notion that being 'tough on crime' sends a message to would-be offenders and shows that the government is 'doing something' about crime is not borne out in practice. Harsh penalties appear to be neither necessary nor effective in preventing crime and in fact may, in many ways, worsen social relations by misdirecting attention away from other – potentially more serious – social harms and by failing to address the social problems that are often associated with interpersonal crimes and harms.

This chapter has drawn together differing local, international and global perspectives on punitiveness and its presence (and absence) in various crime control policies. It has shown that responses to crime vary across geographical and political spaces. Juxtaposed against the punitive approach, the chapter has noted examples of justice systems in which a more moderated approach to punishment has persisted and certain forms of crime (such as corporate crime and genocide) have been exempt from a punitive response. By considering contrasting examples, it is possible to critically evaluate punitive approaches to crime and to question both their inevitability and their effectiveness.

References

Andreas, P. and Nadelmann, E. (2006) *Policing the Globe: Criminalization and Crime Control in International Relations*, Oxford, Oxford University Press.

Baker, E. and Roberts, J.V. (2005) 'Globalization and the new punitiveness' in Pratt, J. et al. (eds) (2005).

Beckett, K. and Western, B. (2001) 'Governing social marginality: welfare, incarceration, and the transformation of state policy', *Punishment and Society*, vol. 3, no. 1, pp. 43–59.

Bondeson, U. (2005) 'Levels of punitiveness in Scandinavia: Description and explanation' in Pratt, J. et al. (eds) (2005).

Bottoms, A. (1995) 'The philosophy and politics of punishment and sentencing' in Clarkson, C.M.V. and Morgan, R. (eds) *The Politics of Sentencing Reform*, Oxford, Oxford University Press.

Cavadino, M. and Dignan, J. (2006) 'Penal policy and political economy', *Criminology and Criminal Justice*, vol. 6, no. 4, pp. 435–56.

Chesshyre, R. (2006) 'This mad rush to lock people up: the furore about sentencing overlooks the grim reality of the British penal system today', *The Observer, Comment*, 18 June, p. 28.

Council of Europe (2003) *European Sourcebook of Crime and Criminal Justice Statistics* (2nd edn), The Hague, Wetenschappelijk Onderzoek-en Documentatiecentrum.

Council of Europe (2006) *European Sourcebook of Crime and Criminal Justice Statistics* (3rd edn), The Hague, Wetenschappelijk Onderzoek-en Documentatiecentrum.

Department for Education and Skills (DfES) (2005) 'Foreword' in *Youth Matters*, Green Paper, Norwich, HMSO; also available online at http://publications.dcsf.gov.uk/eOrderingDownload/Cm6629.pdf (Accessed 20 March 2009).

Doob, A.N. and Webster, C.M. (2006) 'Countering punitiveness: understanding stability in Canada's imprisonment rate', *Law and Society Review*, vol. 40, no. 2, pp. 325–67.

Downes, D. and Hansen, K. (2006) 'Welfare and punishment: the relationship between welfare spending and imprisonment', *Briefing No. 2*, London, Crime and Society Foundation.

Downes, D. and Morgan, R. (2007) 'No turning back: the politics of law and order into the millennium' in Maguire, M. et al. (eds) (2007).

Foucault, M. (1977) *Discipline and Punish*, London, Allen Lane.

Garland, D. (1996) 'The limits of the sovereign state: strategies of crime control in contemporary society', *British Journal of Criminology*, vol. 36, no. 4, pp. 445–71.

Garland, D. (2001) *The Culture of Control: Crime and Social Order in Contemporary Society*, Oxford, Oxford University Press.

Hough, M. and Roberts, J.V. (1998) *Attitudes to Punishment: Findings from the 1996 British Crime Survey*, Home Office Research Study No. 179, London, Home Office.

Hoyle, C. and Zedner, L. (2007) 'Victims, victimization, and criminal justice' in Maguire, M. et al. (eds) (2007).

Hudson, B. (2004) 'The culture of control: choosing the future', *Critical Review of International Social and Political Philosophy*, vol. 7, no. 2, pp. 49–75.

Hutton, N. (2003) 'Sentencing guidelines' in Tonry, M. (ed.) (2003a).

Jones, T. and Newburn, T. (2007) *Policy Transfer and Criminal Justice: Exploring US Influence over British Crime Control Policy*, Maidenhead, Open University Press.

Justice Reinvestment (2008) *Facts and Trends* [online], http://justicereinvestment.org/facts_and_trends (Accessed 5 January 2009).

Maguire, M., Morgan, R. and Reiner, R. (eds) (2007) *The Oxford Handbook of Criminology*, (4th edn), Oxford, Oxford University Press.

Males, M., Stahlkopf, C. and Macallair, D. (2007) *Crime Rates and Youth Incarceration in Texas and California Compared: Public Safety or Public Waste?* Centre on Crime and Criminal Justice [online], www.cjcj.org/files/Crime_Rates_ and_Youth_Incarceration_in_Texas_and_ California_Compared.pdf (Accessed 20 March 2009).

Miller, T.A. (2002) 'The impact of mass incarceration on immigration policy' in Mauer, M. and Chesney-Lind, M. (eds) *Invisible Punishment: The Collateral Consequences of Mass Imprisonment*, New York, The New Press.

Morrison, W. (2005) 'Rethinking narratives of penal change in global context' in Pratt, J. et al. (eds) (2005).

Piper, C. (2008) *Investing in Children: Policy, Law and Practice in Context*, Cullompton, Willan.

Pratt, J. (2008a) 'Scandinavian exceptionalism in an era of penal excess Part I: the nature of roots of Scandinavian exceptionalism', *British Journal of Criminology*, vol. 48, no. 2, pp. 119–37.

Pratt, J. (2008b) 'Scandinavian exceptionalism in an era of penal excess Part II: does Scandinavian exceptionalism have a future?', *British Journal of Criminology*, vol. 48, no. 3, pp. 275–92.

Pratt, J., Brown, D., Brown, M., Hallsworth, S. and Morrison, W. (eds) (2005) *The New Punitiveness: Trends, Theories, Perspectives*, Cullompton, Willan.

Simon, J. (2007) *Governing Through Crime: How the War on Crime Transformed American Democracy and Created a Culture of Fear*, Oxford, Oxford University Press.

Simon, J. and Feeley, M. (1995) 'True crime: the new penology and public discourse on crime' in Blomberg, T. and Cohen, S. (eds) *Punishment and Social Control*, New York, Aldine de Gruyter.

Simon, J. and Jensen, E.L. (1996) 'The rhetoric of vengeance', *Criminal Justice Matters*, vol. 25, no. 1, pp. 8–10.

Solomon, E. (2008) 'Investing in incarceration makes no economic sense', *The Guardian*, 7 May [online], www.guardian.co.uk/society/2008/may/07/prisonsandprobation.socialprogrammes/print (Accessed 20 March 2009).

Tonry, M. (ed.) (2003a) *Confronting Crime: Crime Control Policy under New Labour*, Cullompton, Willan.

Tonry, M. (2003b) 'Evidence, elections and ideology in the making of criminal justice policy' in Tonry, M. (ed.) (2003a).

Tonry, M. (2004) *Punishment and Politics: Evidence and Emulation in the Making of English Crime Control Policy*, Cullompton, Willan.

van Kesteren, J., Mayhew, P. and Nieuwbeerta, P. (2000) *Criminal Victimisation in Seventeen Industrialised Countries*, The Hague, Ministry of Justice.

Wacquant, L. (2005) 'The great penal leap backward: incarceration in America from Nixon to Clinton' in Pratt, J. et al. (eds) (2005).

Walmsley, R. (1999) *World Prison Population List* (1st edn), Research Findings No. 88, London, Home Office.

Walmsley, R. (2006) *World Prison Population List* (7th edn), London, King's College.

Whitman, J.Q. (2003) *Harsh Justice: Criminal Punishment and the Widening Divide between America and Europe*, Oxford, Oxford University Press.

Wilkins, L.T. and Pease, K. (1987) 'Public demand for punishment', *International Journal of Sociology and Social Policy*, vol. 7, no. 3, pp. 16–29.

Zedner, L. (1995) 'Comparative research in criminology' in Noaks, L., Levi, M. and Maguire, M. (eds) *Contemporary Issues in Criminology*, Cardiff, University of Wales Press.

Chapter 3
Conflict resolution, restoration and informal justice

Ross Fergusson and John Muncie

Contents

1   Introduction

As outlined in Chapter 1, it is widely taken for granted that the primary response to crime should be the formal prosecution of offenders and, where appropriate, their punishment in the name of protecting the public. In this process responsibility for defining and responding to crime is taken by official state agencies, ideally acting with impartiality and fairness. However, the investiture of such powers in the state has also long been a cause for concern. Critics have maintained, for example, that formal criminal justice is overwhelmingly counterproductive in relation to its objectives. Social problems, conflicts, harms and antagonisms are an inevitable part of everyday life and their 'ownership' is lost if they are delegated to professionals and specialists promising to provide 'expert solutions'. When professionals intervene, the essence of social problems and conflicts is effectively 'stolen' and re-presented in forms that only aid their perpetuation (Christie, 1977). Formal criminal justice also appears to be mired in recurrent crises: of effectiveness, of lack of public confidence, of arbitrary and unprincipled decision making and of reproducing social inequalities. It is in such negative climates that reformers have also long searched for more inclusive and less destructive means of responding to crime: means that are intended to return 'ownership' of the conflicts, disputes and troubles associated with crime to those most intimately involved; that is, their perpetrators and victims.

This chapter explores various modes of justice that explicitly move beyond formal criminal justice and legal institutions. Section 2 reveals the nature and influence of conflict resolution in various forms of indigenous justice; that is, in the customary practices of Navajo, Zulu, Maori and Kikuyu communities. By the late twentieth century, one of the most visible and widespread 'alternative' forms of conflict resolution was realised in the concept and practices of restorative justice. It was most famously associated with the techniques of 'truth and reconciliation' adopted in 'post-conflict' societies such as South Africa, Ireland and Serbia. The focus on restorative justice in Section 3 offers some reflection on the idea of *global* criminal justice policies and the processes through which national and localised policies may be disseminated internationally. Section 4 provides some means through which a critical understanding and appreciation of conflict resolution and informal justice can be gained.

The aims of this chapter are to:

■ consider a range of informal alternatives to formal systems of criminal justice

■ examine some of the ways in which these informal alternatives have been put into practice

- account for the resurgent interest in informal justice (in the form of restorative justice) that has occurred since the 1990s

- develop a critical analysis of some models and theories of social relations that underpin these 'new' policies and practices

- consider the argument that criminal justice and alternative forms of justice are fundamentally incompatible.

2 Indigenous justice: Navajo, Zulu, Maori and Kikuyu

The term 'indigenous justice' usually refers to those forms of conflict resolution developed by First Nation aboriginal communities such as the Navajo in the USA, the Zulu in South Africa, the Maori in New Zealand and the Kikuyu in Kenya prior to Western colonisation. From the outset, it is important to note that how societies organise their processes of justice is fundamental to the ways in which they strive to maintain stable communities. The foundational principles of different modes of indigenous justice are described by their proponents and practitioners in ways intimately connected to wider philosophies, values and world views that appear to be dominant in these societies.

2.1 *Beehaz-aanii, ubuntu, whanau* and *hapu*

Activity 3.1

Read Extracts 3.1, 3.2 and 3.3 on contemporary expressions of indigenous justice. Make notes on the core values that underpin their social and ontological premises and the specific practices that each describes.

The first extract is by Robert Yazzie, Chief Justice of the Navajo Nation in the USA. He compares Navajo 'horizontal' justice and the concept of *beehaz-aanii* ('the essence of life') with dominant Western 'vertical' justice.

Extract 3.1

A 'vertical' system of justice is one that relies upon hierarchies and power. That is, judges sit at the top presiding over the lawyers, jurors, and all participants in court proceedings. The justice system uses rank, and the coercive power that goes with rank or status, to address conflicts.

Power is the active element in the process. A decision is dictated from on high by the judge, and that decision is an order or judgement which parties must obey or face a penalty. Parties to a dispute have limited power and control over the process. ...

When outsiders intervene in a dispute, they impose moral codes upon people who have moral codes of their own. The subjects of adjudication have no power, little or no say about the outcome of a case, and their feelings do not matter.

Within the horizontal justice model, no person is above the other. A graphic model often used by Indians to portray this thought is a circle. In a circle, there is no right or left, no beginning or end. Every point (or person) on the line on a circle looks to the same center as the focus. The circle is the symbol of Navajo justice because it is perfect, unbroken, and a simile of unity and oneness.

The Navajo word for 'law' is *beehaz-aanii*. It means something fundamental and absolute, something that has existed from the beginning of time. Navajos believe that the Holy People 'put it there for us'. It's the source of a healthy, meaningful life. Navajos say that 'life comes from *beehaz-aanii*', because it is the essence of life. The precepts of *beehaz-aanii* are stated in prayers and ceremonies that tell us of *hozhooji* – 'the perfect state'.

Imagine a system of law that permits anyone to say anything they like during the course of a dispute, and no authority figure has to determine what is 'true'. Think of a system with an end goal of restorative justice, which uses equality and the full participation of disputants in a final decision. If we say of law that 'life comes from it', then where there is hurt, there must be healing.

Source: Yazzie, 1994, pp. 29–30

Our second example concerns the concept of *ubuntu* as central to Zulu indigenous justice. In this extract, Yvonne Mokgoro, Justice of the Constitutional Court of the Republic of South Africa, describes *ubuntu* as follows.

Extract 3.2

Ubuntu, a Zulu word ... has generally been described as a world-view of African societies and a determining factor in the formation of perceptions which influence social conduct. It has also been described as a philosophy of life, which in its most fundamental sense represents personhood, humanity, humaneness and morality; a metaphor that describes group solidarity where such group solidarity is central to the survival of communities with a scarcity of resources, and the fundamental belief is that '*[u]buntu ngumuntu ngabantu, motho ke motho ba batho ba bangwe,*' which, literally translated, means 'a human being is a human being because of other human beings' (Mbigi and Maree, 1995). In other words, the individual's existence and well-being are relative to that of the group. This is manifested in anti-individualistic conduct that threatens the survival of the group. If the individual is to survive within the group, there must be collective effort for group survival. Basically, it is a humanistic orientation towards fellow beings. ...

The meaning of *ubuntu*, however, becomes much clearer when we examine its practical effect on everyday life. For example, a society based on *ubuntu* places strong emphasis on family obligations. Family members are obliged to help one another. ...

Group solidarity, conformity, compassion, respect, human dignity, humanistic orientation and collective unity have, among others, been defined as key social values of *ubuntu*. ...

The Interim Constitution sets the tone for socio-political transformation in South Africa. It created 'a historic bridge between the past of a deeply divided society, characterised by strife, conflict, untold suffering and injustice, and a future founded on the recognition of peaceful co-existence ... for all South Africans' (*South African Constitution* (1993), Chapter 16).

To realize the peaceful co-existence recognized by the Interim Constitution, despite the injustices of the past, there is a need for understanding, not vengeance, and a need for reparation, not retaliation. Specifically, that constitution recognized the need for *ubuntu* and not victimization.

References

Lovemore Mbigi and Jenny Maree *Ubuntu: The Spirit of African Transformation Management,* 1–7 (1995).

South African Constitution (1993) Chapter 16, National Unity and Reconciliation is the postscript of the Constitution.

Source: Mokgoro, 1998, pp. 15–18

The third extract concerns Maori justice and, in particular, the central place of *whanau*, the extended family group, and *hapu*, groups of families, in the dispensation of justice. Juan Tauri and Allison Morris describe Maori law and systems of justice as follows.

Extract 3.3

... essentially, Maori justice processes were based on notions that responsibility was collective rather than individual and that redress was due not just to the victim but also to the victim's family. Understanding why an individual had offended was also linked to this notion of collective responsibility. The reasons were felt to lie not in the individual but in a lack of balance in the offender's social and family environment. The causes of this imbalance, therefore, had to be addressed in a collective way and, in particular, the balance between the offender and the victim's family had to be restored. For example, the agreed outcome might have been the transfer of the offender's goods to the victim or work by the offender for the victim ... The role of the *whanau* (the family group which includes parents, children and other close kin) and *hapu* were of paramount importance to the process. Most decisions, whatever their nature, were customarily made by the *whanau* and *hapu* depending on the importance and nature of the decision (Consedine, 1995).

Reference

Consedine, J. (1995) *Restorative Justice: Healing the Effects of Crime*, Lyttleton, New Zealand, Ploughshares Publications.

Source: Tauri and Morris, 1997, pp. 149–50

Comment

In their different ways, all three of these versions of indigenous justice prioritise some form of collectivised, unified view of the social world. The 'unity and oneness' of the Navajo circle; the way in which being human in *ubuntu* depends on a collective unity; the centrality of families and groups of families among the Maori: all these place the group above the individual. Social solidarity is a core value on which all three forms of indigenous justice are based. Their values place *negotiation* at the centre of justice. Navajo justice gives full and equal rights to all disputants in reaching resolution. *Ubuntu* aims for consensus, not the exercise of power by majorities. Maori justice decisions are made by the *whanau* or *hapu*. These three systems all appear to be fundamentally concerned more with restoration and/or reconciliation than with retribution.

The distinctive values of three apparently unconnected indigenous systems of justice, across three continents, seem surprisingly similar. They are frequently linked by Western academics because of their stark contrast to Western administrative justice. Superficially, they all appear more democratic, less exclusionary and capable of restoring well-being rather than the further infliction of pain (through overt punishment). However, it is important to avoid idealising indigenous justice by confusing the processes by which determinations and settlements are reached with the outcomes of those processes. Chris Cunneen (2006), for example, has warned against generalising and romanticising the characteristics of indigenous justice: punishments may take brutal forms, from exiling offenders to harsh physical punishment such as beating and spearing. Similarly, Kathleen Daly (2002) has argued that reverence for indigenous justice ignores bodily punishments that would be considered objectionable in many other societies. John Pratt (1992) has noted that use of the death penalty was not uncommon among the Maori. For example, one dispute following the alleged killing of a young man was settled among Chiefs by an agreement that a raiding party would destroy the village of the offending tribe (Earle, 1966). The person thought to be the first Maori to visit England had been banished for stealing an axe (Wilson, 1990).

2.2 Kikuyu justice, the *kiama* and colonisation

When Kenyan communities were first colonised, white colonialists' dismissal of indigenous justice as uncivilised was widespread.
The Kikuyu are one of the dominant tribes of Kenya. Their system of indigenous justice was based on the *kiama*, a self-appointed council of local elders with a high level of community involvement, which resolved all disputes. It was viewed as primitive and inferior by European colonials, as the following account shows.

Activity 3.2

Read Extract 3.4, from a book written in 1933 by a Catholic missionary, Father Cagnolo, at the height of British colonial rule in Kenya.

As you read, make notes in answer to these questions:

- What parallels between Kikuyu and Western administrative justice can be identified from this account?

- What distinctive features of Kikuyu justice seem to have no equivalent in Western justice?

Extract 3.4

There are no special law courts. Trials take place anywhere: under a tree, in the squares where dances are usually held, at a cross road, even at the accused's or plaintiff's home.

There are no special judges: all the recognized elders have a right to speak and give judgement on a case.

There are no professional advocates. Both plaintiff and accused plead their own case as best they can, and judgement depends upon their own skill and plausibility at putting their case, packed with a string of proverbs, rather than the truth. Elders correspond to judges, but only those belonging to the ruling class, who have already paid a goat to obtain their office. Amongst these are some gifted with intelligence and excellent oratorical powers. ...

When one man wants to sue another he seeks out three or four elders who are prepared to plead his case. He explains thoroughly to them the object of his suit, and asks them to give information to his opponents and to fix a time and place for the hearing. His adversary also appoints a commission of elders as intermediaries, and the members of the commissions will act as judges when the case is heard. ...

Witnesses, in the real meaning of the word, seldom appear; in any case the attendance would be of very little service. The [Kikuyu] are a people very fond of giving and receiving news, they are great gossips, and every petty detail seems to be known to everyone. Hence when a case comes up for decision, everybody is fully informed about it. On the other hand, as the culprit makes no bones about the number of lies he utters, and his backers are equally unscrupulous, being notoriously bribed or bribable with a hunk of meat, and blushing is an unknown feat among these people, the case proceeds quite cheerfully. ...

The order in which the discussion takes place is really remarkable. One man after another is allowed to speak calmly and quietly. A speaker may be as emphatic as he can, but he must never show anger, for this would weaken his case besides being universally disapproved.

Source: Cagnolo, 1933, pp. 147–9

Comment

This general deprecation of indigenous justice, the implied corruption and dishonesty of the Kikuyu compared to Europeans and the failure to identify parallels with European administrative justice are striking. Obvious parallels include centrality of 'procedure', the ostensibly adversarial nature of the proceedings, the high priority given to dispassionate debate and the payment of an elite quasi-judicial class. But some equally striking contrasts indicate ways in which informal conflict resolution differs fundamentally from European justice, especially the communal and oral nature of the proceedings, the absence of professionals, the importance of the elders being appointed by and 'of' the community, the collective nature of judgment and the high level of community engagement.

These registers of 'difference' are important markers for understanding informal and restorative modes of conflict resolution that have latterly been imported into many Western systems, particularly since the 1980s.

Figure 3.1
Registers of difference: Kikuyu tribunal

KIKUYU TRIBUNAL

3 The coming of Western restorative justice

However strong the connections between informalism (i.e. the belief in informal modes of justice), restoration and indigenous justice, and between formalism and administrative justice, these are by no means simple lines of connection. Alternative conflict resolution, in the form of mediation, arbitration, conciliation and tribunals, for example, has long been used in Western systems to settle disputes through the use of an independent third party and without the need for a formal court hearing. Typically, however, this has been restricted to civil matters or to dealing with cases of corporate malpractice. For example, child labour, environmental pollution, corporate fraud and the marketing of unsafe and life-threatening substances have all long been viewed as matters for regulation or voluntary compliance rather than as matters for the criminal law (**Tombs and Whyte, 2010**).

Attempts have, however, been made to introduce degrees of informalism into criminal proceedings, particularly for young offenders. During the 1970s and 1980s, many juvenile justice practitioners, particularly across North America, Europe and Australia, began advocating diversion, decarceration, deprofessionalisation, decentralisation and delegalisation as more appropriate and humane means of dealing with youth 'in conflict with the law'. One of the most tangible outcomes of these debates in the UK, for example, was the abolition of the juvenile court and the establishment of a Children's Hearings system (for under 16-year-olds) in Scotland in 1971. More generally, a 'destructuring impulse' of this time initiated various movements to challenge the omnipotence of state, bureaucratic and professional power (Cohen, 1985, p. 35). The talk was of developing self-help: community control reminiscent of some semi-mythical tribal past that was free of governmental interference (Abel, 1982).

For numerous reasons, not least an incessant criticism that informal systems preclude the delivery of 'just deserts', visions of, and experiments in, informal justice have typically been short lived (Merry and Milner, 1995). Nevertheless, since the 1980s there has been a substantial growth in interest in restorative justice and victim–offender mediation. These have had a remarkable impact on criminal justice in numerous jurisdictions around the world. The restorative justice movement first gained momentum in societies that attempted to 'rediscover', to varying degrees, the systems of justice of their indigenous peoples, as in Canada and New Zealand, for example. Social theologians and various religious faiths have also sought to recover traditions of communally based restorative justice in which crime is understood as an interpersonal harm rather than as a violation of an abstract legal rule. Some radical advocates have spoken of the potential for replacing legal definitions of crime and formal procedures with processes of reconciling conflicting interests and of healing rifts (de Haan, 1990; Walgrave, 1995). Putting right harms is viewed as the obligation and liability of the parties concerned, with only minimal involvement of the state and its agents.

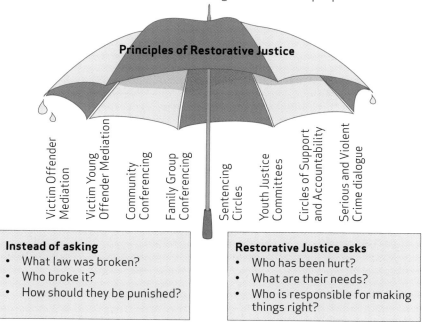

Restorative Justice Umbrella Analogy

Instead of defining crime as breaking the law,
Restorative Justice defines crime as HARM TO PEOPLE.

Instead of responding to this breach with punishment,
Restorative Justice says the response to crime should be MAKING THINGS RIGHT.

People are the victims, not the state.
Crime creates needs and obligations between people.

Principles of Restorative Justice

Victim Offender Mediation
Victim Young Offender Mediation
Community Conferencing
Family Group Conferencing
Sentencing Circles
Youth Justice Committees
Circles of Support and Accountability
Serious and Violent Crime dialogue

Instead of asking
• What law was broken?
• Who broke it?
• How should they be punished?

Restorative Justice asks
• Who has been hurt?
• What are their needs?
• Who is responsible for making things right?

Figure 3.2
Poster produced by a conflict mediation service in Toronto, Canada (Source: Conflict Mediation Services of Downsview, 2002)

A core element of restorative justice is that denunciation of undesirable acts and a shaming of perpetrators is more likely to have an impact on future behaviour than retribution and removal from the community (as in the cases of overtly punitive responses and resort to prison – see Chapter 2). Indeed, a theory and practice known as *reintegrative shaming* is based on the belief that subjecting offenders to expressions of community disapproval, *followed by* repentance and community gestures of reacceptance and forgiveness, is the approach most likely to have positive outcomes (Braithwaite, 1989). According to the theory, reintegrative shaming works and builds on moral conscience and deters others who wish to avoid shame. Because shaming is participatory, it also works to cement community cohesion. This is in sharp contrast to processes of *disintegrative shaming*, which have typically been the norm in both modern Western and communist states. Disintegrative shaming is most evident in criminal court procedures and criminal justice processes, which sever any bond between transgressor and accuser and condemn the convicted offender to stigmatisation and social exclusion (Braithwaite, 1989).

Figure 3.3
The shaming of
prostitutes in China
and drink-drivers in
the USA

Based in part on a case study of shaming in Japan, John Braithwaite
views traditional modes of crime control as self-defeating. In contrast,
reintegrative shaming offers the possibility of preventing future
offending by including the transgressor back into the community.
This again is represented in elements of the burgeoning worldwide
industry of restorative justice. Indeed, supporters of the restorative

justice movement argue that the techniques of reintegrative shaming, restitution, mediation and reparation work on the conscience of the harm-doer in ways that formal legal procedures cannot. Restorative justice holds a greater potential to re-establish the 'deliberative control of justice by citizens' and 'harmony based on a feeling that justice has been done' (Braithwaite, 2003, p. 57).

Both the United Nations and the Council of Europe have given restorative justice their firm backing. The European Forum for Victim–Offender Mediation and Restorative Justice was established in 2000. The Council of Europe has recommended to all jurisdictions that mediation should be made generally available, that it should cover all stages of the criminal justice process and, most significantly, that it should be separate from formal means of judicial processing.

Vivien Stern (2001) has recorded a renewed interest in solidarity, reconciliation and restoration, rather than the colonial prison, as the guiding principles for resolving disputes across many parts of Africa. Arguably, the most influential contemporary example of 'restoration' replacing 'retribution' as the guiding principle in achieving 'justice' is indeed South Africa's Truth and Reconciliation Commission, following the abolition of apartheid. The Commission was charged with investigating past human rights violations, granting amnesty for political crimes and offering reparation to victims. Whatever the political expediency of this strategy, the notion that community relations could be 'healed' only through truth telling, forgiveness and acknowledgement of the harm done to past victims was clearly informed by restorative principles. In 2002, the United Nation's Economic and Social Council formulated some basic universal principles of restorative justice, including non-coercive offender and victim participation, confidentiality and procedural safeguards (see Extract 3.5).

Extract 3.5   UN Resolutions 2002: II. Use of restorative justice programmes

6. Restorative justice programmes may be used at any stage of the criminal justice system, subject to national law.

7. Restorative processes should be used only where there is sufficient evidence to charge the offender and with the free and voluntary consent of the victim and the offender. The victim and the offender should be able to withdraw such consent at any time during the process. Agreements should be arrived at voluntarily and should contain only reasonable and proportionate obligations.

8. The victim and the offender should normally agree on the basic facts of a case as the basis for their participation in a restorative

process. Participation of the offender shall not be used as evidence of admission of guilt in subsequent legal proceedings.

9. Disparities leading to power imbalances, as well as cultural differences among the parties, should be taken into consideration in referring a case to, and in conducting, a restorative process.

10. The safety of the parties shall be considered in referring any case to, and in conducting, a restorative process.

11. Where restorative processes are not suitable or possible, the case should be referred to the criminal justice authorities and a decision should be taken as to how to proceed without delay. In such cases, criminal justice officials should endeavour to encourage the offender to take responsibility vis-à-vis the victim and affected communities, and support the reintegration of the victim and the offender into the community.

Source: United Nations, 2002, p. 57

It is clear that restorative justice is no longer marginal but a burgeoning worldwide industry with local projects proliferating across much of Europe, Africa, North America and Australasia. How such policies proliferate, spread and deserve description as an industry is an issue to which the chapter returns in Sections 3.2 and 3.3.

Unremarkably, such proliferation results in many competing definitions and variants of activities that come to be labelled 'restorative justice'. Yet there remain important common elements. As we noted earlier, central to the concept is that conflicts belong to those directly involved, not to other formally constituted bodies. The victim and the offender are the 'owners', but families and communities are also important partners. Crimes and conflicts are regarded as breakdowns in or violations of good relations between these parties and can be resolved effectively only by and among them. If resolution is to be genuine, effective and meaningful, there needs to be true recognition not only of harms inflicted and damages done, but also of circumstances that brought these about. Until the offender has understood the full consequences for others of his or her actions, resolution is widely viewed as impossible. Equally, if the victim has no understanding of the conditions that caused the offender to act, and no belief that the offender feels genuine remorse, the harm will remain unrepaired, resentment will continue and the dispute will not be closed. But it is not only the victim who is harmed by a crime; families and communities, who live with the anxiety, anger or fear the victim feels, are also believed to be harmed by it (Zehr and Mika, 1997). As we will see in Section 4, this emphasis on personal relations associates restorative justice with many of the values and priorities of some feminist approaches to justice.

Internationally, as we have seen, a wide range of methods and agencies can be (and are) used in pursuit of restoration, including not only reintegrative shaming, but also victim–offender mediation, peacemaking, healing or sentencing circles, community justice panels and many forms of 'conferencing'.

3.1 Indigenous and restorative justice in contemporary New Zealand

Among the most common forms of conferencing is family group conferencing (FGC), which developed in New Zealand and is derived from Maori indigenous justice.

Activity 3.3

Extract 3.6 summarises the response to a robbery and assault that involved a young Maori. The response was based on the FGC method redeveloped in New Zealand through the Children, Young Persons and Their Families Act of 1989. As you study it, make brief notes in response to these questions:

■ What were the critical elements in the apparent success of the process?

■ What traces of the principles of ancient Maori justice methods, introduced in Extract 3.3 in Section 2, and of indigenous justice more generally, are identifiable in the account?

■ What further information would you need to be able to assess confidently the success of the process described?

■ What would you see as the limits to the value of this approach, with regard to other offences, other offenders, different attitudes and different circumstances?

Extract 3.6

Tama was 16 years old when he and two associates (aged 19 and 23) robbed a young man at knife point and assaulted him. Tama had been living rough on the city streets, committing petty offences, and using drugs and alcohol since he ran away from home two years previously, following his mother's re-partnering after his father died. He had lost all contact with his family. Following his arrest he was remanded into the custody of the Department of Social Welfare, while a family group conference (FGC) was arranged. In the absence of immediate family, the youth court coordinator contacted an elder of Tama's Maori tribe.

Four members of his *whanau* attended the conference, as did the victim and his parents, as well as the police and the coordinator. Tama 'dropped his tough façade and cried' as he was embraced by his aunt. His great uncle, a respected tribal elder, opened the conference in Maori (and then in English) with an extended invocation of his birthplace, his ancestors and their land. This was followed by a prayer and a welcome to the victim and his parents, and the officials. A song in Maori affirmed his speech.

Tama admitted his offence, appeared to be moved by the victim's remarks and made a 'sincere and spontaneous' apology to him. Over lunch the families and officials 'mingled in a relaxed way'. Tama and his family then held a private discussion. They acknowledged the seriousness of the attack while also emphasising that Tama was influenced by the other (adult) attackers. They offered to work with the whole *whanau* to develop a supervision plan that would be the subject of a court order. The victim and his family agreed, the police disagreed and the conference was closed.

Still on remand, Tama was allowed to visit his *whanau* in its home town. His mother and forty-three family members came to meet him. They drew up a programme that would isolate Tama from drugs, teach him some skills and provide guidance from Maori tutors knowledgeable in cultural matters. When the Youth Court reconvened, the discussion determined that Tama participate in a forestry camp programme.

Three months later Tama returned to court. His progress report was excellent and 'the change in his demeanour was immediately apparent to all. His chin was up, his voice was confident, and his appearance was clean and tidy'. In the remaining six months he developed forestry skills that led to his employment at the camp. He maintained contact with his *whanau*, and three years later he had not reoffended.

Source: summarised from Stewart, 1996, pp. 83–7 (from which the brief quotations are taken)

Comment

This account captures an apparently successful application of the principles of restorative justice through an FGC. Its success seems to be rooted in:

- the strength of the *whanau*
- its influence over a young person who had become detached from his family

- the standing of Maori elders in the youth justice system

- the involvement of the victim

- the readiness of the full *whanau* to become involved

- the apparent informality of the conference

- the willingness of the family to assume responsibility for managing the offender's conduct

- the apparent sincerity of the offender's apologies

- and perhaps most importantly, the readiness of the judge to balance the preferences of the police against the commitments of the family.

The resemblance to some aspects of indigenous justice are clear, notably the centrality of the *whanau*; the negotiating approach to finding resolution; and the inclusiveness of the proceedings and their rootedness in the tradition, culture and core values of the *iwi* (Maori people or community), especially its social cohesion and solidarity.

Tama's three years without reoffending is the only tangible indicator of the possible success of this FGC. While a longer period without offending would be critical to assessing the success of the process, it would be equally important to consider:

- transcripts of key sections of the deliberations

- the assumptions that are embodied in the quotations

- the durability of Tama's restoration to his *whanau*

- the unmediated views of the victim and his family

- what support the *whanau* provided to Tama before he 'ran away'.

These latter points also begin to indicate possible limits to the appropriateness and success of FGCs. Had Tama been a year older, the FGC process would not have been available. Its suitability had the victim sustained serious injury might also have been in question. FGCs pose special problems when family members are themselves accused, and where there are particularly sensitive and personal issues at stake.

Major tensions between Maori and Pakeha (the Maori name for European settlers) underpinned this upsurge in interest in FGCs in the 1980s. Maori dissatisfaction with the huge over-representation of young Maori males in the criminal justice system was rooted in the legal removal of the rights of *iwi* to manage the conduct of young men. Trevor Bradley et al. (2006) describe the pre-1989 arrangements in terms of the 'virtual exclusion' (p.83) of the cornerstones of Maori social organisation from the processes of dispensing criminal justice to young people. As we noted above, New Zealand's 1989 Children, Young Persons and Their Families Act placed FGCs at the centre of the criminal justice system's response to youth offending. FGCs comprise the young offender, family members, the victim (or their representative), a support person for the victim, the police and a mediator. The meetings are informal and the central role of the family is to talk privately with the offender after the initial hearing, to propose a plan to make good the harm or damage. The plan must recognise the victim's views *and* be beneficial to the offender. If it is approved, sanctions are set – typically community work, a programme of activity or a task intended to restore property or make good the harm. This *may* include an apology.

But how successful have FGCs been in general? Allison Morris and Gabrielle Maxwell's (1998) evaluation research found high levels of satisfaction with FGCs, particularly among offenders and families, many of whom valued feeling involved. And although there were many exceptions, there was 'little doubt that families preferred the process of family group conferences to the processes of courts' (p. 205). Victims were less positive. Half did not attend. More than half who did felt better for attending, and of the quarter of attending victims who felt worse, most attributed this to doubting the sincerity of the offender's apology. Morris and Maxwell concluded that FGCs are restorative in that they 'put things right' for many victims, but that many victims' needs remain unmet and promised outcomes are too often not delivered. Bradley et al. (2006) are more critical. They note that consensus was often not achieved, that professionals sometimes appeared to dominate decision making and that Maori expertise and the involvement of elders were undervalued. These authors refer to 'selective utilisation' of Maori culture and to the way in which aspects of Maori traditions are subject to colonisation and appropriation by 'white justice' (p. 92). In the same vein, Daly (2002) makes the important point that it is tempting to construct white/European-centred origin myths that view restorative justice as the direct product of ancient indigenous forms. FGCs, she suggests, far from being a direct adoption of indigenous Maori practices, are a flexible accommodation and adaptation of some ancient practices to improve their cultural appropriateness.

3.2 Restorative justice in the UK?

Despite these misgivings, the promise of restorative justice through conferencing, particularly for juveniles, has proved irresistible to many Western jurisdictions, including in the UK. The UK, of course, comprises the three separate jurisdictions of England and Wales, Scotland and Northern Ireland. Each has appropriated restorative justice principles for young offenders in different ways. In Scotland the core principles are interwoven with a system that gives a relatively high priority to the welfare of children. In England and Wales restorative justice is blended into a policy context dominated by concerns of crime control and firmly locating responsibility with young people and their parents. In Northern Ireland a National Youth Agency was established in 2001 to implement a new agenda for youth justice based on diversion, human rights and restoration. A Youth Conference Service receives referrals from prosecutors as a diversion from prosecution. It is predicated on the consent of the offender. These quite distinctive versions of restorative justice are, of course, informed by the specific historical context and policy trajectories of each jurisdiction.

The Scottish Children's Hearings system, mentioned at the beginning of Section 3, has its origins in an explicitly welfare-oriented approach to juveniles established in 1968. In common with systems in England and Wales at the time, this gave precedence to the 'best interests of the child', whether they were children who offended or children who were in need of care and protection. On the face of it, Children's Hearings share some of the characteristics of FGCs. Alongside the Reporter (a professional who investigates the case and makes the key determinations, as part of the Scottish Children's Reporter Administration) and the social worker, three members of the local community have key roles (one as chairperson) in Hearings. Young people have a right to attend, while their parents or carers are obliged to. Both are entitled (and sometimes required) to bring their own representative. Hearings can make compulsory provision for care and supervision, including placing an offender in secure accommodation. But Children's Hearings are markedly differentiated from restorative justice proceedings by the absence of the victim. To advocates of restorative justice, they are therefore intrinsically unrestorative. In contrast to the arrangements in New Zealand, Reporters also retain their final powers in determining the disposal, irrespective of the findings from participation in restorative justice (Scottish Executive, 2005).

In Northern Ireland a Criminal Justice Review was established in 1998 as part of the 'Good Friday Agreement'. The Agreement sought a political accommodation to the years of conflict in Northern Ireland and as part of that process the government agreed to a fundamental review of policing and criminal justice. The review recommended specifically that a restorative justice approach should be central to dealing with young offenders. It was from this broader 'post-conflict' consensus that the Youth Conference Service was established in 2003, which placed conferencing for young offenders on a statutory basis (unlike in the other UK jurisdictions) (O'Mahony and Campbell, 2006). The courts must refer all young persons for a conference. An action plan will then be devised, taking into account the nature of the offence, victim needs and community considerations. The plan, which usually involves some reparation or apology, must be consented to by the offender. Initial evaluation of the scheme was largely positive. In contrast to other similar schemes, there was a high level of victim participation (62 per cent) and the process delivered high degrees of victim and offender satisfaction (79 per cent and 71 per cent respectively). The vast majority of both victims and offenders preferred it to court proceedings (Campbell et al., 2005).

In England and Wales the Referral Orders and Youth Offender Panels established through the Youth Justice and Criminal Evidence Act 1999 are the closest English and Welsh legislation has come to institutionalising restorative justice. Referral Orders are mandatory in response to a guilty plea on first offence. They lead to appearance before a Youth Offender Panel, which is considerably less formal than a court. Typically, the panel is made up of members of the local youth offending team and volunteer members of the public. Panels are free to invite a wide range of members of the community to attend, including victims, and friends or relatives of the accused. The panel aims to draw up a contract that will require action on the part of the offender to compensate the victim and deter future offending. Such action might involve 'community service', attendance on a course or restrictions on activities or movement. An apology and reparation are expected whatever the other requirements.

Adam Crawford and Tim Newburn's (2003) evaluation of the Referral Order pilots concluded that they were well received by the professionals responsible for implementing them because of the restorative ideals they promised to deliver. But working with victims was challenging, especially for the police. And achieving standardisation, efficiency and economy sat uneasily with restorative approaches. The evaluation demonstrated some of the tensions between the ideals of restorative justice and its practical implementation. One contradiction concerned the issues of coercion and voluntariness. In most forms of indigenous justice, the offender, the victim and families negotiate a settlement with few, if any, predefined parameters. In that sense, the responses are voluntary. In contrast, Youth Offender Panels mix deliberative activity with that of securing compliance. Loraine Gelsthorpe and Allison Morris (2002) found that reparation is frequently coercive: extracted by professionals under duress to 'close' the process. In another context, Daly's findings, too, led her to conclude that 'a sincere apology is difficult to achieve' (Daly, 2006, p. 140), partly because many offenders are not sincerely sorry.

A second contradiction concerns the reparational value of any subsequent offender programme. Much of the work of community service has no discernible connection to actual harms inflicted or damage done, and hence no capacity to build empathy for the loss or injury experienced by the victim. Furthermore, Crawford and Newburn (2003) noticed that victims were normally absent from proceedings and that the wider community was unrepresented. By breaking the crucial integrity of the offender–victim–community triangle, Referral Orders seemed to undermine the essentially shared nature of successful forms of conflict resolution. Gelsthorpe and Morris (2002) concluded that restorative effects are significantly limited because victims, offenders and their families are never permitted to assume control. In turn, Crawford and Newburn (2003) concluded that Referral Orders are hybrids that attempt to integrate restorative justice ideas and values into an otherwise fundamentally coercive penal system. So long as the prime concern remains dealing with the offender (and making them responsible), benefits to the victim or community are compromised.

It seems clear from these studies that changing crucial, specific aspects of restorative approaches significantly affects their efficacy in altered contexts. Comparing the introduction of restorative justice-sourced methods into mainstream youth justice in England and Wales with approaches in New Zealand and Australia, Gelsthorpe and Morris (2002) noted that, unlike in New Zealand, the powers of professionals and of the courts have never been seriously questioned in England and Wales. Differences in Scotland concerning the optional inclusion of victims raise similar queries. Daly sees this difference as 'reflecting something positive about the conditions of life and modes of governance in [Australia and New Zealand], where there is an openness to addressing social problems and to redressing inequalities' (Daly, 2001, p. 61). Such major differences in the ways in which an apparently common approach, restorative justice, can be manifested in different jurisdictions raises important questions about what happens when policies 'travel'.

3.3 Travelling policies: transfers, learning and translations

Most texts identify indigenous practices in Australia and Canada, as well as New Zealand and the USA, as the founding sources of restorative approaches to resolving conflicts. To some commentators, restorative approaches are 'cultural universals' (Braithwaite, 2003, p.58). Others connect these approaches to the social structures of pre-state and pre-modern societies and to the exceptionally strong bonds between the individual and the social group, or to the absence of institutionalised punishment (Weitkampf and Kerner, 2002). Eugene McLaughlin et al. (2003, p. 2) suggest that the particular colonial histories of these (sub-)continents have resulted in 'highly preserved and partially protected cultures and identities, often associated with special separation on successfully claimed land and carefully circumscribed degrees of self-determination'. This might imply that the predisposition of indigenous cultures to restorative approaches survived most intact in North America and Australasia, rather than being confined to them. The examples of the Zulu *ubuntu* and the Kenyan *kiama* cited earlier are just two among many that have the continuing presence of restorative elements within indigenous forms of justice.

Whatever the explanation for its prominence, there is no suggestion that the restorative approach 'transferred' between these two distant continents. But the contemporary extension of restorative justice to the status of becoming a worldwide policy industry tells a strikingly different story. In the 1980s and 1990s, most European and Anglophone mainstream systems of criminal justice added policies and legislation that claimed to be derived from restorative principles. Some of the groundwork for a restorative approach was already in place. Some commentators find essentially restorative elements in almost all of the world's major religions (Zehr and Mika, 1997; Hadley, 2001). The European Catholic church in particular has actively encouraged its spread (Walgrave, 1998). But restorative justice is unrivalled as the epitome of a specific 'travelling policy' and is the indisputable product of active efforts by 'policy entrepreneurs' (on the supply side) and governments and agencies of criminal justice and welfare (on the demand side). As Trevor Jones and Tim Newburn argue, analysis of the policy process in criminal justice tends to 'overplay the evidence about difference between countries and overlook some highly important *globalising* elements in policy change' (Jones and Newburn, 2007, p. 5, emphasis added). Restorative justice provides unequivocal evidence that criminal justice policies 'travel' globally as a result of active interventions. This occurs on several levels. 'New' policy ideas are developed and promoted by scholars and researchers. Politicians and government agencies actively seek out policy innovations in other countries. The influence of New Zealand's restorative justice on youth justice policy in England and Wales, Scotland and Northern Ireland appears to epitomise this. And as we noted earlier, supranational institutions, such as the Council of Europe, and global institutions, such as the United Nations, seek to shape and even determine government policies. The United Nations' resolutions on restorative justice (United Nations, 2002) and the EU's European network of contact points for restorative justice further exemplify some of the sources of such efforts at 'global governance'.

Many of these processes might be better described as *policy learning* or *policy borrowing*. The simple, deliberate transfer of complete policies, laws and practices from one jurisdiction to another is close to unachievable. The effects and outcomes vary greatly according to jurisdiction and also to the local circumstances in which they are applied. Differences in legislative frameworks and institutional architecture inhibit direct transplantation of policies, and deeply embedded differences of history, tradition and culture may prevent even partial replication. The degree of departure of Referral Orders from restorative justice principles in England and Wales, as reported by Crawford and Newburn's (2003) evaluation, and the important distinctions between FGCs in New Zealand and Children's Hearings in Scotland observed earlier, make this clear. Here the concept of 'policy translation' (rather than that of 'policy transfer') may more accurately reflect the ways in which adaptation and approximation characterise the processes.

4   Evaluating and contesting informal justice

So far this chapter has examined in some detail various practices and procedures associated with indigenous justice, informalism and restorative justice. All appear to promise more participatory and inclusionary means of resolving disputes (including crime) than is possible in formal criminal justice systems. A meta-analysis conducted by Lawrence Sherman and Heather Strang (2007), for example, concluded that although 'restorative justice works differently on different kinds of people' (p. 8), there was evidence that it reduced repeat offending, particularly for violent offenders; provided both victims and offenders with more satisfaction than formal systems of justice; and reduced crime victims' desire for violent retribution.

However, these forms of informal justice have been subject to sustained critique for being replete with contradictions and shortcomings. The most notable of these are the subversion of 'alternative' principles in specific projects and the tendency for these principles to be 'realised' as additions, rather than as alternatives, to formal criminal justice processing. Of particular importance is the much-contested claim that some of these alternatives – notably restorative justice and FGC – constitute a 'feminisation of justice', whereby fundamental precepts of administrative justice are supplanted by modes of conflict resolution that place the person, human need, care and the amelioration of harms at the centre.

This section explores further the nature of these critiques. Alongside the debate about feminisation, we consider different ways in which restorative justice has been critiqued as a contradictory new way of governing populations, either by 'net-widening' through extending the reach of community-based alternative forms of justice, or by particular logics for shaping the ways in which individuals are persuaded to 'govern themselves'. Throughout, we give special attention to the concept of *power*. The critical stances that follow demonstrate in particular how informal justice can embody or mask ways in which prevailing distributions of power are constantly present in the resolution of conflicts.

4.1 Challenging formal justice?

Activity 3.4

To begin this critical appreciation, consider the following questions:

- What are the main features that distinguish informal from formal criminal justice?
- Are these features complementary or fundamentally incompatible?
- Does informal justice promise less state intervention?

Comment

Advocates of informal justice, in whatever form, point to its non-bureaucratic and deprofessionalised nature as evidence of its most progressive possibilities and its credentials in challenging the failures of formal criminal justice. It is not uncommon to find this relation expressed as a series of binary opposites (see, for example, Table 3.1).

Such formulations, of course, are ideal-typical. As you have already seen, such stark differences are frequently expressed in practice as a series of appropriations, reworkings, variations, interpenetrations and negotiations. In most jurisdictions informal justice is contained within (and constrained by) formal criminal justice processes. As Daly (2002) has argued, the stark contrasts as represented in Table 3.1 are neither accurate nor defensible. Restorative justice (and indigenous) processes, for example, can contain both retributive and reparative motives. The insistence on holding the individual offender accountable militates against principles of forgiveness and reconciliation or any sense of collective responsibility. Additionally, there can be no guarantee that the emotions raised by shame, remorse and community disapproval can be considered as always restorative in outcome; they may be profoundly damaging (Harris and Maruna, 2006). Similarly, informal justice also carries with it the possibility of extremely reactionary and coercive practices, particularly the ever-present potential for degeneration into spontaneous or organised vigilantism where self-appointed 'guardians' mete out their own justice.

Table 3.1 Comparing formal criminal justice and informal/restorative justice

Formal criminal justice	Informal/restorative justice
Crime as law violation; an act against the state	Crime as a harm to individuals and communities
Offender defined by deficits	Offender defined by capacity to repair harm and/or resolve conflict
Focus on establishing guilt/innocence	Focus on problem solving
State centred	Non-state, community-based/self-regulation
Victims as marginal to decision making	Victims as central to decision making
Adversarial	Negotiation and reconciliation
Punishment to deter, prevent or exact retribution	Punishment as ineffective and disruptive of community relations
Exclusion	Reintegration
Justice 'owned' by legal professionals	Public access to justice
Procedural justice (due process/reliance on rules/legal safeguards)	Substantive justice (negotiated decision making underpinned by principles of conflict resolution)

Informal justice can also be considered to relegitimise (rather than challenge) formal systems. It is most common to find informal processes being reserved for 'white-collar' and corporate crime or for less serious street offences, while a strong punitive stance is retained towards those offences deemed to be the 'most serious' (this being in direct contrast to Sherman and Strang's, 2007, evaluation 'evidence', referred to earlier, which suggests that repeat violent offenders are among those most likely to react positively to restorative techniques). It is particularly notable that in the UK, but also in New Zealand, the focus of restorative justice has been almost exclusively on juveniles. Moreover, the inclusionary mechanisms of restorative justice may simply allow the state to claim a continued adherence to the 'best interests' of children (as stipulated, for example, by the United Nations Convention on the Rights of the Child), while simultaneously allowing punitive responses that coerce young people or assign greater expectations of responsibility than their youth can sustain. For example, some versions of restorative justice appear to actively encourage individuals to bear sole responsibility for their actions, while at the same time ignoring or disavowing the cultural or structural contexts of their behaviour. For this reason, David Garland (2001, p. 104) argues that restorative justice is typically only 'allowed to operate on the margins of the criminal justice system, offsetting the central tendencies without much changing the overall balance of the system'.

4.2 A feminisation of justice?

Some of the most fundamental challenges to formal justice have long come from feminist theories, which variously note the primacy it affords to administrative procedure, to punitive responses to harms and to a preoccupation with offenders to the detriment of victims (see Chapter 1). These critiques have particular resonance when seen in the context of restorative justice. Emily Gaarder and Lois Presser (2006), for example, have observed that there are, on the face of it, some strong correspondences between some theories of restorative justice and some feminist theory. The centrality of the personal, the crucial nature of interpersonal relations and the prioritisation of care and well-being over abstract principles and rights are common to both. On this view, repairing the damage done by interpersonal harms in individual cases is an essential approach to engendering broader social and criminal justice. Conflicts, abuses and inequalities exist only as the lived relations of individual people and the harms they inflict on one another. Social structures, inequalities and legal frameworks may underpin and exacerbate such harms, but they are realised in and through relations between people. Much domestic violence, in particular, remains invisible to mainstream justice and, even when cases are brought to court, offenders are relatively protected from victims and insulated from fully appreciating the psychological and physical harm they have inflicted. Restorative justice's involvement of the victims' family and friends is viewed as empowering by many feminists, securing their greater involvement in monitoring the victim and deterring repeat offences (Morris and Gelsthorpe, 2000). M. Kay Harris (1991) argues specifically that restorative justice is a feminist vision of justice, because it embodies the principles that all people have equal value as human beings, that harmony and felicity are more important than power and possession, and that the 'personal is political'.

There are, however, other contrasting feminist interpretations. These share a concern that the identification of restorative justice with feminist justice overlooks the centrality of differential relations of power within restorative as in all other forms of justice. They also variously view restorative justice as masking and ameliorating key areas of unequal male power (notably in cases of rape and sexual abuse); as neglecting or managing structural inequalities (e.g. with regard to the economic bases of repeat domestic violence); and as reconceptualising minor crimes in terms of welfare needs, largely to be addressed by mothers, female care workers, and so on. This risks placing domestic harms (alongside white-collar and corporate crimes noted earlier) as 'exceptional' and thereby not warranting the punitive sanctions deployed for 'serious' offences.

The use of FGC in particular raises profoundly contested issues in relation to the sexual abuse of girls and young women by fathers, siblings and uncles. Feminist theories raise serious objections concerning:

- the involvement of (unrestricted numbers of) male relatives of offender and victim in the conference

- the absence of 'due process' to ensure fair, open and equitable hearings for all parties

- the perceived decriminalisation of the offence, which flows from its removal from court proceedings

- the limits placed on the penalties open to FGCs (notably the exclusion of custodial sentences)

- the dishonesty and hypocrisy of implying that the victim can be 'restored' and the harm done 'made good'

- the appropriateness of encouraging young rape victims to condone the restoration of abusers to family and community

- the risks of repeat victimisation in the absence of effective deterrents.

Indeed, Daly (2002) fundamentally challenges the premises that associate restorative justice with feminist praxis, particularly those that construct polar associations between femininity and care, on the one hand, and masculinity and justice, on the other, in response to crime. Such dichotomies fail to recognise the complexity and diversity of cases and contexts. However, much restorative justice is concerned with healing and the personal: so long as it exists as an adjunct to formal justice, it will tend to reproduce the same gendered relations of power as prevail in formal systems. On this reading, only when restorative values provide the bedrock of systems of justice – as *some* would claim for indigenous justice in *some* cultures – will they be able to challenge the dominance of male values and male power.

4.3 A new mode of governance?

One of the greatest claims made for informal justice, and restorative forms in particular, is that it humanises the delivery of 'justice' by directly involving the local community. The notion of 'community' is typically evoked as a more relevant, participatory, responsive and cost-effective means of dealing with offenders and adjudicating on their cases. It was such sentiments that underpinned the development of community-based sanctions (such as community service) in many Western jurisdictions in the 1970s. Diversion from court and from custody became a widely acclaimed strategy for reducing the numbers of offenders, particularly young offenders, subject to the stigma and labelling of judicial processes. Community-based alternatives, such as probation and supervision, were also intended to reduce the use and cost of custody. However, while 'alternatives' burgeoned, so did prison populations. The very existence of apparently benign community-based sentencing options seemed to produce the unintended outcome of increasing the numbers subject to intervention. The relative lower expenditure involved in informal proceedings ironically made it possible to intervene more often. Because coercion was disguised and less visible, the state was able to control more behaviour (Abel, 1982). Stanley Cohen (1979) described such processes as 'thinning the mesh' and 'widening the net'. Allied to his wider 'dispersal of discipline' thesis, Cohen contended that as control mechanisms were dispersed into the community they penetrated deeper into the social fabric. A blurring of boundaries between the deviant and non-deviant and between the public and the private occurred. A 'punitive archipelago' expanded as new resources, technology and professional interests were applied to an increasing number of 'clients' and 'consumers'. Entrepreneurs were drawn into the control enterprise in search of profits. Communities were mobilised to act as voluntary control agents. But, throughout, punitive retribution (in the shape of the prison) remained at the core of the system (see Chapter 2). Cohen argued that the rhetoric of informalism and community empowerment in the 1970s masked what was really going on. Alternatives to formal punitive systems were used primarily at the 'soft' end of the system for petty or 'potential' delinquents or for elites for whom the very fact of exposure and loss of employment was considered to be punishment enough (Levi, 2002). But just as the 'soft' end of the system appeared to be benign, so the 'hard core' (typically male working-class youth) appeared to be more intractable, thereby justifying ever more punitive policies. In the meantime, the wider population has been subjected to increased surveillance and monitoring. Or, as Cohen (1987, p. 364) has put it, we have all become 'the object of preventive social control before any deviant act can take place'.

For Cohen (1985) the real effect of 'community justice' has been to increase the reach and intensity of state control:

■ The criminal justice system has expanded and drawn more people into its reach (wider nets).

■ The intensity of intervention (e.g. based on risk assessment) has increased (denser nets).

■ The 'old' institutions of social control (such as the prison) have not been replaced or radically altered, but supplemented by new forms of intervention (different nets).

In this way, rather than reducing the number of legal interventions, the creation of 'community alternatives' has resulted in the expansion of *both* formal *and* informal processes. Coercion has become disguised within a range of processes of conflict resolution (such as mediations and arbitrations) and masked by nostalgic discourses of 'neighbourhood' or 'community'. State power is thereby said to have increased rather than diminished.

Many of the practices of informal justice, and of restorative justice in particular, can indeed be viewed as constituting a particular 'mode of governance'. George Pavlich (2005, p. 10) identifies them explicitly as 'restorative governmentalities' that 'could be seen as indirect attempts to shape the motivations (and actions) of subjects somehow involved in criminal events ... in which restorative approaches distinguish themselves from the punitive coercions of criminal justice'. On this view, governments are seen to 'govern at a distance' and theories of *governmentality* work to explain how the reach of government is extended by dispersing powers, including through the institutional infrastructures of criminal justice, to agents and groups who work 'on the ground' to shape the lives of communities, particularly those of offenders or those considered to be 'at risk' of offending (see Chapter 4).

Figure 3.4
Blurring community engagement and state coercion? A community payback scheme introduced in London in 2008 in which convicted offenders are made visible by wearing bright fluorescent jackets

Pavlich draws out the particular ways of using power through the rationales and practices of restorative justice, especially how its participants make sense of the processes of conflict resolution in which they are engaged. The focus on 'real people' (rather than abstract legal subjects), on harms (rather than offences against the law), on emotions (as much as facts and material effects) and on resolutions (rather than judgments) requires particular sets of logics. Certainly, on the face of it, *some* power in resolving conflicts is taken away from professionals, institutions and agencies of the state, and taken up by communities, victims and families in FGCs. But in tracing these attempts to shift power, Pavlich (2005, pp. 13–14) finds that 'the attempt to sustain this mode of governance as a viable *alternative* to criminal justice reveals a paradox: while positing itself as a distinct alternative, restorative justice also predicates itself on key concepts within criminal justice'. In particular, 'the assumption of juridical definitions of crime, and an emphasis on individual offenders, commits restorative justice to key tenets of the adversarial mentalities it claims to exceed' (Pavlich, 2005, p. 23).

5   Conclusion

It is apparent that, whereas formal systems are typically bound by well-defined jurisdiction, the remit of informalism can be much broader. Andrew Ashworth (2001) has outlined a number of reservations about informalism (and restorative justice in particular) in terms of its relative lack of accountability and the absence of protection for the offender that appears to be built into non-state forms. Formal law might be less accessible, but at least due process offers opportunities for redress as a right rather than depending on the discretion of others. This raises the fundamental question of whether and when it is appropriate to take the administration of criminal justice out of the hands of the state. Ashworth contends that any response to offending should not be influenced by particular community or victim interests, but should be decided with reference to democratically decided policies that uphold the human rights of both defendants and victims. Without this, the 'rule of law' collapses in the differential priorities of different communities. Ashworth's concern is that fundamental principles of impartiality, proportionality and compensation for wrongs are placed at risk in informal systems. The European Convention on Human Rights, for example, refers to the universal right to a fair, impartial and independent hearing. It is far from clear how quasi-judicial proceedings and tribunals can meet these requirements.

Such criticisms demonstrate in part the pitfalls of both abandoning all aspects of formal criminal justice and the appropriation of informal justice alternatives by formal systems. However, it remains questionable whether any of the criticisms noted above in themselves negate the progressive, transformative and inclusionary potential of alternative conflict resolution.

The study of informal justice does indeed invoke a series of dilemmas and contradictions for the critical criminologist. Alternatives can expose the dangers of coercive state systems, but can also be more intrusive than formal law. Informal justice can represent both a contraction and an expansion of state apparatus. It is premised on the notion of 'returning power to the people', but may also involve the withdrawal of various forms of state protection. As a result, it is not uncommon to find support for informal systems being voiced across political and economic divides. For this reason, it continually evades terminal criticism. For some, it holds a promise of social justice; for others, it is a rational and cost-effective way of achieving governance. It expresses values of harmony over conflict, of equal access over unequal privilege, of participation in decision making over professional appropriation, and of substantive justice over rule-bound procedures (Abel, 1982). Herein lies the claim that whatever their contradictions and limitations, the search for 'alternatives' will continue. When confronted with the continuing exclusionary outcomes of retributive justice, this search remains, for many, a necessity.

Acknowledgement

The authors would like to acknowledge the contribution made by Jane Donoghue while this chapter was in its early drafts.

References

Abel, R. (1982) 'The contradictions of informal justice' in Abel, R. (ed.) *The Politics of Informal Justice*, vol. 1, New York, Academic Press.

Ashworth, A. (2001) 'Is restorative justice the way forward for criminal justice?', *Current Legal Problems*, vol. 54, pp. 347–76.

Bradley, T., Tauri, J. and Walters, R. (2006) 'Demythologising youth justice in Aotearoa/New Zealand' in Muncie, J. and Goldson, B. (eds) *Comparative Youth Justice: Critical Issues*, London, Sage.

Braithwaite, J. (1989) *Crime, Shame and Re-integration*, Cambridge, Cambridge University Press.

Braithwaite, J. (2003) 'Restorative justice and a better future' in McLaughlin, E. et al. (eds) (2003).

Cagnolo, C. (1933) *The* Akikuyu, *Their Customs, Traditions and Folklore*, Nyeri, Kenya, Mission Printing School.

Campbell, C., Devlin, R., O'Mahony, D., Doak, J., Jackson, J., Corrigan, T. and McEvoy, K. (2005) *Evaluation of the Northern Ireland Youth Conference Service*, Northern Ireland Office Research and Statistical Series: Report No. 12, Belfast, Northern Ireland Office, Statistics and Research Branch.

Christie, N. (1977) 'Conflicts as property', *British Journal of Criminology*, vol. 17, no. 1, pp. 1–15.

Cohen, S. (1979) 'The punitive city: notes on the dispersal of social control', *Contemporary Crises*, vol. 3, no. 4, pp. 341–63.

Cohen, S. (1985) *Visions of Social Control: Crime, Punishment, and Classification*, Cambridge, Polity.

Cohen, S. (1987) 'Taking decentralization seriously: values, visions and policies' in Lowman, J., Menzies, R.J. and Palys, T.S. (eds) *Transcarceration: Essays in the Sociology of Social Control*, Aldershot, Gower.

Conflict Mediation Services of Downsview (2002) *Restorative Justice Umbrella Analogy* [online], www.cmsd.org/justice/umbrella.html (Accessed 20 March 2009).

Crawford, A. and Newburn, T. (2003) *Youth Offending and Restorative Justice: Implementing Reform in Youth Justice*, Cullompton, Willan.

Cunneen, C. (2006) 'Reviving restorative justice traditions?' in Johnson, G. and Van Ness, D.W. (eds) *Handbook of Restorative Justice*, Cullompton, Willan.

Daly, K. (2001) 'Conferencing in Australia and New Zealand: variations, research findings, and prospects' in Morris, A. and Maxwell, G. (eds) *Restorative Justice for Juveniles: Conferencing, Mediation and Circles*, Oxford, Hart.

Daly, K. (2002) 'Restorative justice: the real story', *Punishment and Society*, vol. 4, no. 1, pp. 55–79.

Daly, K. (2006) 'The limits of restorative justice' in Sullivan, D. and Tifft, L. (eds) (2006).

de Haan, W. (1990) *The Politics of Redress*, London, Unwin Hyman.

Earle, A. (1966) *Narrative of a Residence in New Zealand*, Christchurch, Whitcombe and Tombs.

Gaarder, E. and Presser, L. (2006) 'A feminist vision of justice?' in Sullivan, D. and Tifft, L. (eds) (2006).

Garland, D. (2001) *The Culture of Control*, Oxford, Oxford University Press.

Gelsthorpe, L. and Morris, A. (2002) 'Restorative youth justice: the last vestiges of welfare' in Muncie, J., Hughes, G. and McLaughlin, E. (eds) *Youth Justice: Critical Readings*, London, Sage/Milton Keynes, The Open University.

Hadley, M.L. (2001) *The Spiritual Roots of Restorative Justice*, Albany, NY, State University of New York Press.

Harris, M.K. (1991) 'Moving into the new millennium: toward a feminist vision of justice' in Pepinsky, H.E. and Quinney, R. (eds) *Criminology as Peacemaking*, Bloomington, IN, Indiana University Press.

Harris, N. and Maruna, S. (2006) 'Shame, shaming and restorative justice: a critical appraisal' in Sullivan, D. and Tifft, L. (eds) (2006).

Jones, T. and Newburn, T. (2007) *Policy Transfer and Criminal Justice: Exploring US Influence over British Crime Control Policy*, Maidenhead, Open University Press.

Levi, M. (2002) 'Suite justice or sweet charity?', *Punishment and Society*, vol. 4, no. 2, pp. 147–63.

McLaughlin, E., Fergusson, R., Hughes, G. and Westmarland, L. (eds) (2003) *Restorative Justice: Critical Issues*, London, Sage/Milton Keynes, The Open University.

Merry, S.E. and Milner, N. (eds) (1995) *The Possibility of Popular Justice*, Ann Arbor, MI, University of Michigan Press.

Mokgoro, Y. (1998) '*Ubuntu* and the law in South Africa', *Buffalo Human Rights Law Review*, vol. 4, no. 15, pp. 16–23.

Morris, A. and Gelsthorpe, L. (2000) 'Re-visioning men's violence against female partners', *Howard Journal of Criminal Justice*, vol. 39, no. 4, pp. 412–28.

Morris, A. and Maxwell, G. (1998) 'Restorative justice in New Zealand: family group conferences as a case study', *Western Criminology Review*, vol. 1, no. 1, pp. 201–11.

O'Mahony, D. and Campbell, C. (2006) 'Mainstreaming restorative justice for young offenders through youth conferencing: the experience of Northern Ireland' in Junger-Tas, J. and Decker, S. (eds) *International Handbook of Juvenile Justice*, Dordecht, Springer.

Pavlich, G. (2005) *Governing Paradoxes of Restorative Justice*, London/Portland, OR, GlassHouse.

Pratt, J. (1992) *Punishment in a Perfect Society: The New Zealand Penal System, 1840–1939*, Wellington, Victoria University Press.

Scottish Executive (2005) *Restorative Justice Services in the Children's Hearings System*, Edinburgh, Scottish Executive.

Sherman, L.W. and Strang, H. (2007) *Restorative Justice: The Evidence*, London, Smith Institute.

Stern, V. (2001) 'An alternative vision: criminal justice developments in non-Western countries', *Social Justice*, vol. 28, no. 3, pp. 88–104.

Stewart, T. (1996) 'Family group conferences with young offenders in New Zealand' in Hudson, J., Morris, A., Maxwell, G. and Galaway, B. (eds) *Family Group Conferences: Perspectives on Policy and Practice*, Annandale, NSW, Federation Press.

Sullivan, D. and Tifft, L. (eds) *Handbook of Restorative Justice: A Global Perspective*, Abingdon, Routledge.

Tauri, J. and Morris, A. (1997) 'Re-forming justice: the potential of Maori processes', *The Australian and New Zealand Journal of Criminology*, vol. 30, no. 2, pp. 149–67.

Tombs, S. and Whyte, D. (2010) 'Crime, harm and corporate power' in Muncie J., Talbot, D. and Walters, R. (eds) *Crime: Local and Global*, Cullompton, Willan/Milton Keynes, The Open University.

United Nations (2002) *Basic Principles on the Use of Restorative Justice Programmes in Criminal Matters: Resolutions and Decisions Adopted by the Economic and Social Council at its Substantive Session of 2002*, New York, United Nations.

Walgrave, L. (1995) 'Restorative justice for juveniles: just a technique or a fully fledged alternative?', *Howard Journal*, vol. 34, no. 3, pp. 228–49.

Walgrave, L. (ed.) (1998) *Restorative Justice for Juveniles*, Leuven, Leuven University Press.

Weitkampf, E. and Kerner, H.J. (2002) *Restorative Justice: Theoretical Foundations*, Cullompton, Willan.

Wilson, O. (1990) *Kororareka and Other Essays*, Dunedin, John McIndoe.

Yazzie, R. (1994) 'Life comes from it: Navajo justice', *The Ecology of Justice* (In Context), vol. 3, no. 8, pp. 29–31.

Zehr, H. and Mika, H. (1997) 'Fundamental concepts of restorative justice', *Contemporary Justice Review*, vol. 1, no. 1, pp. 47–56.

Chapter 4
Risk prediction, assessment and management

Deborah Drake and John Muncie

Contents

1   Introduction

The notion of risk has become a deeply embedded concern of many Western societies. It is commonly discussed in relation to countless aspects of social life on international, local and individual levels. References to risk are found in relation to:

■ personal and global health

■ pollution and the environment

■ industrial or workplace hazards and safety

■ food safety and hygiene

■ financial and economic matters, including personal investments, insurance policies and mortgages, as well as national and international economic relations

■ personal safety and security in private and public spaces

■ policing, crime, crime policy, victimisation and prisons.

Risk is not only associated with dangers, harms and negative outcomes. It is also a feature of thrill seeking, 'adrenaline' sports, life satisfaction and stock-market success. However, the term 'risk' has been used prolifically in a variety of social, financial and political contexts to refer to the calculability or prediction of a potential harm or hazard. It is also a highly politicised and increasingly emotive concept that stimulates

Figure 4.1
A man takes a bungee jump in the Tochal mountain area of Iran

action and prompts discourse and debate. The meaning of the term 'risk', then, has technical and personal, and positive and negative, connotations.

For the discipline of criminology, risk has become a central concept (Brown and Pratt, 2000). Regardless of whether one is interested in pragmatic criminological fields (such as crime prevention and crime avoidance) or more theoretical realms of social reality (such as the possibilities of a 'risk society'), the concept of risk has risen to some prominence. It invites investigation from a variety of vantage points: including legal, political, psychological, sociological and geographical perspectives.

The aims of this chapter are to explore:

■ the 'late modern risk society' thesis

■ how risk is constituted locally, globally, personally and governmentally

■ the way in which the concept of risk is used in criminal justice contexts

■ how risk interconnects with themes of power and of harm and violence.

Section 2 examines the prevalence of risk discourse in a global context. It reveals how the concept has been theorised by the late modern risk thesis, most associated with the work of Ulrich Beck and Anthony Giddens. Section 3 explores the degree to which risk assessment and risk management have come to be pervasive in a restructuring of many Western criminal justice systems since the 1970s. Section 4 then offers some means by which the theorisation and application of 'risk mentalities' can be subject to critical appraisal.

2   The prevalence of risk

Since the 1970s, a discourse of risk has come to permeate global concerns for security and safety. Fears of nuclear radiation, terrorist attack, global warming, identity theft, migration, unsafe foodstuffs, economic meltdown, the repercussions of waging war, transnational organised crime, 'natural' disasters, environmental pollution, and so on, appear to be all-pervasive. Some of these risks are, of course, far from new, but what *is* new is the perception that in a globalised world certain risks have taken on more threatening connotations. Some risks (e.g. terrorism, global warming, economic uncertainty) are seen as being *out of control* – out of governmental control and out of our control. Everywhere we are presented with images of risk: not only suggesting

Figure 4.2
Goddard's cartoon of
reactions to risk

"Some bloke wants to know if we've carried out
a thorough risk assessment?"

an apparent collapse in traditional orderings, a withering away of
self-control and social cohesion and the potential threat of imminent
danger, but also requiring fundamental shifts in how we relate to and
can make sense of the social world.

2.1 The 'late modern risk society' thesis

For some authors, such as Beck and Giddens, the changing nature of
social life is symptomatic of a (global) transition from one form of
society to another: from what were seen as the old certainties of class
structures that characterised industrial capitalism to the diffuse
boundaries, uncertainties and anxieties of a 'risk society'. They suggest
that there has been a transition from the scientific sureties of modernity,
which were characteristic of the late nineteenth and early twentieth
centuries, to the uncertainties of a 'late modern' present. The terms 'late
modern' and 'high modern' are typically used by these authors in
preference to that of 'postmodern': 'High modernity is characterised by
widespread scepticism about providential reason, coupled with the
recognition that science and technology are double-edged, creating new
parameters of risk and danger as well as offering beneficent possibilities
for human kind' (Giddens, 1991, pp. 27–8).

Beck and Elisabeth Beck-Gernsheim (2003, p. 22) have argued that the risk society holds implications for every individual: namely, that there is 'a struggle for a new relationship between the individual and society'. They state that:

> We live in an age in which the social order of the national state, class, ethnicity and traditional family is in decline ... The choosing, deciding, shaping human being who aspires to be the author of his or her own life, the creator of an individual identity, is the central character of our time.
>
> (Beck and Beck-Gernsheim, 2003, pp. 22–3)

For these authors, social life has come to be characterised by an individualised 'risk consciousness' in which communities and identities have become fragmented and atomised. In the modern age, risk was seen as something that could be measured, calculated and predicted. Although in the 'late modern' age it is still seen as such, risk is also accompanied by increasing uncertainty, indeterminacy and contingency (Kemshall, 2003). Beck (1992), in particular, has argued that the risk society, more so than at any other point in history, is characterised by local and global ambiguity and fearfulness. This underlying sense of insecurity, Beck argues, is brought about primarily through manufactured risks and the inability to contain them effectively. Humanly produced risks (such as the Chernobyl nuclear disaster, global warming or environmental pollution) generally emanate from Western countries, but have adverse implications across the globe. Further, these manufactured risks 'evade established systems of security and welfare' (Beck, cited in Mythen, 2007, p. 797). This is in contrast to natural hazards, which, Beck argues, are not as globally threatening because they have a more local impact and can be constrained by both time and structural factors (Mythen, 2007). As Hazel Kemshall (2003, p. 9) has stated, 'No longer is nature the source of risk, it is nature itself which is threatened by risk'.

The risk society is, therefore, best described as a pessimistic awareness of the dangers inherent in our social world: 'In other words, we now think of the negatives – the risks – associated with the possibilities of modernity, rather than the benefits' (Hudson, 2003, p. 43). Further, Kemshall argues that 'The risk society's central feature is the "precautionary principle", better to be safe than sorry' (Leonard, cited in Kemshall, 2003, p. 9).

The 'late modern risk society' thesis significantly shifts the concept of risk from its neutral and quasi-scientific connections with insurance and its positive connections with entrepreneurial 'risk taking', towards the negative suggestion of (all-pervasive) danger. To calculate risk is now to estimate future dangers and to act accordingly, whether this involves decisions to invade, prosecute, withhold consent, eat certain foods, and so on. Given the ubiquitous nature of the concept, it can be applied to virtually any behaviour or event in any global context. In this sense, the 'concept of risk emerges as a key idea for [our] times because of its uses as a *forensic resource* ... danger would once have been the right word but plain danger does not have the aura of science or afford the pretension of a possible precise calculation' (Douglas, 1990, pp. 3–4, emphasis added).

A 'risk society' is also defined by its efforts to manage risk (O'Malley, 1998). As a concept, and as a political philosophy, it is driven by a renewed search for order and stability through the scientific endeavour to hypothesise, identify, measure, test and, above all, predict the future in terms of 'known' probabilities (Dean, 1999). The managing of risk involves the 'joined-up' modernisation of various state agencies in the pursuit (or imposition) of greater stability and predictability in human social life.

Activity 4.1

Risk is a part of everyday life, but to what extent are we actually 'at risk' of positive or negative life events, such as winning the lottery or being struck by lightning? The April 1996 issue of *DISCOVER* magazine presented statistics for 'A Fistful of Risks'. Try the following quiz to determine your Risk Awareness Quotient (RAQ). The statistics are based on trends in the USA. The correct answers are given at the end of the quiz.

Extract 4.1

Rate your risk quiz

Remember that risk calculation is an inexact predictor of future events. It reports on averages and not on individual circumstances. The past is not always a good indicator of what will happen in the future!

1   What is your risk of home repossession in the next 12 months?

   1 in 24

   1 in 345

   1 in 720

2   Which of the following is most likely to happen to you?

   Being struck by lightning

   Being infected with flesh-eating bacteria

   Being injured in a lift

3   Which of the following is most likely to kill you in the next 12 months?

Drinking detergent

Dog bite

Snake bite

4   Which of the following is least likely to happen to you?

Winning the Irish Sweepstakes [lottery] jackpot

Contracting the Ebola virus, if you're an African

Dying in an earthquake or a volcano

5   Which of the following accounts for the most childhood accidental deaths?

Fire

Choking

Poisoning

6   Which of the following takes the most off your life expectancy?

Driving once without a seat belt on

Drinking one diet soft drink

Smoking one cigarette

7   What are the chances that, in the next 12 months, you will be murdered?

1 in 50,000

1 in 32,000

1 in 11,000

8   What is the risk of your being wiped out (with nearly everybody else) next year by a catastrophic comet, meteor or asteroid impact?

1 in 750,000

1 in 20,000

1 in 15 million

Answers

1   The risk of home repossession is 1 in 345.

2   The risk of being:

Infected with a flesh-eating bacteria: 1 in 700,000

Struck by lightning: 1 in 750,000

Injured in a lift: 1 in 6 million.

3   The likelihood of dying by:

Dog bite: 1 in 20 million

Detergent: 1 in 23 million

Snakebite: 1 in 36 million.

4   The likelihood of these events happening to you is:

Irish Sweepstakes: 1 in 5,245,786

Earthquake or volcano: 1 in 11 million

Ebola virus: 1 in 14 million (for an African).

5   Childhood accidental deaths:

Fire: 15%

Choking: 3%

Poison: 1%.

6   Your life expectancy is reduced by:

6 seconds when driving without a seat belt

9 seconds by drinking one diet soft drink

12 minutes by having one cigarette.

7   1 in 11,000.

8   1 in 20,000.

Source: adapted from Rate Your Risk Quiz *(undated)*

Comment

The quiz above illustrates that the likely occurrence of the risks associated with various everyday activities is generally quite low. However, the preoccupation with risk in many Western societies persists in an effort to create a sense of stability and predictability in our lives.

The 'risk society' is a society of paradox. Risk can be a euphemism for profound pessimism in a world where experts and politicians cannot be trusted, where 'nobody knows' and where dangers and threats are so inestimable that we are left with social inertia and paralysing fear: a 'riskiness of everything and the certainty of nothing'

(O'Malley, 1999, p. 139). But it can also be a society in which the calculating and managing of risks become a key preoccupation. Here the furtherance of scientific knowledge and technological development holds a promise to make the 'unknowable future' knowable once more. However, contemporary uncertainty can also encourage nostalgic rediscoveries of the past in the pursuit of faith-based knowledge and morality alongside new politics of authority. Beck's (1992) route out of these contradictions is to accept and embrace the new uncertainties; open them up to democratic public debate; scrutinise where and how risks and hazards are generated, and by whom; and encourage a healthy scepticism of any protagonist of the 'scientific solution' and of 'scientific certainty'. For Giddens (1994), too, the idea of risk need not be intrinsically negative; it also opens up new opportunities and necessitates the rethinking of traditional political agendas.

Figure 4.3
The risks of everyday life?

2.2 Risk, justice and crime control

In criminology and criminal justice the discourse of risk has become a significant part of both policy and academic inquiry. It is found in various aspects of offender profiling, offender management programmes, crime prevention, crime avoidance and community safety strategies, and in informing decisions over inmate security, pre-sentencing reports and prison parole (Kemshall, 2003). As Gordon Hughes (1998, p. 7) has argued, 'In the context of crime there is increasing emphasis placed on the management of risk rather than the prevention of crime per se. The idea that crime can be effectively prevented seems to be in the process of being replaced by a widespread recognition that at best crime, given its routine social normality and presence, may be better understood as a risk to be managed'. Offenders and potential offenders, victims and potential victims: all are increasingly judged with reference to classification systems ranking them from low to high risk. Moreover, George Rigakos (1999) maintains that risk prevention strategies tend to self-generate. With each response to a risk factor, a new risk is created by the technology, practice or policy originally designed to inhibit the risk. The cycle of risk, then, is perpetual.

Richard Ericson and Kevin Haggerty (1997) have argued that risk discourse cultivates insecurities and presents risk-based 'expert knowledge' as the only available solution. New technological and behavioural strategies can then be promoted as the main route to greater public security. The vocabulary of risk assures a constant attention to 'cultural pressure points'. Parents, teachers, clergy, social workers, policy makers, politicians, police and the media are constantly 'risk aware' and are often 'risk averse': making judgements and decisions on the basis that some future risk might be imaginable and always on guard for indications of danger (Schehr, 2005). It is a way of understanding and acting that might be viewed as just as likely to engender mistrust and suspicion as to ensure future security.

3   Technologies of risk

The import of risk discourse and strategies of risk assessment and risk management into systems of criminal justice is reflected in myriad complex ways. This section is based on the following eight assumptive trajectories and draws out the logical connections between them.

1   Penal welfare provided the parameters of debate over the purpose of criminal justice in most Western societies for much of the twentieth century (Garland, 2001). Social insurance, offender rehabilitation and social work – predicated on the concept of 'need' – were its hallmarks. Due to rising crime rates and re-evaluations of the role of a welfare state, by the 1970s this modernist agenda was largely perceived to have 'failed'. The emergence of risk filled the vacuum.

2   Policy makers began to accept the idea that crime was normal and ubiquitous. It could not be eradicated. The best that could be hoped for was that crime could be managed, in particular, by identifying and targeting those most 'at risk' of offending or reoffending in certain categories.

3   This new mentality of 'damage limitation' came to view crime less as a form of rule breaking by those of individual or social pathology (as criminology had traditionally maintained) and more as a risk to be calculated by us all, whether as offenders or as victims.

4   It followed, then, that crime management could no longer be the sole preserve of governments. Families, communities and businesses were all identified as having a role to play in crime prevention. Self-governance and public participation have become widely encouraged. The state, it has been argued, has begun to govern more 'at a distance', relying on 'joined-up' partnerships, free market solutions, deregulation and privatisation, rather than traditional centralised structures (Rose, 2000). This shift is also expressed in the practical and discursive terms of 'crime reduction partnerships', 'inter-agency cooperation', 'active citizenship' and 'self-help' initiatives that are now common across many Western societies –

including the USA, Australia, Sweden and the Netherlands, as well as the UK.

5   In contrast, other risk strategies are explicitly 'expert led' or 'scientifically led'. As a core concern is less one of 'curing' the individual offender and more one of minimising risks and reducing costs, the most salient risk factors that might lead to criminal behaviour in the future need to be identified. Longitudinal research, particularly when replicated over time and across different jurisdictions, has claimed that risk factors can be clearly identified and that, as a result, the most effective means to achieve crime reduction can be formulated.

6   Risk profiling can identify likely offenders and where crime is most likely to occur so that particular groups of people and particular places can be more effectively subjected to surveillance, policed and managed; and potential victims can know which people and places to avoid.

7   Risk (or actuarial) assessment – based on clinical calculations of future probabilities – can also be applied to known offenders to determine their level of risk of reoffending. The assessment tools typically comprise standardised inventories of risk, which can then be used to assign a 'reconviction score' to an offender and in turn to suggest the most appropriate intervention, whether that be, for example, some form of parenting correction, cognitive behavioural therapy or preventive detention. For some, this suggests possibilities for reinvented, individually targeted forms of rehabilitation.

8   All interventions require monitoring and evaluation so that governments can know 'what works' and can allocate resources appropriately. To do so requires the managerial tools of setting performance targets, putting structures of accountability in place and measuring 'success' through criminal justice audits. Policy, in these terms, is then capable of being 'rational', 'non-ideological' and 'evidence led'. Auditing for effectiveness becomes a continual self-justifying process (see Figure 4.4).

The presence of these rationalities in various 'technologies' of crime control is outlined in the rest of this section and critically assessed in Section 4.

Figure 4.4
The never-ending cycle of risk management (Source: Olzak, 2007, Figure 1)

3.1 Actuarial justice

The emergence of the terms 'risk management' and 'prevention' in criminal justice reflects the growing importance of what has been termed a new penology of 'actuarial justice'. This shift first took place in the USA in the 1980s in response to demands for more accountability and rationality in correctional policy. Jonathan Simon was one of the first to identify how actuarial assessments of risk were making a radical impact on public and political mentalities (Simon, 1988). The 'old' disciplinary society of correcting and punishing individuals appeared to be challenged by a 'new' risk society in which the primary aim was to identify 'risky populations' on the basis of aggregate data and informed calculations of future probabilities. For Simon, the ideological power of this 'actuarial risk society' resides in its depoliticisation of social problems and its ability to neutralise political and moral resistance. In subsequent analyses, Simon, together with Malcolm Feeley (Feeley and Simon, 1992, 1994), focused directly on how actuarial logic is capable of radically altering the discourses, objectives and techniques of crime control. They argue, for example, that the rehabilitative rationales of criminal justice have been increasingly challenged by an actuarialist language of calculating risk and estimating the statistical probability of offending: much in the manner of insurance tables, which predict the likelihood of having a house fire, house flooding or serious illness.

Appropriate interventions are then modelled on psychological profiling and on predicted estimates of current and future 'risk', rather than, say, on assessments of rehabilitative 'need'. Through the use of aggregate data, criminal justice, it is contended, becomes more concerned with the targeting and managing of specific (pre-criminal) categories of people. Management of these groups is realised through the application of increasingly sophisticated risk assessment technologies and prediction tables. In turn, this shift also enables the system to construct its own measures of success and failure (meeting targets) and to predict its own needs (efficient allocation of resources).

Feeley and Simon's thesis does not deny the continuance of traditional disciplinary forms of intervention, such as the prison, but the purpose of these, they claim, has significantly changed from one of correction to one of containment and incapacitation (see Chapter 2). Further, actuarialism logically connects with global processes, such as the proliferation of neo-liberal, market-driven socio-economic policies that have reduced welfare expenditure and protection and have produced surplus populations (the 'underclass'), which then have to be contained and controlled. In short, actuarialism has helped to legitimise a 'waste management' response to difficult and troubling populations.

Activity 4.2

In thinking about the impact of actuarialism, consider the following questions:

- How far do you think actuarialism is a radical new departure for criminal justice in the twenty-first century?

- In what ways is risk management compatible with punitiveness (as discussed in Chapter 2)?

Comment

Feeley and Simon (1992, 1994) acknowledge that the impact of actuarialism is far from hegemonic, but are convinced of its novelty and potential to overturn traditional criminal justice objectives such as rehabilitation and deterrence (see Chapter 1). Pat O'Malley (1992), on the other hand, argues that actuarialism has long held a place in penal and social policy. What is novel is a shift away from *social* forms, such as social insurance and the welfare state, to *market* forms of actuarialism, such as private insurance and private security. The precise form in any one jurisdiction is determined primarily by the character and success of broader political programmes to which it is aligned. Neither does the emergence of a precautionary (prudentialist) risk management discourse necessarily preclude the coexistence of punitive technologies. Both prudentialism and punitivism emphasise that the individual should take full responsibility for their actions. Penal incapacitation (despite its cost) and risk management can be viewed as integral and mutually supportive strategies that are consistent with a broader climate of marketised neo-liberalism. Further, O'Malley notes a series of risk reduction or insurance-based strategies in which the burden of managing risk is held by individuals themselves. In other words, crime prevention becomes the responsibility of private individuals who, through self-interest and 'liberated' from an over-protective state, will be able to take active steps to insure themselves against personal harm or property loss and damage. Investment in security measures becomes an essential element of a newly constituted 'risk-averse' citizenship.

3.2 Risk prediction and risk profiling

> More than anything else, early intervention is crucial … recent
> advances in our knowledge have offered the promise that we might be
> able to achieve it. … We also know a lot more about how to protect
> people against these risks. … we can now be reasonably confident that
> we can identify likely problems at a very early stage.
>
> (Blair, 2006)

These are the words of the then UK Prime Minister, Tony Blair,
announcing in 2006 that criminality could be predicted at a very early
age, indeed even pre-birth, and that we now know what works to
prevent it. Such ideas were by no means original, but were given added
impetus at the time by renewed political interest in the Cambridge Study
of Delinquent Development and the ability to identify and measure the
risk factors that will propel people into 'a life of crime'. In 1961, a sample
of 411 working-class boys aged 8 was selected from six primary schools
in Camberwell, London. Girls were not included. Twelve of the sample
were from minority ethnic communities. They were contacted again
nine times over the following forty years (Farrington et al., 2006) to
examine which of them had developed a 'delinquent way of life' and
to identify the common characteristics of those who had continued a
'life of crime' into adulthood. About a fifth of the sample had been
convicted of criminal offences as juveniles and over a third by the time
they had reached the age of 32. But half of the total convictions were
amassed by only twenty-three young men – less than 6 per cent of the
sample. Most of these 'chronic offenders' shared common childhood
characteristics (such as impulsivity, low intelligence, convicted parents,
family breakdown). Based on this data, the Cambridge Study has
consistently identified various individual, family and environmental
predictors ('risk factors' or 'profiles') of future criminality. An initial list
of 150 potential factors was eventually reduced to thirty-nine of the
most statistically significant. The most prevalent *individual* factors are
low intelligence, personality and impulsiveness. The strongest *family*
factors are criminal or anti-social parents, poor parental supervision and
disrupted families, while at the *environmental* level, peer association,
areas of deprivation and schools with high delinquency rates are the
best indicators (Farrington and Welsh, 2007). On this basis it is
contended that future 'chronic offenders' could have been predicted
with reasonable accuracy at the age of 10 (Farrington, 1994).

Longitudinal surveys are the necessary research tools to examine links
between risk factors and offending. These typically begin with a survey
of large samples of children and young people, with repeated interviews
over significant periods of time (usually more than five years). David
Farrington and Brandon Welsh (2007) identify over thirty such studies

that have been carried out or are still in process over the past sixty years, mainly in cities in the USA (e.g. Chicago, Pittsburgh, New York, Philadelphia and Denver), but also in Australia, New Zealand and Scandinavia. Although not all of these studies are methodologically comparable, they do confirm that a cluster of individual, family and community circumstances are associated with quantified estimates of anti-social and criminal behaviour as recorded in self-report and official criminal statistics. As a result, Farrington (2000) has claimed the existence of a 'globalisation of knowledge' in which a 'risk factor prevention paradigm' has not only a local but also a global (or, at least, a Western industrialised) applicability. In policy terms, this identification of the most prevalent risks has come to be crucial in the formulation of 'early intervention' strategies in order to 'nip offending in the bud' and to prevent the onset of 'criminal careers':

> A key advantage of the risk factor prevention paradigm is that it links explanation and prevention, fundamental and applied research, and scholars and practitioners. Importantly, the paradigm is easy to understand and to communicate, and it is readily accepted by policy makers, practitioners, and the general public. Both risk factors and interventions are based on empirical research rather than theories. The paradigm avoids difficult theoretical questions about which risk factors have causal effects.
>
> (Farrington, 2000, p. 7)

The more such surveys have been carried out and the more their methodologies have become sophisticated, the more complexities have emerged regarding the particular weight that might be given to some factors over others, how they might combine in particular circumstances and whether there is a linear relationship between identified risk and subsequent behaviour. As most of such studies acknowledge, the risk factor prevention paradigm reveals correlations, patterns and links, but does not necessarily establish causes. For example, a UK-based study of 1957 14- to 15-year-olds in Peterborough in 2000 combined individual personality factors (self-control, morality, dispositions) and family circumstances with lifestyles and community contexts. It found a 'strong interaction' between individual characteristics and high-risk lifestyles (alcohol and drug use, association with delinquent peers in public spaces). These findings suggested three distinct groups of young offenders: *propensity induced* (the 'maladjusted'), *lifestyle dependent* (related to peer group pressure) and *situationally limited* (well-adjusted individuals who may nevertheless occasionally offend, depending on the situation). Such research established that it is the relation between individual and family factors, coupled with situational contexts, which allows us to identify the complex parameters of risk (Wikström and Butterworth, 2006). Further research in Pittsburgh, USA, based on over

1500 interviews with boys aged 7, 10 and 13 in 1987 and 1988 and repeated over the following twelve years, found a significant interaction between types of people and the nature of the area in which they lived. The Pittsburgh Youth Study concluded that a key risk factor was the socio-economic status of particular neighbourhoods. Those with some of the lowest individual risk factors nevertheless offended more frequently if living in the most deprived neighbourhoods (Wikström and Loeber, 2000).

Other studies, however, have found it difficult to isolate specific risk factors, whether based on personality, family or community. Research by Colin Webster et al. (2006), into young people growing up in poor neighbourhoods in Teesside in the north-east of England, for example, concluded that risk-based assessments may not always be reliable. Their in-depth interviews with 185 young people revealed that over 50 per cent, who would be considered 'high risk' if the Cambridge Study's methodology were to be applied (e.g. large disharmonious families, poor parental supervision, truanting, low educational achievement), had no history of offending and no contact with the youth justice system. These researchers contended that the adoption of standardised risk identification tends to negate the complex dynamics of (unpredictable) personal biographies, denies the material significance of locale and overlooks the broader context of labour market conditions and related opportunity structures. Other researchers have argued that risk factors are not necessarily universal but may be offence, gender and 'race' specific (Kemshall, 2003).

The longitudinal Edinburgh Study of Youth Transitions and Crime, involving a cohort of 4100 children and young people who started secondary school – aged around 12 – in the city of Edinburgh in 1998, focused more on continuance than onset of offending (McAra and McVie, 2007). However, after allowing for the impact of individual, family and community factors, this study concluded that the deeper that children and young people penetrate youth justice systems, the less likely they are to 'desist' from offending. In other words, these researchers noted that the key risk factor propelling young people into and through youth justice systems is not their individual personalities or 'dysfunctional' families, but police targeting and subsequent labelling and stigma as they passed through the judicial process. Here the key to reducing offending was considered to lie more in minimal intervention and maximum diversion than in early intervention.

Recurrent commentaries on the risk factor prevention paradigm have revealed that the links between risk factors and criminal pathways are inherently complex and problematic. The paradigm tells us more about *what* factors are linked to (known) offending, but not *how* and *why* such factors might be linked. Risk factors can impact differentially; it is difficult to know which might have more weight than others at particular times and with particular population groups. The paradigm also 'misses' valuable data about different qualitative *perceptions* of risk that could be gleaned from juvenile justice practitioners or from young people themselves (Pitts, 2001; Armstrong, 2004; Case, 2007). By applying *generalised* probabilities to individuals, the risk factor prevention paradigm can produce substantial numbers of 'false positives': that is, a mislabelling and inaccurate identification of putative offenders who may then be subject to unwarranted degrees of intrusive intervention (Smith, 2006). Risk factor research is based on known or self-confessed offenders. It has never been seriously applied to understanding crimes of the powerful and state crime. It tends to reaffirm the 'failings' of (some) working-class male youth in industrialised Western societies. Kevin Haines and Stephen Case (2008, p. 8) argue that it transforms 'the dynamic, interactive process of offending into the static effect of developmental anomalies by conceiving of diverse (psychological, emotional, social, structural) factors as if a unitary phenomenon which can be ascribed a statistical value'.

Activity 4.3

Consider the following questions:

■ Why do you think that the application of a risk factor prevention paradigm has become a defining characteristic of criminal justice since the 1990s?

■ What might be considered the major limitations of this approach? Can 'risk' be measured by aggregate data?

■ How might a risk factor prevention paradigm be put into practice? What particular criminal justice interventions does it suggest?

Comment

Measures of risk prediction have become the bedrock not only of risk assessment but also of identifying how the likelihood of offending might be reduced (protective factors) through particular focused interventions. Numerous authors (e.g. Farrington, 1996; Utting, 1996; Sherman et al., 1997; Graham, 1998) have maintained that the 'most hopeful' methods of tackling crime and anti-social behaviour (derived in the main from experimental research in the USA and Canada) are those that involve a series of 'early interventions'. The key influence was that of the Perry pre-school programme in Michigan. This experiment began in the 1970s and provided sixty African American 3- to 5-year-olds with high-quality nursery education. Their development was compared to a control group who did not have such support. Twenty years later, 30 per cent of the experimental group had been arrested at least once, compared to 50 per cent of the control group. At the age of 40, programme group members had also achieved higher levels of schooling, better records of employment and higher annual incomes (Schweinhart et al., cited in Farrington and Welsh, 2007).

On the basis of such programmes (and their evaluation), successful modes of intervention, it is claimed, include: pre-school intellectual enrichment and child skills training programmes (individual factors); parental education, day care and parent management training (family factors); and teacher training and school-based discipline management (environmental factors). Moreover, it is argued that the overall approach is 'evidence led', predicated not on some vague philosophical aspiration (such as rehabilitation, restoration, welfare or justice), but on a proven capacity to reveal 'what works' through scientific research. What is also noticeable about such research findings, however, is how they reduce what might be considered a requirement of a just and compassionate society – family support, job training, after-school activity programmes, and so on – to being viable (and resourced) only if connected to a crime prevention rationale. Nevertheless, in the context of criminal justice driven by punitive values, advocates of the risk factor prevention paradigm can present their thesis as a progressive and pragmatic solution:

> Since most prolific offenders start early, an important policy aim should be to prevent the early onset of offending. Cognitive-behavioural skills training programmes, parent training, pre-school intellectual enrichment programmes and home visiting programmes are effective. Because offenders tend to be deviant in many aspects of their lives, early prevention that reduces offending will probably have wide-ranging benefits in reducing accommodation problems, relationship problems, employment problems, alcohol and drug problems, and aggressive behaviour. Hence, there is enormous scope for significant cost savings from effective early intervention programmes.
>
> (Farrington et al., 2006, p. vi)

3.3 Evidence-led policy and the 'what works' industry

Offender profiling and risk assessment have also been turned to as a means of overcoming the 'nothing works' pessimism that had pervaded much of criminal justice, and particularly probation,

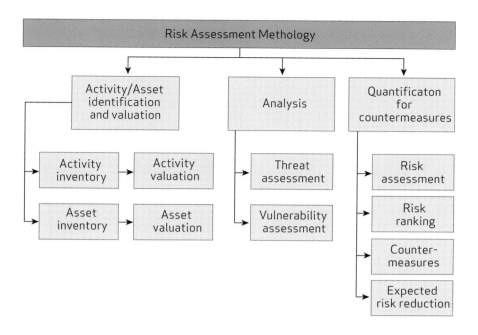

Figure 4.5
A risk assessment
methodology
formulated by the
security industry
(Source: Gordon
Herrald Associates,
undated, Figure 1)

since the 1970s. Gradually, the case has been made that *some* forms of intervention can be successful in reducing *some* reoffending for *some* offenders at *some* times. A core element (illustrated in Figure 4.5) is the methodology of risk identification, evaluation (given as 'valuation' in the figure), assessment, ranking and the formulation of countermeasures.

Optimism in one such countermeasure was generated by the work of the Canadian researchers, Robert Ross, Elizabeth Fabiano and Crystal Ewles (1988). Their 'reasoning and rehabilitation' project was designed to retrain high-risk adult probationers via a cognitive skills training programme. The results showed a recidivism rate that was reduced by some 50 per cent for those on the programme compared to regular probation. As a result, they claimed that some rehabilitation programmes can 'work' remarkably well when properly resourced. In a meta analysis of over 400 research studies on the effectiveness of such 'treatments', Mark Lipsey (1995) claimed that when intervention is focused around behavioural training or skills issues and sustained over a period of at least six months, a 10 per cent reduction in reoffending can be expected. Focused and structured supervision programmes combining behavioural and skills training, training in moral reasoning, interpersonal problem-solving skills training and vocationally oriented psychotherapy have all been cited as successful.

This new 'rehabilitative orthodoxy' claims that highly structured programmes that compel offenders to address their behaviour are capable of success. In turn, this has facilitated the rapid development of highly intensive interventionist approaches, whether directed at preventing crime through 'nipping it in the bud' or at reducing further offending by encouraging individual responsibility. Both are justified by reference to the capacity of such treatments to 'work' in risk management terms. That is, they:

■ are based on classificatory systems that enable the most intensive programmes to be targeted at 'high-risk' offenders

■ focus on the specific factors associated with offending

■ use a structured learning style that requires active participation on the part of the offender

■ develop high programme integrity

■ match the level of risk, based on offending history, with the level of intervention

■ use cognitive behavioural interventions, which help to improve problem solving and social interaction, but which also address and challenge the attitudes, values and beliefs that support offending behaviour.

Much contemporary theory and practice in crime prevention, desistance and recidivism, then, combine techniques of risk calculation (backed up by evaluation research) with a re-emergent 'rehabilitative' commitment to 'changing people'. In what has proved to be a hugely influential piece of research, Lawrence Sherman and colleagues prepared a report in 1997 for the US Department of Justice outlining 'what works', 'what fails' and 'what might be worth pursuing' in the practice of crime prevention. Based on a review of more than 500 evaluations of crime prevention practices, the authors devised lists of successes and failures. For example, they argued that some rehabilitation programmes; early, focused intervention; some prison-based therapeutic community treatments; and the incapacitation of 'high-risk' offenders all 'work' to reduce 'crime in the community', whereas, Scared Straight programmes (prison visits), correctional boot camps, juvenile wilderness programmes and unstructured counselling do 'not work'. This review is now almost universally accepted as incontestable 'policy relevant' knowledge.

However, the extent of adoption of this evidence has been somewhat mixed. For example, the report by Sherman et al. (following the work of the Cambridge Study) makes it clear that early intervention in the form of home visits by health professionals 'works' best to prevent the onset of delinquency. Ten years after Sherman et al.'s report, boot camps in the USA, though reduced in number, still formed a core component of the correctional system in the USA, while many 'welfare' aspects of parental and family support were being cut back. This disjuncture suggests that at the level of policy implementation, considerations of what is deemed to 'work' are driven as much by political priorities as by any adherence to social scientific research.

Nick Tilley (2003) has also warned of the methodological and scientific shortcomings of scientific evaluations based on experiments which are then uncritically employed to inform policy. He suggests that the quest for a universal, globally replicable 'what works' paradigm is both misguided and unachievable. A more 'realist' approach would be to ask the rather more complex and contingent question of 'what works for whom, in what circumstances and contexts, and how?' What works today may not tomorrow. What works with some people in some places will not with others. Indeed, attempts to replicate the positive outcomes of the Canadian reasoning and rehabilitation project have not always been successful. An evaluation of cognitive skills programmes for adult male prisoners in the UK between 1996 and 1998 found no difference in reconviction rates between those who attended the programme and those who did not (Falshaw et al., 2003).

Activity 4.4

Consider the following questions:

- What are the strengths and weaknesses of a 'what works' paradigm in identifying and responding to offending?

- Does the scientific testing and implementation of various programmes inevitably lead to a more rationalised and efficient (and uncontroversial) criminal justice system?

Comment

The discourse of 'what works' appears as practical and non-ideological. It promises future policy reform that is free from politics and is geared to prevention rather than crude punishment. It also seems to be simple common sense. How can anyone claim to act otherwise and advocate policies that are demonstrable failures? Yet criminal justice reform is also clearly driven by assessments of what is politically and publicly popular. In practice, 'what works' is not just a rational, objective and neutral process; it is also driven by political, institutional and economic imperatives. 'What works' research itself has been rather inconclusive. It has only rarely been conducted on a fully scientific basis – that is, by using randomised trials with control groups: the 'gold standard' for medical research – and appears to standardise modes of understanding and intervention that take little note of diverse personal biographies and changing social circumstances. Such research also appears to be used selectively and only when it seems to confirm predetermined governmental policies (Pitts, 2001). From a practitioner point of view, 'what works'-based formulae tend to negate professional autonomy and trap decision making within an inflexible, technocratic and predetermined ranking of risk (Webb, 2001). In a more fundamental sense, social, economic and political issues become redefined as problems to be *managed* rather than as issues to be *resolved*. In countries like the USA since the 1980s and particularly in England since the 1990s, the political symbolism of toughness appears to have taken precedence over the practical questions of effectiveness, efficiency and economy. If there is an emergent globalised paradigm of crime prevention and crime control, it appears to be driven as much by a politically motivated 'punitiveness' as by an objective and disinterested science (see Chapter 2).

3.4 The application of science

A key component of risk management lies in its claim to scientific inquiry through its insistence on 'evidence-led' practice. This in part was the impetus for the establishment of the Jill Dando Institute of Crime Science in London in 2001. *Crime science* (a term first coined by a journalist and broadcaster) is influenced primarily by the notion that the offender is a 'rational actor' and that offending is directly related to available opportunities and situational contingencies. A major concern is to use science and technology to change opportunities rather than to change people (Pease, 2005). Crime science is a key part of a technical 'what works' network, which also includes the National Institute of Justice in the USA and the Campbell Collaboration of academics worldwide dedicated to applying the research methods of medicine and health to study crime prevention and crime control. An International Crime Science Network was established in 2004, attracting membership from the USA, Australia, New Zealand and the Netherlands, as well as the UK. The founding director of the Institute of Crime Science, Gloria Laycock (2005), has outlined its distinctive features, involving not only the prevention and detection of crime and disorder on the basis of evidence, but the empirical testing of hypotheses through the collection and analysis of data. Crime science, Laycock maintains, is informed by forensic science, crime mapping, cost-benefit analysis, DNA identification, genetic and psychological risk identification, offender profiling, computer science and technologies of behavioural control. All of these technologies, it is claimed, enable objective assessments of crime and criminality to be made by experts untainted by political or ideological concerns (see Chapter 5).

Figure 4.6
Forensic psychology and forensic science have captured public and political imaginations in their portrayal of successful crime fighting as being dependent on expert knowledge and technology

Activity 4.5

It is difficult to underestimate the impact that the possibility of a scientific solution has had on public and political perceptions of crime control. Read the following extract from an article published in *The Guardian* newspaper in 2007. As you read this extract, consider the following questions:

■ How is the concept of risk being used in the article?

■ What are the ethical dilemmas involved in 'risk screening'?

■ What segments of society would be most 'at risk' for being 'actively risk managed' by this policy?

■ How might this policy be seen as harmful, and to whom?

Extract 4.2

Every child to be screened for risk of turning criminal under Blair justice plan

Alan Travis

A new-style '11-plus' to assess the risk every child in Britain runs of turning to crime was among a battery of proposals unveiled in Tony Blair's crime plan yesterday. The children of prisoners, problem drug users and others at high risk of offending will also face being 'actively managed' by social services and youth justice workers. New technologies are to be used to boost police detection rates while DNA samples are to be taken from any crime suspect who comes into contact with the police.

The 'early intervention' approach is part of a package of proposals on security, crime and justice produced by Downing Street which underline the scale of criminal justice reform Mr Blair believes is still needed despite passing 53 law and order bills since he came to power in 1997.

The shadow home secretary, David Davis, focused his criticism on the extension of the DNA database to any crime suspect and the early intervention plans for children. He described the proposal to assess every child for risk of offending as the 'nanny state gone mad' while he said the Conservatives would have 'great and grave concerns' about any extension of the DNA database.

A Home Office spokeswoman said the universal checks on children would look at factors including attainment at school, truancy rates, and substance abuse.

...

Early intervention

- Vulnerable children and 'those at risk of criminality', including those whose parents are in prison and/or among the 300,000 problem drug abusers, are to be 'actively case managed' by Children's Trust social services staff and youth justice workers from 'the earliest possible point'.

- Universal checks on every child throughout his or her development to help 'service providers' identify those most at risk of offending throughout their development, including at 11 when they go to secondary school.

- Preventative programmes to tackle social exclusion, drugs and alcohol abuse.

Source: *The Guardian*, 28 March 2007

Comment

Evaluations of 'what works' in crime identification and crime prevention can never be a pure science. The unpredictability and variability of local contexts and the complexity of the social and the political in general militate against standardisation and uniformity. The idea of 'risk screening', it has been argued, is not scientifically legitimate and is ethically questionable. It is evident that such logic can be used to justify intervention because of the existence of 'characteristics associated with offending', rather than on evidence of actual wrongdoing. There is no reliable test for criminal risk (McConville, 2003, p. 253). Identifying people who are at risk of committing a crime is not the same as proving intent or causation. Policies that seek early detection of criminal suspects through risk analysis, it has been argued, are a better means of labelling people (Becker, 1963) than they are an accurate predictor of future criminal behaviour. Why, then, does risk play such a significant role in so many Western crime control policies? Richard Sparks argues that risk is not merely a means through which potential harms and dangers can be identified. The rise of risk analysis also concerns:

> ... often fevered politics that swirl around questions of risk and the battles that determine which risks are selected for particular attention, which categories of person and which places come to be regarded as bearers or containers of intolerable levels of risk, and so on ... Risk is never the dry, technocratic matter that it initially appears. Instead each system of risk management creates as its counterpart a blaming system.

> (Sparks, 2003, p. 160)

Although the extract suggests that a goal of criminal risk screening is early intervention, it not clear what this would involve. Beneath the surface there is the suggestion that the state is seeking an unprecedented level of surveillance and control over individuals. The notion that future criminality can be predicted in a scientific way and intervened in by government agencies seems to contradict the commitments of democracy. Arguably, it is the cost-saving benefits of identifying *individual* choice and risky lifestyles as the main causes of crime that are too tempting for 'late modern risk society' governments to ignore. It allows a selective targeting of resources on 'identified' individuals and families and thereby avoids any demand for universal provision.

4   Interrogating risk

Given some of the issues raised above, this section broadens the exploration of the usefulness of the concepts of 'risk' and 'risk society' in informing understandings of crime, justice, harm, power and violence in a globalised world. Although it is undeniable that the concept of risk has permeated many aspects of different societies around the world, and the notion of the risk society captures some aspects of the transition to late modern Western social life, there are also limitations to its universality. Gabe Mythen (2007) has catalogued six main criticisms:

1   'Natural' and 'manufactured' risks are inseparable. The natural and the social have long been intertwined and it is difficult to untangle the effect of one on the other.

2   Risk is not experienced universally in the same way. There are higher levels of risk associated with impoverished living conditions. For example, in Western societies, the poor are more likely to be at risk of health problems, unemployment, and so forth. Similarly, in economically disadvantaged countries there is greater exposure to AIDS and environmental pollution. The concept of risk 'reinforces rather than transforms patterns of inequality' (Mythen, 2007, p. 800).

3   The differential impact of manufactured risks on disadvantaged populations and countries is obscured by the assertion of a universal impact of global dangers.

4   Cultural understandings of risk are not easily generalisable. 'Different risks mean different things to different people' (Mythen, 2007, p. 800).

5   A dystopic view of risk precludes the possibility that risk taking can bear fruitful rewards (e.g. in the fields of medicine, in alternative approaches to justice and in leisure activities).

6   There is no convincing evidence of an all-embracing 'world risk society'. From a global perspective, risk has multiple meanings across multiple landscapes and cannot be essentialised to a singularly Western understanding of the concept.

4.1   Risk, rights and discrimination

As this chapter has already discussed in relation to actuarial justice, risk prediction and crime science, a political shift of direction has occurred, moving away from attempts to understand the causes of crime towards viewing crime as another risk to be accurately measured and managed (Garland, 2000). By transforming the problem of crime into subsets of threats to personal, local or national security (each with its own strategies for managing risk), there is less of a burden on governments to solve the crime problem.

Governments play a central role in selecting which risks we should concern ourselves with, including which categories of person and which places and situations need to be recognised as most threatening. In this way, only certain harms and dangers (such as street crime, anti-social behaviour or terrorism) are highlighted, whereas others (such as state crime, environmental damage or political violence) are de-emphasised. Orienting the problem of crime around the problems of risk and dangerousness has been crucial to the restructuring of criminal justice, especially in the USA and England and Wales. As we noted at the beginning of Section 3, in some ways state control over crime and social order has been eroded and passed on to other agencies or individuals (e.g. to private security companies or to technologies of personal protection). Risk, then, can be seen as a vehicle through which governments have diffused some of their responsibility for social life and public safety (Loader and Sparks, 2002). Yet in other respects the very process of decentralising government control over crime – by shifting to a focus on risk – has only redirected attention back towards the role of government. Sparks (2003, p. 160) argues that 'a more heated politics of crime and punishment is now prevalent precisely because the state's capacity to deliver security is so much in question'.

The shift to a focus on risk in crime policy also includes a moral shift towards a blame culture. As Kemshall (2003, pp. 143–4) argues, a key trend in a risk-based approach to crime control includes 'a rational approach to understanding crime causation and crime control that results in a moral blamism of those who fail to exercise the correct "choice" and acceptable levels of responsibility'. Here the rise of risk coupled with the emphasis on individualism, which is so much a feature of many Western (and neo-liberal) countries, marks a sea change in conceptions of rights. Ericson et al. argue that individual rights have become constricted and that 'rights will only be granted to those who meet their ethical obligations of self-sufficiency' (Ericson et al., 2000, p. 554). That is, there is a two-tiered risk system. Simon (1987) notes that there is a risk system of affluence, which relates to, for example, automobile insurance, occupational health and safety and financial investments. This risk system is non-blaming and routine and has the pretence of equal rights. The other risk system, by contrast, is one of poverty. This system is punitive, stigmatising and discriminatory. The poor are seen as 'risk posers, as drawers upon systems rather than contributors to them' (Hudson, 2003, pp. 58–9). Within the risk system of poverty, individual rights are curtailed or withdrawn because the poor themselves are viewed as a 'risky population', which needs to be controlled and managed (Simon, 1987).

The discriminatory potential of a risk paradigm applies not only to local issues in Western societies, but also to the way in which economically disadvantaged countries can be marginalised in the global marketplace. For example, financial advisory firms identify and provide e-commerce information on safe and high-risk countries in order to allow online businesses to make informed choices about the countries in which they may pursue business opportunities. Similarly, the interaction between risk, state power and corporate power can create barriers to global trade for developing countries (Anderson, 2004). Moreover, developing countries can sometimes be disadvantaged in international trade agreements due to their 'high-risk' status (Nogués, 2002). Although potential 'harm' to so-called safe countries can be managed through risk prediction methods, the harm that may come to deprived countries as a result of being either excluded from trade relationships or marginalised within trade agreements is rarely taken as seriously. It is evident, then, that the identification of risk can be a value-laden process, which systematically favours some social conditions and disadvantages others.

4.2 Hybrid strategies of crime control

Risk mentalities and risk technologies do not exist in isolation. They may challenge, but arguably never eclipse, the state's claim to a monopoly of violence and its sovereign right to punish. As a result of its own contradictions and its location alongside competing penal rationales, the 'risk society' also heralds a series of 'curious hybrids' in crime control in which the discursive and material realities of crime prevention, community safety, actuarial justice, risk prediction, profiling, crime science, evidence-based policy, managerial efficiency, self-policing, erosion of state authority, responsibilisation of individuals, punitiveness and population monitoring can somehow mutually coexist (Cohen, 1985; Hope and Sparks, 2000). Alongside risk assessment, prediction and management there typically exist claims for *punitive sovereignty* and *community safety* (Stenson, 2000).

Punitive sovereignty maintains that only those who meet their obligations of responsible citizenship are deserving of freedom under the law. Within this strategy, crime control is managed through such measures as zero-tolerance policing, Anti-social Behaviour Orders, increasing mandatory prison sentences and three-strikes legislation (see Chapter 2). In some contrast, claims for community safety call for a greater responsibilisation of local communities. They encompass social crime prevention strategies, community safety partnerships, mediation, community policing and restorative justice initiatives (see Chapter 3).

In the 1980s, a school of left realism based at Middlesex University set out its crime control stall, against what it then termed 'administrative criminology', by arguing that the structural factors – especially relative deprivation – that give rise to offending must also be acknowledged and confronted. For left realists, 'good jobs with a discernible future, housing estates of which tenants can be proud, community facilities which enhance a sense of cohesion and belonging, a reduction in unfair income inequalities, all create a society which is more cohesive and less criminogenic' (Young, 1994, pp. 115–16). Confronting crime, it was argued, requires tackling social inequality, poverty and differential life chances, including increasing educational and employment opportunities, available housing, health care provision, skills training and family support initiatives. The focus here is on challenging the processes that cement disadvantage and promote social exclusion (Young, 1999). North American realists, such as Elliot Currie (1986), have also advocated policies that would precipitate a move from a neo-liberal market society to what Currie describes as a 'sustaining society'. Currie advocated a number of macro policies based on full employment and a concerted strategy for reducing the extremes of social and economic inequality, as well as micro programmes based on comprehensive child and family support. In short, for left realists, an effective crime prevention strategy lies outside of the current concerns of the risk paradigm. In stark contrast to the evidence-led scientific paradigm, it involves a broad and inclusive notion of community safety and support: a reinvention of the 'social'.

Hughes et al. (2002) have also argued that an overtly 'anti-social' stance appears to be promoted by the new scientific and actuarial criminologies: in particular, the way in which complex social issues are reduced to 'simple' control strategies that can be readily implemented by practitioners, policy makers and governments. Hughes (2007) has critiqued 'the naivety' of crime science for its promoting of the universal applicability of its policy prescriptions (ignoring contingencies of time and place), its reducing of complex social processes to statistical artefacts and its rejection of any criminology that does not offer easily implemented ('quick-fix') technical solutions. A preoccupation with risk can indeed suggest a 'nightmare', 'asocial' future of readily identifiable 'risky' citizens whose actions can be controlled only by pre-emptive intervention, social exclusion and the fortifying of places of 'normal' commerce and interaction.

Within these hybrid strategies of crime control it is evident that previous approaches to the crime problem, such as offender rehabilitation, improved crime detection and theories of crime causation, have become less of a focus. But taken collectively, it is also clear that they reflect an expanded use of what Stanley Cohen (1985) referred to as inclusionary and exclusionary social control. That is, some people are included and protected by these crime control strategies and others are targeted, stigmatised and excluded. Thomas Blomberg and Carter Hay summarise Cohen's visions of the future of social control:

> ... these patterns suggest a vision 'not too far from Orwell's' – [Cohen] foresaw the pursuit of a utopian city in which social control increasingly spirals to greater levels. Our entire cognitive and social existence will be subject to greater inclusionary controls and in those cases where deviance persists nonetheless, the system would be provoked into using an increasingly more punitive and rigid set of exclusionary controls.
>
> (Blomberg and Hay, 2007, p. 178)

Activity 4.6

Think about the following questions:

- How might risk-based justice be mediated by other social control rationales?

- Which harms remain uncontrolled by these hybrid (risk, punitive, community safety) strategies?

Comment

Despite its apparent ubiquity, it is important to note that risk-based justice is only one managerial response to harms, dangers and crime. Neither does 'risk talk' necessarily imply just statistical risk assessment and the power to predict. Discourses and practices of risk are multiple, not just statistical, and can be mobilised in different ways in different parts of social and criminal justice and in different jurisdictions (O'Malley, 1998). Talk of a new emergent 'risk society' may also be misleading. Class consciousness may not have been replaced (as is claimed) by 'risk consciousness'. Long-standing inequalities within and between nations remain. Most jurisdictions have also quite evidently not abandoned retributive justice in the pursuance of acting on the scientific principles of what may work to prevent future harms and offending. The practice of criminal justice remains typically symbolic, political and moral, as well as actuarial and pragmatic. It is awash with emotive, political, moralising and expressive enterprise. Because of this volatile mix, Hughes (1998) has claimed that it will always be possible to imagine alternative futures in which prevention and control might be resocialised and rehumanised, and not simply subjected to a standardised, actuarial management.

5 Conclusion

The rise of risk marks an important shift in criminal justice thinking and practice. The emergence of terms such as 'risk management' and 'crime prevention' in criminal justice reflects a new approach to crime control that places greater emphasis on individual responsibility in offending and in personal crime prevention. Although traditional disciplinary forms of intervention such as the prison persist, their purpose has come to be more focused on containment, risk classification and management than on meeting offender needs. Offender profiling, risk classification and the technologies of risk have been turned to as means of overcoming the 'nothing works' pessimism that emerged in the 1970s. But hybrid risk-based strategies of crime control are not technocratic, value-free mechanisms for managing the social fact of crime. Instead, they reflect inclusionary and exclusionary mechanisms of social control that reinforce and recreate social inequalities. Discourses and practices of risk have multiplied across political spheres, social institutions and jurisdictions. The proliferation of risk and risk thinking needs to be critically considered and carefully observed. The increased use of the concept of risk in managing the apparent dangers of everyday life focuses public attention on particular threats to personal safety and security and diverts attention away from other – potentially more damaging – social harms and violations.

References

Anderson, P.N. (2004) 'What rights are eclipsed when risk is defined by corporatism? Governance and GM food', *Theory, Culture and Society*, vol. 21, no. 6, pp. 155–69.

Armstrong, D. (2004) 'A risky business? Research, policy, governmentality and youth offending', *Youth Justice*, vol. 4, no. 2, pp. 100–16.

Beck, U. (1992) *Risk Society: Towards a New Modernity*, London, Sage.

Beck, U. and Beck-Gernsheim, E. (2003) *Individualization: Institutionalized Individualism and Its Social and Political Consequences*, London, Sage.

Becker, H. (1963) *Outsiders*, London, Macmillan.

Blair, T. (2006) *Our Nation's Future: Social Exclusion*, Speech, 5 September [online], www.pm.gov.uk/output/Page10037.asp (Accessed 20 March 2009).

Blomberg, T.G. and Hay, C. (2007) 'Visions of social control revisited' in Downes, D., Rock, P., Chinkin, C. and Gearty, C. (eds) *Crime, Social Control and Human Rights: From Moral Panics to States of Denial. Essays in Honour of Stanley Cohen*, Cullompton, Willan.

Brown, M. and Pratt, J. (eds) (2000) *Dangerous Offenders: Punishment and Social Order*, London, Routledge.

Case, S. (2007) 'Questioning the "evidence" of risk that underpins evidence-led youth justice interventions', *Youth Justice: An International Journal*, vol. 7, no. 2, pp. 91–106.

Cohen, S. (1985) *Visions of Social Control: Crime, Punishment, and Classification*, Cambridge, Polity.

Currie, E. (1986) *Confronting Crime: An American Challenge*, New York, Pantheon.

Dean, M. (1999) 'Risk: calculable and incalculable' in Lupton, D. (ed.) *Risk and Socio-cultural Theory*, New York, Cambridge University Press.

Douglas, M. (1990) 'Risk as a forensic resource', *Daedalus*, vol. 119, no. 4, pp. 1–16.

Ericson, R. and Haggerty, K. (1997) *Policing the Risk Society*, Toronto, University of Toronto Press.

Ericson, R., Barry, D. and Doyle, A. (2000) 'The moral hazards of neo-liberalism: lessons from the private insurance industry', *Economy and Society*, vol. 29, no. 4, pp. 532–58.

Falshaw, L., Friendship, C., Travers, R. and Nugent, F. (2003) 'Searching for "what works": an evaluation of cognitive skills programmes', *Findings No. 206*, London, Home Office.

Farrington, D. (1994) 'Human development and criminal careers' in Maguire, M. et al. (eds) (1994).

Farrington, D. (1996) *Understanding and Preventing Youth Crime*, Social Policy Research Findings, No. 93, York, Joseph Rowntree Foundation.

Farrington, D. (2000) 'Explaining and preventing crime: the globalisation of knowledge', *Criminology*, vol. 38, no. 1, pp. 1–24.

Farrington, D., Coid, J., Harnett, L., Jolliffe, D., Soteriou, N., Turner, R. and West, D.J. (2006) *Criminal Careers up to Age 50 and Life Success up to Age 48: New Findings from the Cambridge Study in Delinquent Development* (2nd edn), Home Office Research Study, No. 299, London, Home Office.

Farrington, D. and Welsh, B. (2007) *Saving Children from a Life of Crime: Early Risk Factors and Effective Interventions*, Oxford, Oxford University Press.

Feeley, M. and Simon, J. (1992) 'The new penology: notes on the emerging strategy of corrections and its implications', *Criminology*, vol. 30, no. 4, pp. 449–74.

Feeley, M. and Simon, J. (1994) 'Actuarial justice: the emerging new criminal law' in Nelken, D. (ed.) *The Futures of Criminology*, London, Sage.

Chapter 5
Surveillance and social ordering

Roy Coleman

Contents

1   Introduction

It has become commonplace in the advanced societies of the twenty-first century to talk about the ubiquity of surveillance (see Chapter 1). Whether or not we are aware of it, most of us are subject to a vast array of information gathering fuelled by an alleged 'need to know' about a range of interconnected life experiences related to our travel, home life, consumer behaviour, work record, leisure pursuits, criminal propensities or associations. In its many guises, surveillance may ascertain 'who we are' – to register and authenticate our identity; it may seek to monitor our location in a particular space (electronic or physical) and our reasons for being there; it may seek to ascertain our motives, both short and long term, as citizens, consumers, workers, and so on; it may inquire about our social status as credit worthy, as 'deserving' or 'undeserving' of goods and services. Surveillance also attempts to know our bodily movements through public, private, local, national and international space; it may be called upon to aid the prediction, pre-emption or containment of 'risks', behaviours and events (see Chapter 4). In short, surveillance renders aspects of social life visible for the purposes of managing stability in social relations. It appears as a central means to achieve a very broadly defined notion of 'security' in the twenty-first century through 'the informatisation of life' (Monahan and Wall, 2007, p. 154).

In turn, the means, extent and purpose of surveillance are subject to intense ongoing debate. Some argue in a positive vein that surveillance provides a means to deter crime, manage 'risks' and reduce harms. Others retort that surveillance amplifies social risks and social divisions, and infringes fundamental civil liberties. Wherever one is positioned in this debate, surveillance matters because it is never a neutral exercise. It is based on the assumption of generating categories of suspicion in attempting to identify deviations from prescribed norms, thereby aiding the ordering of social relations. This chapter is designed to illustrate that surveillance is a form of power with various strands.

The aims of the chapter are to explore:

- whether and to what extent privacy, individual freedom and civil liberty are under threat from surveillance

- whether or not surveillance 'works' with respect to its stated aims

- how criminologists have 'made sense' of 'surveillance societies'

- how surveillance is implicated in processes of social ordering and the reinforcement of social divisions

■ the potential of surveillance to become a global phenomenon

■ whose 'justice' is being protected and whose denied by the proliferation of surveillance technologies and rationalities.

Following this Introduction, Section 2 considers two examples of surveillance as expressed through population monitoring: the use of CCTV and biometric profiling. The typical debates around surveillance query whether it enhances security or invades privacy and whether technology can be relied on to address social problems and harms, including crime. Section 2 develops the debate further by drawing attention to how the techniques of surveillance also produce and reproduce categories of people who might be considered (literally) 'out of place'; that is, how people are 'sorted' into categories of 'worthiness' or 'riskiness'. Section 3 explores the various theoretical tools and concepts that criminologists have employed to understand the meaning of the proliferation of surveillance spaces and techniques. Section 4 examines some of the indices and prospects for 'global surveillance', and Section 5 considers the differential positioning of groups and individuals in relation to surveillance practices. Throughout, you will be asked to consider how far the practices of surveillance are embedded in pre-existing relations of power, and how they help to construct particular social and spatial understandings of 'crime', 'security', 'order' and 'justice'.

2   Surveillance as a social issue

Whatever its context, surveillance raises social questions and, in doing so, invites us to move beyond understanding forms of monitoring as mere technological 'solutions' to social problems. Instead, developments in surveillance, such as CCTV and DNA matching, are implicated in what it means to be 'social' and whether we are to be targeted for inclusion within or exclusion from the boundaries of a social collectivity. As we shall see, surveillance is very much about the monitoring of social norms, along with the consequences this inevitably has for meanings of 'participation' and 'justice' within society.

Figure 5.1
'Spit and Run: You'll still get caught' is a scheme operating in Yorkshire and London

Activity 5.1

Consider the two cases of 'surveillance' from the UK, outlined in Extracts 5.1 and 5.2. The first details the proliferation of electronic monitoring and CCTV since the 1990s. The second raises the issue of widespread DNA profiling to monitor targeted populations.

While studying these cases, ask yourself how far such technologies might work to improve our safety and security or how far they constitute an unacceptable degree of intrusion into our private lives. Also begin to ask yourself how far surveillance is not confined to particular advanced Western states, but is capable of crossing international borders and is truly becoming a global phenomenon.

Extract 5.1

Surveillance system tracks faces on CCTV

Bobbie Johnson

British researchers say they have developed a new technology that will allow police to track suspicious individuals over CCTV more efficiently.

The system, which uses computer software to monitor and break down live television images, is able to track a moving face through a crowd.

Engineers at British defence company BAE Systems, which is working on the technology, claim it is even able to automatically follow a target even if they change their appearance by changing their clothes or hiding beneath a hat.

...

The Integrated Surveillance of Crowded Areas for Public Security (Iscaps) project is part of a joint initiative with Europe to develop security systems for potential deployment around the continent.

The scheme, which is partially funded by the European Commission, started just months before the London bombings in July 2005, which claimed 56 lives. CCTV pictures were crucial in identifying the bombers after the attack had taken place, but proved little help in preventing the actions of the bombers.

A Home Office study in 2005 found that CCTV was largely ineffective at preventing crime, but claimed [many] of the problems were due to lack of proper monitoring. Only half of surveillance control rooms were staffed for 24 hours a day.

The development comes as law enforcement officials step up their attempts to keep tabs on those suspected of terrorist offences.

Source: *The Guardian*, 12 October 2007

Extract 5.2

Where's the debate on the DNA database?

Diane Abbott

A government-funded inquiry is calling for the DNA profile of people, who have not actually been convicted of a crime, to be removed from the national DNA database. Britain has the largest DNA database in the world. There are over 4.2 million people on it. But a million of those people have never been convicted of anything. And 50,000 of them are children. Millions of these profiles are given to private companies without the consent of individuals. Yet the DNA database has mushroomed with no basis in legislation. And members of parliament have never been given the opportunity to vote on it.

Perhaps, if the database did have some legislative foundation, there would have been a chance to put in place the safeguards which are lamentably lacking from the current system. Forty per cent of black men are on it, but only 9% of white men. This bears no correlation to relative arrest or conviction rates. And the police seem determined to hold on to their power to put people on the database in a completely arbitrary way.

I saw this when a friend had her 14-year-old daughter's DNA sample taken because she happened to get a lift home in a car which was stopped by the police. No one was charged, no offence had been committed, but the police took it upon themselves to take a DNA sample from her. They tried to suggest to the parents subsequently that it was mandatory for them to do this. It was only when I took up the case with government ministers that they admitted that it was at their own discretion. Six hundred and forty five rapists have been caught using the DNA database. But I doubt that many of them were 14-year-old girls. Yet the police had the power to criminalise my friend's daughter with no appeal and no safeguards.

Professor Sir Alec Jeffreys, the man who actually invented DNA fingerprinting, is concerned. He says:

> The national DNA database is a very powerful tool in the fight against crime, but recent developments such as the retention of innocent people's DNA raises significant ethical and social issues. The real concern I have in the UK is what I see as a sort of 'mission creep'. When the DNA database was initially established, it was to database DNA from criminals so if they re-offended, they could be picked up. Now hundreds of thousands of entirely innocent people are populating that database.

Source: *The Guardian*, 30 July 2008

Comment

From these cases we see that surveillance is bolstered by allusions to technical efficiency in relation to public well-being. However, information gleaned from surveillance constitutes a form of power in placing people into categories; for example, as 'worthy' or 'unworthy' and as 'responsible' or 'irresponsible'. Surveillance systems 'are both socially shaped and have social consequences, some of which go beyond the intentions inscribed in their shaping' (Lyon, 2001, p. 25). Think of public CCTV cameras being installed for 'crime prevention', but also becoming useful for other non-criminal related uses (such as monitoring crowd movements). This is known as 'function creep' or 'expandable mutability' (Norris and Armstrong, 1999, p. 58), where the intended practice of any surveillance technique morphs outwards into areas other than those initially anticipated.

Indeed, these two cases raise a number of fundamental issues (as discussed below), which can be encapsulated in debates over (a) protection and privacy; (b) technological 'fixes'; and (c) social sorting and social ordering.

2.1 Protection and privacy

Surveillance is often seen as a form of invasion, undermining the privacy of the self through what powerful others (governments, law enforcers, public agencies and corporations) can legitimately know about individuals and for what purposes. In 2007, Privacy International sought to assess how much protection and privacy citizens around the world have from both corporate and government surveillance. Privacy International is a human rights group that was formed in 1990 to act as an overseer of surveillance and privacy incursions by governments and corporations. The group has campaigned across the world to protect people against such intrusion. From a survey of forty-seven countries, Privacy International reported that surveillance is becoming increasingly and, for them, alarmingly 'endemic', particularly in the UK, the USA, Russia and China. Of the forty-seven countries, these were the most subject to surveillance. Privacy International also found that 'extensive surveillance' exists in countries such as Denmark and Australia, and Israel demonstrated a 'systematic failure' to uphold safeguards against intrusive surveillance practice. None of the countries surveyed 'consistently upholds human right [*sic*] standards' (Privacy International, 2007a). The report points to an acceleration of surveillance. In turn, this raises questions about how information will be used, and by whom; and what rights of access citizens have to information kept on them. Concerns such as these usefully point to the way in which data can be unprotected, contain errors, become lost, be used inappropriately and be disseminated without consent. Moreover, surveillance – whether by states or corporations – can, at certain historical moments, be tied to what is termed the 'asymmetrical loss of privacy' (Andrejevic, 2007, p. 7). As a form of 'seeing' and 'knowing', surveillance enables the increasing visibility of some individuals and agencies, thus reducing their privacy, as in the case of children on the DNA database and of suspected (if not actual) criminals. At the same time, surveillance renders other individuals and agencies more impervious to scrutiny – thereby protecting privacy or denying accountability. This is particularly true with respect to companies that compile and trade information about the population and then invoke their own right to privacy – with resources to defend it – as a means of preventing the population from accessing that information.

Figure 5.2
A surveillance camera outside the British Parliament, but who is watching whom in the 'surveillance society'? Whose privacy is being invaded and whose is relatively protected by current surveillance arrangements?

Up until May 2009, MPs in the British Parliament had also successfully fought off public scrutiny – through evoking 'privacy' and 'security' – of their salaries, expenses and allowances accrued from taxpayers' money. Such scrutiny is theoretically allowable in the UK under the Freedom of Information Act (2000), but can be countered by powerful bodies who may argue that 'transparency will damage democracy', as was argued by the Head of the House of Commons Fees Office, Andrew Walker (Brooke, 2009, p. 4). 'Privacy' is therefore not an absolute, but is better viewed as a concept that can be utilised differentially: some individuals and agencies may be better placed to protect their privacy from surveillance than others.

2.2 The technological 'fix'

The efficiency of surveillance systems and whether or not they work on their own terms has provided another critical line of inquiry. However, questions of efficiency may be, and often are, irrelevant to the development and installation of surveillance practice. For example, the introduction of CCTV in the UK in the 1990s was not preceded by evidence of its impact on crime and disorder. In fact, assessments of its efficiency came much later, after the widespread installation of cameras. In the early twenty-first century a comprehensive review of studies on camera surveillance acknowledged that there 'is little substantive research evidence to suggest that CCTV works' in crime prevention (Nacro, 2002, p. 6). Furthermore, public support for CCTV has been 'inflated' by unsophisticated surveys (Ditton, 1998). Deploying the technology can lead to increases in anxiety and the displacement of crime to areas not covered by surveillance (Ditton, 1998). This leaves many unanswered questions as to why CCTV in the UK – particularly in urban centres – has proliferated unlike anywhere else in the world, especially when it has a marginal relationship to 'crime prevention' (Coleman, 2004).

From Extract 5.1 it can be deduced that the unrolling of surveillance technologies need not be supported by research evidence. This finds support in areas other than CCTV. Such an area is DNA testing and biometric forms of surveillance (Nelkin and Andrews, 2003). Biometric surveillance refers to the measurement of the body to corroborate identity and thus manage movement and access. Fingerprints, iris scans, hand geometry and facial recognition technology 'offer what many believe to be the most reliable ways of perfecting ... tokens of trust' (Lyon, 2007, p. 125). Increasingly, these forms of surveillance are being conjoined with identity cards (which are discussed further in Section 4.1). DNA surveillance takes parts of the body as a source of identity to be collected and stored. Identity verification here is associated not with what one has or knows (a smart card, password or PIN number), but with what one is in relation to the body: one will always be what one is in relation to body parts. In many countries of the advanced world an increasing array of individuals are being DNA fingerprinted – raising questions of social discrimination, mistaken samples and loss of privacy (Poudrier, 2003). The official discourse around biometrics and DNA profiling proffers the utility of these with assurances concerning security, expediency and effectiveness: these forms of bodily surveillance can solve or prevent crimes, thwart immigration fraud or target ill health. But it has also been argued that the move towards DNA databases is discriminatory (Dyer, 2007).

In 2009, the world's largest database – operating in England, Wales and Northern Ireland – was increasing by about 30,000 a month and held 5.1 million profiles, accounting for 9.1 per cent of the total population. 15.6 per cent of those on the system had not been convicted of any crime (Dyer, 2007). Disproportionate numbers are from minority ethnic communities, with estimates that over half of all black men would be on the database by 2010 (Doward, 2007). Debates around these issues point to the importance of 'function creep'. Some (including forensic experts, judges and senior police officers) argue for DNA registration at birth for all citizens (Doward, 2007). On the latter point, it is argued that a universal database would not only increase efficiencies in solving (even forestalling) crimes, but would be non-discriminatory because everyone would be on it. However, in December 2008 the European Court of Human Rights condemned the British Government for allowing the 'indiscriminate' application of police power to take and retain DNA indefinitely, regardless of the offence or whether a conviction results after someone has been stopped and DNA sampled by police (Travis, 2008).

2.3 Social sorting and social ordering

The concerns noted above – particularly in respect of privacy – do not relay the whole story about surveillance and why it matters. Torin Monahan (2006a, p. 2) argues that these critical paths to exploring surveillance – as important as they are – sideline, even hide, the 'deeper motivations and logics behind surveillance and security'. In its many guises, surveillance aims to place people into categories underpinned by notions of 'worth' or 'risk'. Surveillance therefore has a relational link to assigning social status, with the consequence of promoting the life chances of some while curtailing those of others. But who defines the categories and what are their purposes?

The promise of enhanced security, safety and stability begs further questions: does surveillance reduce social harms? Is it just as likely to generate them? If so, how? If one finds oneself on a DNA database – even without committing a crime – does this affect life chances in terms of job prospects? Whose 'security' and 'safety' are we talking about? If surveillance cameras are largely ineffective at preventing crimes (as Extract 5.1 indicates), why do societies like that of the UK continue with them? Evidence suggests that CCTV is a factor in managing particular spaces; for example, consumption zones and shopping malls, where certain activities, behaviours and demeanours can be monitored and filtered out – such as signs of non-consumption in the form of homelessness or congregating youths (Coleman, 2005; **Mooney and Talbot, 2010**). Thus, surveillance practice is also connected to the maintenance of specific socio-spatial borders. These borders may be formal or informal and their creation and monitoring through surveillance raises questions concerning the ways in which notions of 'justice' and 'participation' in social life are rendered meaningful. Not only does surveillance contribute to order by intervening in peoples' lives, it also disseminates ideas about its targets ('the watched'), their behaviour and their status within the social order. As a process of 'social sorting', surveillance 'obtains personal and group data in order to classify people and populations according to variable criteria, to determine who should be targeted for special treatment, suspicion, eligibility, inclusion, access and so on' (Lyon, 2003a, p. 20). Surveillance delineates 'status' and therefore has implications for life chances and social positioning. This line of argument requires exploration of surveillance as a 'related but not entirely coordinated set of practices geared to the construction and maintenance of social order' (Lacey, 1994, p. 28).

What the two cases we have considered in Extracts 5.1 and 5.2 make clear is that surveillance practice does not necessarily have a rational foundation, let alone a publicly debated one. As a result, we also need to consider how surveillance 'works', not in a technical-evaluative sense but in relation to its political, economic, symbolic and emotional drivers. This does not mean that all surveillance technology is necessarily 'bad', but it does require us to ask how it is used, why it is used and with what consequences for social order. Furthermore, in asking such questions we need to be mindful of the issue of whom it 'works' for, and in what sense. This may have less to do with efficiency and more to do with some groups consolidating their power by managing 'risks' and assuaging 'insecurity' as they perceive these categories in relation to their interests. Understood in this way, surveillance reflects and reinforces power dynamics inherent in social relationships.

3 Theorising surveillance

Although it is commonplace to describe societies of the advanced world as surveillance societies, this rather general descriptor undermines an understanding of surveillance as a spatial practice – that is, it has particular purchase in some spaces and less in others; it reflects, modifies and reinforces power relations in space. As suggested above, surveillance is embroiled in managing movement within, between and beyond spatial borders – it also reinforces common perceptions and understandings of what particular spaces are for (the activities they support, and the resources and rights they forge in relation to particular groups and individuals).

3.1 The proliferation of surveillance spaces

Many writers have attested to the idea that 'the rise of surveillance society may be traced to modernity's impetus to coordinate or control' (Lyon, 2001, p. 49). Michel Foucault tied late twentieth-century surveillance within the spatial enclosures that emerged with the modern European prisons between 1760 and 1840. Carceral punishment heralded a constant surveillance of inmates under a new kind of disciplinary power – rendering bodies more observable and acquiescent to control. A form of spatial and temporal control via hierarchies of surveillance and classification sought to inaugurate discipline and routine over a prisoner's body. This surveillance gaze was asymmetrical in that those subject to it were at once the objects of 'knowledge' pertaining to their behaviour, but were also unable to verify how, where and when this knowledge through surveillance was being gathered. The panoptic principle – where the few can exercise surveillance over the many – meant that a handful of surveillants (prison guards) could control, monitor and contain hundreds of prisoners and ensure a more intense, 'efficient' and automatic functioning of power in which subjects (inmates) were encouraged to self-police and discipline their own conduct, under conditions of constant watching (Foucault, 1977).

As you have already read in Chapter 1, the power of this panoptic surveillance gradually became operative in other enclosed spaces, bringing forth the 'the utopia of the perfectly governed city' (Foucault, 1977, p. 198). Here, surveillance proliferated in new spaces such as schools, hospitals, workplaces, barracks and asylums, fostering modes of inspection, categorisation and regulation that – in Foucault's terms – render the creation of a 'disciplinary society'. What once constituted a drive to control illegalities (crime) was applied to a whole range of behavioural and spatial contexts where 'the norm' reigned supreme and surveillance offered the possibility of countering many forms of non-illegal 'deviation' whether in the workplace, the school or the family (see Chapter 1). Controversially, panoptic surveillance was designed to encourage a 'docile' citizenry – self-inspecting and self-correcting in relation to predominant social norms. But Foucault also asserted that where there is surveillance there is also resistance (Foucault, 1977). In other words, as developments in surveillance emerge they also encounter forms of contestation, alongside the ability (for some individuals and groups) to negotiate and even evade surveillance targeted at them. We will return to this issue in Section 5.

Throughout the twentieth century, spaces subject to surveillance proliferated with the adoption of community corrections, Neighbourhood Watch schemes, private security and the use of public surveillance cameras. Stanley Cohen (1985) critically traced such developments by noting a number of related processes in this 'dispersal of discipline'. First, the move to informal, private and communal controls 'widens the net' of the formal system, bringing about 'an increase in the total number of deviants getting into the system in the first place'. Second, a 'thinning of the mesh' results in 'old and new deviants being subject to levels of intervention (including traditional institutionalisation) which they might not have previously received' (Cohen, 1985, p. 44). Third, the dispersal of social control blurs the 'old' boundaries between formal/informal and public/private forms of control, resulting in 'more people [getting] involved in the "control problem" [and] more rather than less attention ... given to the deviance question' (Cohen, 1985, p. 231). For Cohen, surveillance not only continues to expand into the minutiae of social life, it also brings with it new forms of expertise and control that we not only encounter in our daily lives, but on which we even come to depend (as parents, workers, travellers, consumers, workers or sexual beings) (see also Chapter 3).

Activity 5.2

The theoretical concepts of 'panopticism' (Foucault) and the 'dispersal of discipline' (Cohen) can conjure up dystopian images akin to George Orwell's *Nineteen Eighty-Four*. But what are the broader social implications of being 'watched over'? Is surveillance out of (our and its own) control?

Comment

As discussed above, the development of surveillance has multiplied its spaces of operation – blurring the formal/informal and the public/private. In Cohen's writing it works towards visions of both inclusion (the normalisation of conduct inside communities) and exclusion (proliferating stigma, banishment and separation of deviants from particular spatial contexts and social entitlements). The notion of panoptic control and its diffusion introduces the idea of the unseen observer (for some, the motif of modern surveillance) and the relentless classification of bodies, thoughts, gestures and actions that modern surveillance produces. Surveillance appears to be self-sustaining, generating its own justification. In fictional accounts, such as Orwell's, the extent to which surveillance measures actually work towards deeply dystopian goals are over-emphasised. On the other hand, Orwell's vision points us to aspects of surveillance that we recognise: the mutation of information/knowledge; the undermining of human autonomy and the increase in individual fragmentation through seemingly endless classification procedures; processes of exclusion aimed at the already disenfranchised; as well as ongoing debates about centralised control (and loss) of surveillance data. There is little room for the interplay of resistance and human agency in such fictional accounts, although resistance is clearly a feature in surveillance practice (see Section 5 below): surveillance always seems to 'work' to 'capture' the human soul, rendering it, in Foucault's (1977) terms, 'docile'. Moving beyond accounts such as *Nineteen Eighty-Four* we encounter great leaps in (a) computing technology and (b) the rise of other powerful agencies (corporations, the workplace and the internet) working alongside governments and nation states in the enactment of surveillance. If Foucault's general idea of the panopticon is to be retained, it will need to be refined, leaving room for tensions and contradictions in surveillance practice. It will also need to be grounded in the specific power plays of given spatial arrangements. In this sense, the power of surveillance works to finely tune, sort and regulate our 'participation' in the social world along the fault lines of social class, gender, 'race', age and sexuality.

3.2 The panoptic sort

With the advent of computer databases in the late twentieth century, which speed up and increase the volume of surveillance knowledge, 'the cadre of professionals' has grown, 'based upon the ability to draw finer and finer distinctions between segments of the public' (Gandy, cited in Andrejevic, 2007, p. 28). The 'panoptic sort', as Oscar Gandy calls it and which was discussed briefly in Chapter 1, is a 'complex discriminatory technology' that collates 'information about individual status and behaviour to be potentially useful in the production of intelligence about a person's economic value' (Gandy, 1996, p. 133). However, these processes of sorting and judging are increasingly carried out automatically – without apparent human intervention. Automated surveillance and the use of interlocking databases make information from surveillance transferable across distant spaces or institutions. Mark Poster (1996) called this the 'superpanopticon' where many of us – perhaps unwittingly – partake in our own surveillance during bank transactions, for example, or when surfing the internet, making telephone calls or using interactive television (see Section 3.4 below). We leave electronic traces of action that databases sort into categorical identities, constructed remotely as it were – and simulated by computer tracking and matching. Classifications of 'dangerous'/'safe', 'suspect'/ 'innocent' or 'wanted/'not wanted' are engraved into databases. The 'superpanopticon' is even less verifiable to the subjects of surveillance than the panopticon – we simply have no way of knowing on this global scale how, where and when data about us is stored, how our identities are fabricated and, then, how our 'data-double' is used.

Networks of computers can also be used for 'data mining'; that is, the extraction of information 'directed towards the generation of rules for the classification of objects' (Gandy, 2007, p. 149) – such as the classification of high- and low-value customers, and high- or low-risk of criminality (based on databases of police stops, searches or arrests). Data mining can be used for prediction of future behaviour and for increasing the profits of corporations, based on knowledge of consumer behaviour in the name of 'efficiency'. The computerisation of surveillance thus engenders what David Lyon (2001, p. 16) calls the 'disappearance of the body', as social relations (for some) become stretched over time and space: 'Disembodied and abstract relationships are maintained not so much in human memory as in data banks and networked computer systems'. Face-to-face contact – although clearly not disappearing altogether – is often displaced by electronic mediation and institutional remoteness. Surveillance produces partiality in knowledge of its subjects: we are 'known' more from the abstractions produced and stored by surveillance practice and less from encounters as embodied persons in a social context.

Picking up on these points, many writers have identified 'new' modes of control that are quantitatively and qualitatively different from 'older' surveillance practice as reflected in societies concerned with the anticipation of risk and where 'to be suspected' one only has to 'display whatever the characteristics the specialists responsible for the definition of preventive policy have constituted as risk factors' (Castel, 1991, p. 288; see also Chapter 4).

3.3 Simulated surveillance

William Bogard (2007, p. 97) takes this further in arguing that many features of the new surveillance exist as 'simulated surveillance' because, for him, they involve 'observation before the fact' and have the goal of pre-ordering and pre-emption. The proliferation of profiling exemplifies this and exists across a range of social sites, including policing, insurance, banking, teaching and advertising. Profiling is an attempt at pre-emption in that it diagnoses and targets, in advance, problematic behaviour, individuals or groups. As Bogard (2007, p. 97) puts it in relation to policing, 'If your skin colour, sex, age, type of car ... matches the computer profile each officer carries while on duty, you're a target, whether you have actually done anything wrong or not'. For many, 'such systems are profoundly reductive; they utilise no other logic than whatever is programmed into their software' whereby 'access is accepted or denied; identity is either confirmed or rejected; behaviour is either legitimate or illegitimate' (Norris, 2003, p. 276). In terms of policing, profiling prescribes 'typical' offender behaviour or patterns of suspicious conduct. The offender or deviant is simulated from patterns of appearance, spatial movement or behaviour. This triggers a form of action, not necessarily in response to an offence or deviation that has actually occurred, but in response to the appearance of a *risk* that an offence or deviation *might* occur. Bogard stretches the Foucauldian idea to its limit in inviting us to view surveillance as transformed into complex networks, all-encompassing in their ability to design out danger and conflict. In this scenario, power itself is so amorphous in its targeting and decentralised in its non-location, that it is seemingly impossible to resist or identify any particular power interests served by 'simulation'. As Bogard (2006, p. 118) puts it, 'There are too many virtual connections, too many observers of observers, too many points of recording: all products ... of the networks themselves'. And as Lyon (2001, p. 118) has observed, in Bogard's work the environment in which we find ourselves 'no longer requires control, the environment *is* control'.

Figure 5.3
Steve Bell cartoon lampooning politicians for granting police greater surveillance powers, seemingly without regard for accountability and oversight

Activity 5.3

How far do you agree that panoptic surveillance is now a technical exercise, all-pervasive and undifferentiating in its targeting and in the consequent outcomes on life chances?

Comment

In Bogard's scenario the social world is devoid of hierarchies and conflict. He downplays structural inequalities fostered and reinforced, in part, by the targeting and effects of surveillance. Such perspectives are based on 'the premise that everyone is equally subject to the same surveillance regime' or database (Norris, 2003, p. 277). But surveillance databases (i.e. their modes of classification) are socially constructed, reflecting the priorities and goals of powerful surveillance agencies, which in turn reflect the spaces they seek to maintain. In the realm of crime control, entry on to databases depends on previous discretionary decisions about whom and what is targeted as problematic and what counts as crime and harmful behaviour. Surveillance databases are built and maintained within particular spatial settings that prioritise particular norms and values. For example, within the spaces of increasingly privatised cities dedicated to commercial vitality, surveillance regimes developed around CCTV and private security are, to a significant degree, privately developed, funded and managed by urban entrepreneurs dedicated to the monitoring of, and intervention in, non-consumerist activity, thus producing unequal patterns of spatial targeting and exclusion directed at homeless people, categories of youth and racialised 'others' (Coleman, 2004). Networks of surveillance, then, are grounded in identifiable and structured social relations that they both reflect and reinforce. In contrast to the argument that we are in the midst of a 'new surveillance', research also suggests that the use of technologies such as CCTV is underpinned by CCTV operators 'who bring with them taken-for-granted assumptions about the distribution of criminality within a given population' (Norris and Armstrong, 1999, p. 118). It is often politically marginal and low- or no-income groups that come to be systematically defined as 'risky' and therefore as targets for surveillance. This is made clear in the face-to-face surveillance of police stop-and-search practice in the UK, where black people are up to seven times more likely than white people to be stopped, searched and detained by police on the streets as a result of police discretion and 'common-sense' racial profiling (Newburn, 2007).

3.4 Synoptic surveillance

In light of technological and media advancements, many writers have indicated that in the twenty-first century we are all subject to some degree of surveillance (Haggerty and Ericson, 2006b): it has become multidirectional, rendering many spaces visible – particularly spaces that are the preserve of the powerful – in ways they never were before. Kevin Haggerty and Richard Ericson state that surveillance in the late twentieth and early twenty-first centuries has resulted in the proliferation of greater social visibility in a manner that flattens social hierarchies 'as people from all social backgrounds are now under surveillance' so that 'the many are able to watch and judge the powerful' (Haggerty and Ericson, 2006b, pp. 6, 28). This is deemed to be so because of the rise of the 'surveillant assemblage' (Haggerty and Ericson, 2000), which encompasses the advances in information and data gathering we have noted so far. For these writers, such an assemblage is rhizomatic: the result of infinitesimal offshoots, interconnections and flows of data across borders and between institutions that produce an outcome whereby 'it is increasingly difficult for individuals to maintain their anonymity', allowing, it is argued, 'for the scrutiny of the powerful by both institutions and the general population' (Haggerty and Ericson, 2000, pp. 619, 617). How is this so?

Following these arguments, some writers have emphasised that traditional panoptic surveillance (where the few see the many) has been supplemented by synoptic surveillance (where the many see the few). This is particularly associated with the rise of, and access to, database technology, the internet and the mass media generally in the late twentieth century (Mathiesen, 1997; Lyon, 2006a). The rise of synoptic surveillance may point to evidence of the flattening of the social world, where access to, and utilisation of, surveillance is spread across different social groupings. It is thought that this has at least two effects. First, Lyon argues that scopophilia (the love of looking) has become a cultural condition evidenced in the growth of surveillance-based reality media that inflicts a wider public visibility on celebrities, politicians and criminals. Thus, 'the question of why people permit themselves to be watched [and "accept" the surveillance society] may be paralleled by the question of why people want to watch', at least in the realms of what passes for 'entertainment' (Lyon, 2006a, p. 48). Second – and as mentioned above – synoptic surveillance enables scrutiny of 'the demeanour, idiosyncrasies and foibles of powerful individuals' (Haggerty, 2006, p. 30).

These are debatable points in surveillance studies and so questions remain: are we all subject to the same degree of surveillance and with the same social consequences irrespective of our class, gender, 'racial' or age backgrounds or our sexual orientation? Is the obliteration of anonymity – 'the disappearance of disappearance' as Haggerty and Ericson (2000, p. 619) call it – a ubiquitous and valid notion? Can we think of circumstances in which some groups maintain relative protection over their level of anonymity because of their social, political or economic position? We have already touched on questions as to whether the extent and quality of surveillance aimed at the powerful (and the information garnered from this and its uses) is the same as that aimed at relatively powerless groups. However, the power of synopticism can also be explored with respect to how this form of surveillance encourages particular understandings and perceptions of crime, harm and violence in societies. In other words, with the expansion of broadcast television, surveillance has 'become a more public and collective phenomenon' helping to 'create a new type of watching public' (Doyle, 2006, p. 218). As the many are encouraged to watch the few, 'a shared experience' that arouses 'collective sentiments' is thus created (Doyle, 2006, p. 218).

Figure 5.4
ITV's serial *Police, Camera, Action* typically features police footage and occasional media footage relating to bad driving and to crime on the roads

Activity 5.4

Consider the production of reality TV shows that offer a window on the problem of crime (such as BBC's *Crimewatch*, Fox's *America's Most Wanted*, ITV's *Police, Camera, Action*, and so on). Do these kinds of programmes offer us a dispassionate and neutral form of knowledge with regard to the 'problem of crime' and who commits crime, and where? What kinds of messages do such programmes relay about the powerful – in this case the police and forces of law and order?

Comment

The proliferation of synoptic surveillance exemplified in the growth in reality TV programmes on the subject of crime and punishment typically draws on accredited surveillance experts (police, security personnel and crime profilers), surveillance testimonies and camera footage, with the result that crime is depicted in a particular way: through atypical and individually murderous events, or interpersonal violence and petty offences focused on the street in the world of the public. Such mass encoding represents events and people in ways that ascribe supposedly commonly held social values. This is achieved through over-typifying and over-emphasising some behaviours and activities as the source of socially harmful behaviour, while underplaying other social harms. This raises questions about how we are encouraged to 'see' (in moral, emotive and cultural terms) different segments of the population through the mass media in a way synonymous with powerful definitions of 'crime', 'order' and 'disorder'. This in turn can encourage the identification and monitoring of others (e.g. in drawing attention to long-standing 'enemies' or folk devils in the form of 'deviants' around whom the possibility exists to mobilise social forces for order maintenance and expansions in panoptic control). In this sense, we can understand synoptic and panoptic forms of surveillance as interconnected. But, as already suggested, they are also differential in the way in which they are connected, targeted and received among the wider population. Surveillance does not merely reflect or 'find' difference or deviation from commonly defined social norms, but actively shapes and reinforces particular norms, values and ways of thinking that configure what or who is 'different'. This certainly seems to be the case with surveillance in its synoptic guise. We are – through 'infotainment' – encouraged to watch and digest the pursuit and punishment of precategorised and predefined aspects of social harm (**Neal, 2010**).

For Thomas Mathiesen (1997, p. 230), the media inculcates a process of surveillance aimed at presenting 'a general understanding of the world' in which the 'personal and the individual, the deviant, the shuddering, the titillating' are emphasised. Mathiesen also argues that synoptic surveillance – particularly in its negative portrayal of threats, deviations, rising crime and the perceived insufficient protection from these behaviours – reinforces panoptic surveillance, in particular the perceptions and interests of the forces of law and order. Fear-inducing tales of criminality and terror are often the basis for establishing expansions in real-world panoptic surveillance, thus unintentionally endorsing calls for more street cameras, more prisons, more data checks, greater police powers, and so on. We can think of the repetitive image-driven reportage of the events of 9/11 in the USA and 7/7 in the UK and the impact this had on surveillance debates, 'anti-terrorism' campaigns and the perceived need for greater controls. Again, the important point is that surveillance – whether panoptic or synoptic – is partial. It contributes as much to our 'understanding' of, and exposure to, events in the world as it creates 'a spiral of silence' in relation to what we do not see and are not told or informed about (Mathiesen, 2004, p. 103). For example, in synoptic terms corporate wrongdoing or 'crime', committed in pursuit of legitimate goals, along with the negative consequences of a range of corporate action hardly feature. Whether in terms of the few observing the many or the many observing the few, harmful corporate actions (deaths at work, environmental pollution, and so on) scarcely figure in comparison to other arguably less harmful activities, such as conventionally defined crimes (Tombs and Whyte, 2007). Furthermore, violence in the world of the private domestic sphere, where two women are murdered each week in the UK, receives little or no attention (Bindel, 2008).

As noted earlier, surveillance increasingly proliferates into formal and informal spaces, which in turn drives the self-surveillance of deviance. This process is both differential and gendered, as illustrated in the ways in which women's magazines, such as *Cosmopolitan*, *Women's Own*, or *Marie Claire*, provide a synoptic framework for female self-surveillance in relation to practised codes of femininity (e.g., beauty tips), domestication (house and child rearing) and body management (weight watching). It may be that not only are articles and images in such magazines important here, in relaying codes of feminine 'attainment' and 'deviance', but that so too are the kinds of advertisements they carry. In this gender-specific environment, how is surveillance different for women as compared to men, in terms of its practice and outcomes?

Articles and images in women's magazines delineate feminine appropriateness in relation to domestic roles, bodily cleanliness, dietary habits, dress sense and sexual performance. Popular women's magazines idealise what it is to be feminine through (self-)surveillance directed at the body. Feelings of failure to live up to prevalent feminine codes of appropriate body size, shape or demeanour may lead to self-denial or shame. Delineating 'conventional feminine behaviour' encourages surveillance directed towards 'the discipline of perfecting the body as an object'. This can have harmful results, as found, for example, in cases of anorexia nervosa and bulimia (Bordo, 1993). For Susan Bordo, the fact that women's magazines are underpinned by a discourse of 'liberation' and 'empowerment' renders them insidious: 'to feel autonomous and free while harnessing body and soul to an obsessive body-practice is to serve, not transform, a social order that limits female possibilities' (Bordo, 1993, p. 179). Sandra Lee Bartky (1988, pp. 81–2) emphasises how self-surveillance in this context operates as 'obedience to patriarchy' underpinned 'with a pervasive feeling of bodily deficiency'. This means considering how stereotypes relayed synoptically for female consumption both reflect and discipline 'popular anxieties' that frame surveillance regimes for the attainment of femininity. While some have argued that women's magazines encourage surveillance as self-loathing, other feminist writers have countered that the genre is more complicated in that magazines allow space for debate (however limited) about women's issues – including sexuality, work and motherhood – that are not necessarily stereotypical (Wolf, 1993).

Informal surveillance processes of this kind are geared towards a relatively hidden form of 'policing' of the normative borders between the 'feminine' and the 'unfeminine'. Feminists have noted that the inability to live up to normative expectations prescribed in modes of informal surveillance can result in violence and coercion aimed against the deviant (hence 'unfeminine') woman in both informal (domestic) and formal (criminal justice) settings (Deveaux, 1994).

4   Crossing borders: global surveillance?

We have observed that, 'When surveillance topics are controversial it is often because defining, creating, crossing or failing to cross a border of some form is at issue' (Marx, 2005, p. 29). This section considers the formalisation of borders and how information about people is collated, stored, retrieved and then passed – particularly when using computer technology – across public and private boundaries and institutional and international borders. This can be true for financial information as well as for information held on police databases or in major consumer organisations. Surveillance is not merely tied to specific institutions and place locations; it is potentially, if not actually, a global phenomenon over which most of us have little or no control in terms of information collection, dissemination and usage (Webb, 2007). Indeed, for example, under the Mutual Legal Assistance Agreement signed by the European Union and the USA in 2003, US law enforcers have access to bank accounts throughout the EU in investigating serious crime. For John Torpey (2007, p. 52), 'modern states and the international state system of which they are a part' have always 'expropriated from individuals and private entities the legitimate "means of movement", particularly though by no means exclusively across international borders'. Thus, in collating information about (and 'knowing') identities and checking these at border points (international border points, commercial/financial points of transaction, police searches either on the streets or via databases, and so on), surveillance also enables and disables identities and mobilities in time and space.

4.1 Identities (and ID cards)

Whatever their form, identity (ID) cards act to signify citizenship within a designated national space. They attempt to perform the 'reliable identification of each member of the population to which they are issued, for example as citizens of a country, immigrants, refugees, or welfare recipients' (Stalder and Lyon, 2003, p. 83). However, not all countries have embraced ID cards and if they have, they have not done so in a uniform manner. National ID cards have a central purpose in aiding state servants to ascertain who belongs and who does not belong to a designated nation state. They are heralded as a once-and-for-all assurance of identity. This is because they are thought to be based on 'smart' electronic technology. Such smart technology means that ID cards can be machine-read and linked to networked and searchable databases; they can carry on them biometric (bodily) forms of identity assurance (such as fingerprints and eye scans) and they can be used for any range of purposes beyond a discrete policing function.

However, far from being panaceas in securing identity surveillance, practices such as these are prone to generate new risks, such as the possibility of error in the system that in turn generates false identification or a failure to identify. Even a 'foolproof' system would not prevent all criminal or political violence. Most of those involved in the 9/11 attacks on the USA, for example, had no previous criminal records and were in possession of valid visas. Thus, the checks that ID cards perform (including background checks against a list of suspects) would not have produced positive results because the individuals concerned were not on the radar of suspicion in the first place (Stalder and Lyon, 2003).

Surveillance practices such as ID cards are also not introduced in a vacuum but in social climates imbued with pre-existing discriminatory practices. For example, as part of crime control strategies, policing agencies have always targeted some groups disproportionately more than others – based on age, 'racial' profile, class location or sexuality (see Chapter 6). In both European and North American domains, police stop-and-search procedures have, in historical terms, differentially targeted poor, minority ethnic groups (Wacquant, 1999). How would the mandatory introduction of ID cards counter this? For some – particularly proponents – ID cards act as a leveller: we would all carry them, therefore discrimination based on ethnic features, for instance, would be eliminated. This may possibly be the case when immigrants apply for work or welfare – the card denotes entitlement without negotiation with officials. However, ID cards encode information such as workplace, address, gender and ethnicity and are part of the drive of pre-emptive surveillance identified earlier. Felix Stalder and David Lyon (2003a, p. 89) have argued that, 'however well-intentioned the introduction of ID cards, the resulting classifications of ethnic groups will produce categories of suspicion that will capture innocent persons in their net'. The risk that more, rather than fewer, people will be caught in the net of surveillance could be compounded in this scenario by moral panic around particular forms of crime or terrorism identified in official and media circles with particular social or ethnic groups (as indicated in Activity 5.4). Such risks emanating from the use of ID cards can, in some contexts, contribute to more life-threatening forms of social harm. In Iraq in 2007, the US military collected biometric data from hundreds of thousands of Iraqi citizens with the aim of containing insurgents. It is feared by Privacy International (2007b) that such data will increase the killing of members of religious sects by those from different sects – as is already the case – on the basis of identification papers showing religious affiliation and place of residence. Similarly, during the genocide in Rwanda in 1994, the word 'Tutsi' stamped on an ID card became a virtual death sentence for thousands of people (Imperial War Museum, 2008).

Figure 5.5
Amnesty International campaign raising awareness of the dangers of racial profiling found in the 2001 US PATRIOT Act, which allows US law enforcers to use physical characteristics (e.g. skin colour, hair type, dress style) as predictors of criminal acts

ID cards are to be introduced in the UK by 2017 and will – as in other countries – include biometric data from eyes, fingers, hands or faces. The Identity Cards Act 2006 states that, from 2010, renewal of a UK passport will require attendance at an 'enrolment centre', where fingerprints and photographs will be conjoined and any number of the 200 questions, which the Home Office has devised to examine an applicants' identity, origin and entitlement to remain a UK citizen, will be asked. EU rules also stipulate the operation of a similar scheme for all member states, to include retention of information on a database (Hayes, 2008). However, proponents of biometric profiling argue that its reliance on unique body parts as identifiers makes it harder to engage in identity theft. As with other forms of surveillance, however, cases of fraud and mistakes in the technology do occur and will have a differential impact on particular groups. For example, poorer people with ID cards could be at particular risk of ID theft because their cards could be their only form of identity, unlike more affluent holders of multiple credit cards and other means of identification associated with work and travel. Thus, those who have greater means of ensuring their identity will be at less risk from mistakes when machines incorrectly read ID cards and when ID cards are stolen or lost, whereas poorer people will be left with little or no means of identifying themselves (Watt, 2008). If ID cards are meant to render visible that which seeks to remain invisible, then a question remains in relation to how this squares with the desire of suicide bombers in wanting to be known for their actions – evident in the fact that they leave videos and carry forms of identity – albeit after the fact.

Maureen Webb (2007) has argued that ID cards and other forms of identity registration have both an inclusionary and an exclusionary logic – the latter generating risks for those who do not have the card, ID documents or data profiles (because these could be lost or stolen or are not possessed on conscientious grounds), or who may not participate (through poverty or choice) in the types of activities on which data are collected. In all these cases the spectre of being a 'non-person' is created – at least from the vantage point of a surveillance regime. It has been argued that in such cases of 'non-personhood', 'one will be, by definition, a risk. And one will be *at* risk, since the state will deal with one aggressively, granting few, if any legal safeguards' (Webb, 2007, p. 101, original emphasis). Again, we can see that the act of transgressing or refusing a surveillance regime connected to gender, 'race' or class invites the possibility of social ordering through other means – namely those of coercion.

4.2 Mobilities (and airport surveillance)

Like shopping malls, airports are designed for transient control where, according to Mark Salter (2005, p. 43), 'architecture, confession and hyper-documentation' intersect in 'supporting the sovereign power of the state to compel subjects to docility and obedience'. The difference between this and Foucault's panoptic surveillance in prisons is in the latter's regard for 'the regulation of limited movement through repetition'. Airports, on the other hand, also rely on obedience, for 'the regulation of mass movement and the discrimination of desirable and undesirable travellers' (Salter, 2005, p. 42). First, on arrival at airports travellers are required to self-sort into categories for inspection: citizens, foreigners and refugees. Second, this is followed by the 'confessional' where border agents ascertain past and future intentions coupled with an examination of passports and other documents. The confessional has an obvious weakness, as seen in the case of those involved in the 9/11 bombings, for example, who placed themselves in a state of war with the nation and therefore did 'not feel the compulsion towards confession' (Salter, 2005, p. 47). Third, risk profiling, or 'hyper-documentation', also comes into play, whereby interlinking pieces of information about individual travellers are run through databases to be tracked and sorted. Since 2001, this area, too, has relied on biometrics and cross-sharing of information.

As noted in Section 2, biometric technology and facial recognition have received extensive coverage in promising a dependable surveillance instrument. However, the reliability of face recognition technology has been challenged by David Birch (2002) in his study of Heathrow Airport (which takes more than one million passengers weekly). Ten individuals who are the real targets of security checks pass through the screening system and are correctly identified by the cameras. Thus, a success rate of 99.9 per cent using face recognition cameras will also throw up about 990 cases of false positives (0.1 per cent of one million). The argument here is that to verify and disallow 1000 false positives in a week is simply unworkable because it would prove expensive and over-burden the system. The research therefore concludes that facial recognition technology, as used in CCTV, may possibly create feelings of safety but, in objective terms, levels of safety have not changed. Furthermore, as noted earlier, discriminatory practices more often than not can become an integral feature of surveillance systems. Thus, research suggests that facial recognition systems find it easier to identify African Caribbean, Asian and older people, who will therefore be more likely to trigger an alarm (Introna and Wood, 2004).

Figure 5.6
A Registered Traveller airport boarding pass for 'privileged passengers'. In return for providing personal information prior to travelling, Registered Travellers become known to the airport/ airline and therefore receive special dispensation privileges (such as foregoing routine security measures)

Automated systems at border controls give rise to the risk of racialised profiling, leading to a form of categorical suspicion exemplified in the phrase 'flying while Arab' (Lyon, 2003a, p. 99), much in the way that 'travelling while Irish' operated as a signifier of suspicion in the UK in the 1970s. In using biology and physical appearance as means of identification, biometrics legitimises group differentiation and racialisation in the name of security. Arguably, the furtive nature of the technology and the ease with which it can be used leave little room for escaping the gaze of the authorities while failing to enhance public protection and security.

Further, we often think of airports as places that provide easy access to effective global mobility. But as intense surveillance spaces, airports provide this access differentially – reproducing social divisions and inequalities in mobility. For example, paid-up members of pre-approved traveller schemes such as INPASS, operating in a minority of airports in the USA, enjoy faster movement through the airport – as 'preferred customers' or 'low-risk' passengers able to traverse elite business corridors. 'For some people to move faster, it is sometimes necessary to make the mobility of others slower ... [For] these others this may mean more direct forms of scrutiny, such as strip searches, interrogation, incarceration, and deportation, and more sustained forms of immobility' (Adey, 2006, p. 207). The Registered Traveller scheme enables users to buy their way into surveillance programmes: they allow themselves to be profiled into databases, which provides them with a 'low-risk' status and speedier mobility. Those with slower velocity may, out of frustration, seek to pay to become Registered Travellers, thus expanding the databases. Pre-emptive, less visible systems work alongside these practices. Since 9/11, airlines flying to the USA have been obliged to hand over data pertaining to the names and the ticket and passport information of flyers – before the flight takes off. This data is – within fifteen minutes of flights departing – relayed to US Customs and Border Protection where it is cross-checked with other databases, such as the FBI (Federal Bureau of Investigation) wanted persons lists. Surveillance and inspection thus take place prior to travellers reaching their destinations (Adey, 2006).

Private entities and corporations (in the case of airports, shipping companies, and so on) 'participate in the regulation of movement at the behest of states' (Torpey, 2007, p. 56). In 2007, a Passenger Name Record (PNR) agreement between European states and the USA allowed data to be made available to the US Department of Homeland Security (DHS). Information included religious beliefs, political opinions and sexual habits. As Ben Hayes (2008, p. 16) has stated, when taking a flight from the UK to Amsterdam, for example, 'up to 35 categories of personal information that you supply could find themselves in the US DHS inbox'.

5 Evading and contesting surveillance

This section explores further the extent to which surveillance is all-pervasive, global in its reach and uniform in its effects.

Activity 5.5

Can you think of any ways in which individuals and agencies might be able to avoid and/or are in a position to be able to contest being made visible by surveillance?

Comment

Surveillance technologies are contradictory in that they create spaces and possibilities for the evasion of monitoring and resistance to it: for example, we may be inclined to be less than fully truthful in disclosing information or we may exercise discretion in how we use the internet. Lawbreakers, both powerful and powerless, do avoid or try to outfox surveillance measures. Claims that surveillance is multidirectional, casting its scrutinising gaze evenly across social hierarchies is, as we have already seen, too simplistic a view. Lyon (2007, p. 48) has noted that, 'surveillance expresses an ongoing theme, [in] that those who establish some means of watching over others are demonstrating that they do not trust those being watched'. However, some social actors – by means of socio-cultural, ethnic or gender status or political acumen – are clearly 'trusted' more than others to be left relatively free from surveillance scrutiny. Social position – that is, where one is situated in the hierarchy of power – can also allow a degree of surveillance avoidance. The kind of questions to which this gives rise might include the following. Is the monitoring of violent men in the private sphere given equal time and resources in both panoptic and synoptic terms? Does surveillance of professional groups, such as doctors, befit the levels of responsibility and power they exercise over patients? Does surveillance of corporate actors include the decision making involved in credit management in the banking system?

Surveillance across different spatial settings is experienced and enacted differently. As we have seen, surveillance for some may be organised and perceived in a way that is non-burdensome or beneficial; for others, it is bound up with a system of 'detection, judgement ... and punishment, aimed at limiting freedom and channelling behaviour' (Gilliom, 2006, p. 125). As John Gilliom argues, how we understand surveillance needs to take account of 'how differently situated people – welfare mothers, prisoners, students, middle class professionals – speak of and respond to their various surveillance settings' (Gilliom, 2006, p. 126).

The ability to evade and contest surveillance should also be situated in relation to a person's social standing and the power of a surveillance regime in relation to those under its gaze. Powerfully situated actors are materially or ideologically better able to 'neutralise, permanently or temporarily, the moral bind of the law' (Cohen, 2001, p. 60).

Surveillance regimes often enforce this 'moral bind of the law', but it can also be negotiated (in terms of whether or not surveillance occurs) and is heavily dependent on access to material resources and cultural capital. In addition, individuals may have the comfort of choosing voluntary participation within a surveillance regime in return for given 'rewards' (as we have seen, for instance, in the case of airport fast-tracking). In advanced capitalist societies, such as that of the UK, legal and political structures allow for some groups to negotiate regulatory surveillance over 'their' domain (as is the case with professional bodies such as the General Medical Council or the police force). Other groups and agencies may be in a position to cultivate close relations with surveillance and regulatory agencies in and around government. These asymmetries in the ability to negotiate surveillance and press moral and political claims on regulatory agencies can, in part, explain why in the UK, for instance, the likelihood of an employer being monitored with regard to implementing the minimum wage is once every 330 years (Bunting, 2008). Furthermore, although the monitoring of worker 'performance' and 'efficiency' is commonplace (Ball, 2003), the average rate for inspection of workplaces in the UK by health and safety officers is once every twenty years.

On the other hand, social campaigning groups and activists use surveillance tactics to expose corporate polluters or to capture state misdemeanours (such as police misconduct). As forms of counter-surveillance, these kinds of activities are also mirrored in the use of information technology to propagate dissent and resistance to oppressive forms of government. However, as forms of resistance they operate in a field of asymmetrical power relations. Take the example of using information technologies to express dissent in authoritarian regimes – most evident in countries such as Iran, China and Burma. Chat rooms, blogs and websites have been used in these countries to discuss and expose abuses of liberty (torture, imprisonment, arbitrary arrest). This information is then disseminated to the rest of the world. In an age of media censorship, campaigners such as Amnesty International rely on such web forums to galvanise public support and push for political pressure to challenge oppression in such countries. However, as Amnesty has observed, asymmetries of power come into play in the ability of powerful actors to silence dissent by closing down and censoring websites (with the resultant arrest and imprisonment of those found using them) (Allen, 2006). The notion that the internet enables 'free expression' is tested more seriously here (than is the case when those in the West are monitored and discriminated against by advertisers). Yahoo, Google and Microsoft have all bowed to pressure from the Chinese state to limit internet access to Chinese citizens, even handing over information identifying names and email addresses of those using the internet to spread 'political content' (Allen, 2006; **Neal, 2010**). Global IT companies have also supplied China with technologies to monitor internet use. The point made here is not that resistance is futile, but that it takes place within pre-existing asymmetries of power where social forces and specific institutional/corporate interests are a factor to be reckoned with. This produces contradictory results in specific locations. In the case of China (where markets are being developed), Yahoo stated that it had to obey local law; in the USA (where markets are relatively established), Google fought and won a legal wrangle over the Bush administration's attempt to gain access to its vast data banks pertaining to individual internet use (Johnson, 2006). Finally, both the form and the extent of a surveillance regime, and the possibilities and means to contest it, are not globally homogenised and will depend on different legal oversight measures, economic circumstances, political priorities, gender and 'racial' relations, and cultures as they exist in different countries (Lyon, 2007).

6 Conclusion

This chapter has focused on surveillance not as a self-contained entity, but as a set of technologies fused with social ordering practices that reflect and maintain terrains of power across diverse spatial settings. Surveillance maintains spatial borders (both formal and informal) and the behaviour and movement within and between spaces – and it is also implicated in the regulation of attempts to transgress or change commonly defined meanings characteristic of social space. In this sense, surveillance has been explored as a socially tangential technology that is uneven in its quest for 'visibility' and differentiating in its targeting and effects.

A core paradox of surveillance is that wider public access to information and civil rights (and thereby the achievement of a greater 'justice') is accompanied by means to impose coercive control when warranted by particular circumstances (and thereby exacerbating existing, or creating new, 'injustices'). Moreover, the trajectory of surveillance towards the arguably practised goals of risk prevention, pre-emption and prediction is transforming the landscape of 'justice' (see Chapter 4). Apart from undermining traditional practices of criminal justice and due process, it is also transforming wider patterns of social 'entitlement' in relation to how participation (particularly for the already marginalised) is practised and managed in social life. In Cindy Katz's words, surveillance often 'marks a retreat from politics' (Katz, 2006, p. 26) and a failure to debate how 'justice' and 'injustice' are generated within social orders. Instead, surveillance often concentrates on individualising responsibility and apportioning 'blame'. Therefore, the naturalisation of surveillance may displace questions of the political–economic underpinnings of 'crime' and 'terrorism', as well as forms of social harm that contemporary surveillance rarely casts its gaze upon (Coleman, 2004). Who is monitored, through what means, why, for what purpose and with what effects – these are questions that have led us to focus on the complex interrelationship between the practice of surveillance and the values and interests underpinning social order. Furthermore, we have asked what, if anything, is being secured by surveillance. Simply viewing surveillance as a gateway to improving 'public safety' is myopic. Instead, we have probed the extent to which surveillance is integral to the process of constructing social understandings of 'crime', 'security', 'order' and 'justice'. Consequently, surveillance is as much ensconced in reflecting and reinforcing social relations and social divisions – in work, migration and consumption – as it is in fighting crime and terrorism.

References

Adey, P. (2006) '"Divided we move": the dromologics of airport security and surveillance' in Monahan, T. (ed.) (2006b).

Allen, K. (2006) 'Today, our chance to fight a new hi-tech tyranny', *The Observer*, 28 May [online], www.guardian.co.uk/technology/2006/may/28/news.humanrights1 (Accessed 5 April 2009).

Andrejevic, M. (2007) *iSpy: Surveillance and Power in the Interactive Era*, Kansas, KS, University of Kansas Press.

Ball, K. (2003) 'Categorising the workers: electronic surveillance and social ordering in the call center' in Lyon, D. (ed.) (2003b)

Bartky, S.L. (1988) 'Foucault, femininity, and the modernisation of patriarchal power' in Diamond, I. and Quinby, L. (eds) *Foucault and Feminism*, Boston, MA, Northeastern University Press.

Bindel, J. (2008) 'Two women killed each week', *The Guardian*, 2 July [online], www.guardian.co.uk.commentisfree/2008/jul/02/ukcrime.women (Accessed 5 April 2009).

Birch, D. (2002) 'A world away from the reality' *The Guardian*, 24 January, [online],
www.guardian.co.uk/technology/2002/jan/24/onlinesupplement
(Accessed 5 April 2009).

Bogard, W. (2006) 'Surveillance assemblages and lines of flight' in Lyon, D. (ed.) (2006b).

Bogard, W. (2007) 'Surveillance, its simulation, and hypercontrol in virtual systems' in Heir, S.P. and Greenberg, J. (eds) (2007)

Bordo, S. (1993) *Unbearable Weight: Feminism, Western Culture and the Body*, Berkeley, CA, University of California Press.

Brooke, H. (2009) 'Unsung hero', *The Guardian*, 15 May, pp. 4–6

Bunting, M. (2008) 'Fair wages are a fantasy in the brutal underside of Cowboy Boss Britain', *The Guardian*, 5 May [online], www.guardian.co.uk/commentisfree/2008/may/05/workandcareers.gordonbrown (Accessed 7 May 2009).

Castel, R. (1991) 'From dangerousness to risk' in Burchell, G., Gordon, C. and Miller, P. (eds) *The Foucault Effect: Studies in Governmentality*, London, Harvester Wheatsheaf.

Cohen, S. (1985) *Visions of Social Control: Crime, Punishment, and Classification*, Cambridge, Polity.

Cohen, S. (2001) *States of Denial: Knowing About Atrocities and Suffering*, London, Polity.

Coleman, R. (2004) *Reclaiming the Streets: Surveillance, Social Control and the City*, Cullompton, Willan.

Coleman, R. (2005) 'Surveillance in the city: primary definition and urban spatial order', *Crime, Media and Culture: An International Journal*, vol. 1, no. 2, pp. 131–48.

Deveaux, M. (1994) 'Feminism and empowerment: a critical reading of Foucault', *Feminist Studies*, vol. 20, no. 2, pp. 223–47.

Ditton, J. (1998) 'Public support for town centre CCTV schemes: myth or reality?' in Norris, C., Moran, J. and Armstrong, G. (eds) *Surveillance, Closed Circuit Television and Social Control*, Aldershot, Ashgate.

Doward, J. (2007) 'Civil rights fears over DNA file for everyone', *The Observer*, 27 May, p. 2.

Doyle, A. (2006) 'An alternative current in surveillance and control: broadcasting surveillance footage of crimes' in Haggerty, K.D. and Ericson, R.V. (eds) (2006a).

Dyer, C. (2007) 'Anger over call to widen DNA database', *The Guardian*, 6 September, p. 12.

Foucault, M. (1977) *Discipline and Punish*, London, Allen Lane.

Gandy, O.H. (1996) 'Coming to terms with the panoptic sort' in Lyon, D. and Zureik, E. (eds) (1996).

Gandy, O.H. (2007) 'Data mining and surveillance in the post-9/11 environment' in Heir, S.P. and Greenberg, J. (eds) (2007).

Gilliom, J. (2006) 'Struggling with surveillance: resistance, consciousness and identity' in Haggerty, K.D. and Ericson, R.V. (eds) (2006).

Haggerty, K.D. (2006) 'Tear down the walls: on demolishing the panopticon' in Lyon, D. (ed.) (2006).

Haggerty, K.D. and Ericson, R.V. (2000) 'The surveillant assemblage', *British Journal of Sociology*, vol. 51, no. 4, pp. 605–22.

Haggerty, K.D. and Ericson, R.V. (eds) (2006a) *The New Politics of Surveillance and Visibility*, Toronto, University of Toronto Press.

Haggerty, K.D. and Ericson, R.V. (2006b) 'The new politics of surveillance and visibility' in Haggerty, K.D. and Ericson, R.V. (eds) (2006).

Hayes, B. (2008) 'Surveillance society', *Red Pepper*, issue 157, June, pp. 14–18.

Heir, S.P. and Greenberg, J. (eds) (2007) *The Surveillance Studies Reader*, Maidenhead, Open University Press.

Imperial War Museum (2008) *Through My Eyes: Stories of Conflict, Belonging & Identity. Rwandan Genocide* [online], www.throughmyeyes.org.uk/server/show/nav.23319 (Accessed 7 May 2009).

Introna, L.D. and Wood, D. (2004) 'Picturing algorithmic surveillance: the politics of facial recognition systems', *Surveillance and Society*, vol. 2 no. 2/3, pp. 177–98; also available online at www.surveillance-and-society.org/articles2 (2)/algorithmic.pdf (Accessed 20 March 2009).

Johnson, B. (2006) 'Google stands up to White House in row over privacy on web', *The Guardian*, 9 November [online], www.guardian.co.uk/technology/2006/nov/09/news.usnews (Accessed 5 April 2009).

Katz, C. (2006) 'The state goes home: local hypervigilance of children and the global retreat from social reproduction' in Monahan, T. (ed.)(2006b).

Lacey, N. (1994) 'Introduction: making sense of criminal justice' in Lacey, N. (ed.) *A Reader in Criminal Justice*, Oxford, Oxford University Press.

Lyon, D. (2001) *Surveillance and Society: Monitoring Everyday Life*, Buckingham, Open University Press.

Lyon, D. (2003a) 'Surveillance as social sorting: computer codes and mobile bodies' in Lyon, D. (ed.) (2003b).

Lyon, D. (ed.) (2003b) *Surveillance as Social Sorting: Privacy, Risk and Digital Discrimination*, London, Routledge.

Lyon, D. (2006a) '9/11, synopticon, and scopophilia: watching and being watched' in Haggerty, K.D. and Ericson, R.V. (eds) (2006b).

Lyon, D. (ed.) *Theorizing Surveillance: The Panopticon and Beyond*, Cullompton, Willan. (2006b).

Lyon, D. (2007) *Surveillance Studies: An Overview*, Cambridge, Polity.

Lyon, D. and Zureik, E. (eds) (1996) *Surveillance, Computers and Privacy*, Minneapolis, MN, University of Minnesota Press.

Marx, G. (2005) 'Some conceptual issues in the study of borders and surveillance' in Zureik, E. and Salter, M.B. (eds) (2005).

Mathiesen, T. (1997) 'The viewer society: Michel Foucault's panopticon revisited', *Theoretical Criminology*, vol. 1, no. 2, pp. 215–34.

Mathiesen, T. (2004) *Silently Silenced: Essays in the Creation of Acquiescence in Modern Society*, Winchester, Waterside.

Monahan, T. (2006a) 'Questioning surveillance and security' in Monahan, T. (ed.) (2006b).

Monahan, T. (ed.) (2006b) *Surveillance and Security: Technological Politics and Power in Everyday Life*, London, Routledge.

Monahan, T. and Wall, T. (2007) 'Somatic surveillance: corporeal control through information networks', *Surveillance and Society, Special Issue Part 1*, vol. 4, no. 3, pp. 154–73; also available online at www.surveillance-and-society.org/articles4(3)/somatic.pdf (Accessed 20 March 2009).

Mooney, G. and Talbot, D. (2010) 'Global cities, segregation and transgression' in Muncie, J. et al (eds) (2010).

Muncie, J., Talbot, D. and Walters, R. (eds) (2010) *Crime: Local and Global*, Cullompton, Willan/Milton Keynes, The Open University.

Nacro (2002) *To CCTV or not to CCTV? A Review of Current Research into the Effectiveness of CCTV Systems in Reducing Crime*, London, Nacro.

Neal, S. (2010) 'Cybercrime, transgression and virtual environments' in Muncie, J. et al (eds) (2010).

Nelkin, D. and Andrews, L. (2003) 'Surveillance creep in the genetic age' in Lyon, D. (ed.) (2003b).

Newburn, T. (2007) *Criminology*, Cullompton, Willan.

Norris, C. (2003) 'From personal to digital: CCTV, the panopticon, and the technological mediation of suspicion and control' in Lyon, D. (ed.) (2003b).

Norris, C. and Armstrong, G. (1999) *The Maximum Surveillance Society: The Rise of CCTV*, Oxford, Berg.

Pallister, D. (2009) 'Jacqui Smith says DNA profiles of 800,000 innocent people will be axed', *The Guardian*, 4 May, p. 6

Poster, M. (1996) 'Databases as discourse; or, electronic interpellations' in Lyon, D. and Zureik, E. (eds) (1996).

Poudrier, J. (2003) 'Racial categories and health risks: epidemiological surveillance among Canadian First Nations' in Lyon, D. (ed.) (2003b).

Privacy International (2007a) *Leading Surveillance Societies in the EU and the World 2007: The 2007 International Privacy Ranking* [online], http://pi.gn.apc.org/article.shtml?cmd[347]=x-347-559597 (Accessed 5 April 2009).

Privacy International (2007b) *Federal Republic of Iraq: Constitutional Privacy Rights* [online], www.privacyinternational.org/article.shtml?cmd[347]=x-347-559528 (Accessed 5 April 2009).

Salter, M. (2005) 'At the threshold of security: a theory of international borders' in Zureik, E. and Salter, M.B. (eds) (2005)

Stalder, F. and Lyon, D. (2003) 'Electronic identity cards and social classification' in Lyon, D. (ed.) (2003b).

Tombs, S. and Whyte, D. (2007) *Safety Crimes*, Cullompton, Willan.

Torpey, J. (2007) 'Coming and going: on the state monopolization of the legitimate "means of movement"' in Heir, S.P. and Greenberg, J. (eds) (2007)

Travis, A. (2008) '17 judges, one ruling – and 857,000 records must be now wiped clear', *The Observer*, 5 December, p. 6.

Wacquant, L. (1999) 'How penal common sense comes to Europeans: notes on the transatlantic diffusion of the neo-liberal doxa', *European Societies*, vol. 1, no. 3, pp. 319–52.

Watt, N. (2008) 'ID cards may put poorer people at risk of fraud', *The Guardian*, 16 May, p. 11.

Webb, M. (2007) *Illusions of Security: Global Surveillance and Democracy in the Post-9/11 World*, San Francisco, CA, City Light Books.

Wolf, N. (1993) *Fire with Fire: The New Female Power and How It Will Change the 21st Century*, London, Chatto and Windus.

Zureik, E. and Salter, M.B. (eds) (2005) *Global Surveillance and Policing: Borders, Security, Identity*, Cullompton, Willan.

Chapter 6
Transnational policing and security

Louise Westmarland

Contents

1   Introduction

This chapter addresses some fundamental yet recurring questions, such as 'What is policing?'; 'What is policing for and how is it transformed by "transnational", "international" or "supranational" developments?'; and 'What are the connections and contradictions between the demands for local and global security?' As scholars have been reminding us for at least the past three decades, such questions take us far beyond visible patrol work; indeed, beyond those activities that we might normally ascribe to 'the police'. One of the reasons for this 'expansion' of policing is linked to general influences of 'globalisation' and to the supposed growth in criminal opportunities and its prominence in political agendas across the world. Added to this are international terrorist threats highlighted by the 'war on terror' and the dissolving 'borders' of crime and crime control. As the preceding chapters have shown, one of the central concerns of criminal justice, in its many forms and guises, is the control of certain people, actions and outcomes.

To pursue these themes, this chapter explores the increasingly troublesome connections between the local and the global in terms of the policing and security of three elements:

1   'criminal' populations or individuals

2   actions deemed to be illegal in particular jurisdictions or contrary to the well-being of the society and citizens of those jurisdictions

3   the outcomes of the actions or preventative measures taken by the authorities that are given the responsibility for the policing and security of particular jurisdictions.

As the chapter will show, it is clear that there are ambiguities surrounding the definition of apparently straightforward terms, such as 'transnational' and 'international' policing, and the differences between these. This is further complicated when issues of national and international 'security' and 'cross-border' cooperation, as opposed to 'supranational' control, are raised. At the centre of these debates is the question of who has the power to attempt to control 'transnational criminal' activities, people and places, and what is the legitimate remit of the agents of the state, such as the police and, increasingly, 'private' security forces that operate outside usual state boundaries. A key issue for this chapter, therefore, is whether we are witnessing the break-up of a state monopoly on policing.

The aims of this chapter are to explore:

■   the relationship between 'the police' and policing

■   the history of police cooperation across borders and how this operates

- why 'international', 'transnational' and 'supranational' policing are issues and how the terms differ in meaning

- the ways in which increasing privatisation of policing and security affects or interacts with trans/international policing and security

- the main issues surrounding 'transnational' policing and how these differ from discussions of 'normal' policing, which are concerned with, for example, legitimacy, corruption and accountability

- whether transnational policing contributes to 'postmodern' policing and whether it will lead to the end of 'state'-led policing as it currently exists.

The chapter examines a number of themes concerning policing, which aim to go beyond borders and expand on the idea of 'local' policing. The discussion follows two main directions. The first is the way in which a 'globalising' world, with an increasing threat of insecurity, has created the possibility, if not of a 'world police', at least of a world of cooperation across nation state boundaries. The second refers to the privatisation of policing and how the 'security' aspect of policing is ambiguous in the sense not only of the 'local', but also of the 'global'. Whether security can be bought and to what extent the power of international, private or even state police can be guaranteed are questions the chapter addresses.

Figure 6.1
Local police are often seen as the 'thin blue line' because their roles of crime fighting and prevention and, as this image suggests, maintaining public order, are generally viewed as a state monopoly

Section 2 explores the nature of policing and looks at distinctions between 'public' and 'private' policing. Section 3 gives a brief overview of the history and development of cross-border police cooperation, while Section 4 begins to examine contemporary cross-border cooperation in law enforcement. Sections 5, 6 and 7 go on to explore the relationship between international, transnational and supranational policing and security and the effects of the blurring of internal and external security mandates.

2   What is policing?

To begin thinking about the issues noted above, it is useful to break them down into a number of basic questions, such as 'What is the relationship between "the police" (as in the state-funded and accountable, front-line "street patrol" officer) and "policing"?' One of the definitions of front-line policing is that it is the '24/7', 'who can we call?' first-response service. This describes the broad role that the public police have claimed for themselves: as a 'cover-all', emergency agency and as the legitimate body of physical control: state-run police are sanctioned to use reasonable physical force where this is deemed to be necessary (Westmarland, 2001), supervised by senior police leaders who are democratically overseen (by the Home Office in the UK), if not directly elected (as in the USA). They are also subject to rules and discipline and usually to a public complaints procedure should their behaviour fall short of that expected.

Activity 6.1

Think about some of the ways in which people are 'policed' in everyday life, such as:

- at home, within the family

- at work, in factories or offices

- in public places, such as the street or shopping mall

- using leisure facilities.

Now read the following two extracts and consider the way in which 'policing' operates at a local level and how 'private' spaces are controlled, and the resources this entails.

Extract 6.1

Crime reduction: improvements to how we deal with domestic abuse

Since 2003, Thames Valley Police has made a number of significant improvements to how it deals with domestic abuse.

These include:

All domestic abuse incidents are now graded as 'urgent' as a minimum. This means that police officers aim to respond within at least one hour unless circumstances require a more immediate response.

Force policy on domestic abuse states that officers must positively intervene in all domestic abuse incidents. When considering the level of intervention, the arrest of the alleged perpetrator must always be considered. Officers must be able to justify why they have not arrested. This has led to a considerable increase in the number of people arrested for domestic abuse-related offences.

Source: Thames Valley Police, 2009

Extract 6.2

Following a decade of rapid expansion within its leisure infrastructure ... Manchester City Centre now attracts crowds of up to 100,000 people on Friday and Saturday evenings. A liberal estimate is that approximately thirty to forty officers are engaged on public order duty at these times, whilst the crowds are simultaneously controlled by an estimated 1,000 bouncers working per night. Similar comparisons can be drawn in towns and cities throughout the UK. For example, Nottingham City Centre, which regularly attracts 50,000 weekend night-time visitors, [is] 'policed' by over 400 bouncers, but only twenty to twenty-five police officers.

Source: Hobbs et al., 2003, p. 43

Comment

These different 'private' arenas pose varying problems for the 'forces of law and order' at the micro, local level. To take the example of violence in the home, it has been argued that this has not been 'policed' very adequately in the past (Hoyle, 2000; Walklate, 2008). Similarly, control of the workplace is often carried out 'in house', with little involvement from state agencies. It seems that, increasingly, shopping malls, leisure facilities and the places where these meet public spaces, such as the street, are being patrolled by private companies rather than by traditional, visibly identifiable public service police. These spaces are sometimes described as 'semi-private' in that they are open to the public but are regulated by laws and rules of private property (see Shearing and Stenning, 1983; Wakefield, 2003). Questions have been posed by critical commentators and academics (see, for example, Walker, 2000; Den Boer, 2002; Sheptycki, 2002) about the extent to which (and to whom) these agencies are accountable.

Figure 6.2

Night club security staff, or 'bouncers', often work on the street, rather than inside the venue itself; thus, 'public' spaces also come within their surveillance

As Table 6.1 shows, in England and Wales the number of private security 'police', in the broadest sense of the term, is almost double the number of sworn, public officers – almost a private army. Despite the introduction of a registration scheme and regulatory body, the Security Industry Authority (SIA), the scheme is largely voluntary for companies that employ 'in-house' security staff, although organisations that provide security personnel (such as 'bouncers', for example), and their individual workers, have to be registered. The UK Government has handed over control to a corporate rather than a legislative body, which lacks the power of similar organisations in Europe (Button, 2007; Zedner in Crawford, 2008). In Spain and Belgium, for instance, state-controlled legal regulatory systems include training, licences and 'stringent character requirements for owners, managers and staff' (Button, 2007, p. 117).

Table 6.1 Plural policing in England and Wales, 2007: policing beyond the police

Occupational group	Number
Police officers	141,731
Police staff	75,989
Community support officers	15,391
Designated officers	1616
British Transport Police	2520
SIA licensed security guards	122,369
SIA licensed door supervisors	100,416
SIA licensed cash in transit guards	10,421

Source: Crawford, 2008, p. 165, Table 7.3

It seems that the growing numbers of security workers are taking the place of 'sworn' police officers, with full powers of arrest, training in legal issues, and so on. This raises again the question of what policing is and what is its purpose. This issue is, of course, not new. Private policing – in some form – has always coexisted with public policing:

> Most currently accepted theoretical generalisations on the state of British policing conclude that there is an innovative and ongoing blurring of the boundaries between the public and the private sectors. Many make reference to the practice of the private purchase of police services from public police forces, and some explicitly claim that this is a relatively recent innovation, growing in frequency. Yet this practice is not new; it has been a feature of public policing throughout the period of the 'criminal justice state' (c. 1825–1975) ... Accounts of policing which stress the relationship between privatisation and 'late modernity' thus need to be questioned.
>
> (Williams, 2008, p. 190)

These issues raise questions that continually trouble commentators who theorise about policing. Here the debate is about state-funded, 'public' policing, but as Activity 6.1 above has suggested, there are other forms of 'police'. Just looking at the list of agencies given in Table 6.1, it is clear that, in England and Wales alone, there are several public regulatory agencies apart from standard state policing, as most narrowly defined.

The 'mass private property' hypothesis, as termed by Clifford Shearing and Philip Stenning (1983) (and revisited by Michael Kempa et al., 2004), argues that previously public spaces, such as shopping malls and places of public entertainment, increasingly are being controlled, monitored and subjected to surveillance, leading to the exclusion of 'unwelcome' people and activities. This leads to questions about whether the proliferation of policing, quasi-professionalisation and privatisation has created an over-policed society. As Adam Crawford and Stuart Lister have argued, the agencies that are now involved in the governance and patrol of these public/private spaces can be described as the 'extended policing family' because these '"supplementary" forms of visible *policing* patrol offer a tangible response to the public's quest for symbols of order and authority' (Crawford and Lister, 2006, p. 165). They quote Sir Ronnie Flanagan's official review of the future of policing, which states that 'Policing is not simply the preserve of the police. Modern policing is carried out in partnership with a wide range of local agencies' (Flanagan, quoted in Crawford, 2008, p. 147). This is partly a result of the UK government's aim to encourage all such agencies to work in partnership, using 'joined-up policing' in order to address a wide range of social problems that the police, on their own, cannot hope to address. The following sections of this chapter explore ways in which these conceptions of 'police' and 'policing' are further broadened when considered in international, transnational and global contexts.

3   History of cross-border police cooperation

One of the ways in which the distinctions between 'international' and 'transnational' can be understood is to look at how policing developed both within nation states and in terms of international cooperation. This also includes the process whereby internationally mobile private armies travel to 'hot spots', ostensibly to provide 'security'. The origins of the first organised, paid police organisations had very local foci. In London, for example, the Bow Street Runners provided one of the models for the first uniformed force (Emsley, 2001). The 'new' police of 1829 were established because, as London developed and became more 'civilised', the propertied classes demanded 'security' and protection for themselves and their possessions. Later, a core concern of the police was with law enforcement and peace keeping throughout England (Emsley, 1996) as the demands of capital for security widened.

What processes were involved in moving beyond local or national boundaries? It might be expected that developed European countries that had colonial and internationally held capitalist interests would be most effective as expert 'exporters' of world policing as a result of their experience of defending their interests in other parts of the globe. Surprisingly, however, the origins of international cooperation on crime and security emerged from the desire to protect the independence of the state, rather than to increase sharing of information and resources. A system known as the Westphalia system (see Box 6.1) was established

The TOWNS-END.

Mr. Townsend, Police-Officer, Bow-Street.

Figure 6.3

Established in Bow Street, London, the 'thief takers', or 'Bow Street Runners', were one of the models for Robert Peel's 'new police'

following the Thirty Years War (1618–1648) because states were keen to maintain autonomy within their borders and therefore agreed not to cross the borders of other states. The Peace of Westphalia led to what is sometimes seen as the origins of the modern system of sovereign states that came into existence by mutual recognition of each other's unalienable jurisdictions.

Box 6.1   The Westphalia system

Following the Peace of Westphalia (1648) and subsequent treaty, states began to recognise geographic boundaries, the right to govern their own sovereign spaces and to see each other as independent entities.

The various European states now formed a pattern of independent and interdependent sovereignties where internal issues such as religious tolerance, law and territorial ownership would be respected.

These principles of internal sovereignty were based on feudal, religious, and dynastic ideas rather than what could be recognised as modern democratic ideas.

Because states now saw themselves as independent and reliant on each other's cooperation to maintain this position, concepts of internationally agreed laws and diplomacy evolved.

In effect, neighbouring countries wanted internal 'security' for their goods and people. The early concern of individual states was to protect their borders from incursions by other forces of law and order: the Westphalia system formalised the rights of states to maintain their borders.

In Peter Andreas and Ethan Nadelmann's view (2006), this was a further development of the way in which international crime control evolved. They argue that the early days of general international lawlessness were displaced by the needs of capital (to protect world trade), and the norms and consensus of world politics made it no longer acceptable or desirable that the 'high seas' (which were the means of import/export) should be so insecure. As they explain, what was to become the British Royal Navy expanded in the 1690s, thus increasing their ability to 'police the high seas and its growing empire'. As a result:

> Pirates and their collaborators were hunted down, colonial administrators admonished to enforce the new antipiracy laws ardently, and foreign leaders warned to cease sponsoring pirate expeditions and to crack down on unauthorized pirates operating within and from their territories. Those who failed to comply often found British and other European naval forces crowding local harbours to lend force to their demands.
>
> (Andreas and Nadelmann, 2006, p. 23)

Figure 6.4
International lawlessness and trouble on the 'high seas' was policed by what was to become the Royal Navy

---

Box 6.2   Criminalisation of activities

Following the abolition of slavery in Britain and France, the British Government used both force (the Royal Navy) and diplomacy (which involved agreements with the governments of other states) in order to search for slaves, drugs, and goods. The following provide a brief dateline of international cooperation on the prohibition of slavery and drugs:

1833: Slave trade abolished in Britain

1848: Slave trade abolished in France

1904: 'White slave' trade (people trafficking for sex) abolished via the International Agreement for the Suppression of the White Slave Trade

1961: Opiates and coca: United Nations Single Convention on Narcotic Drugs (amended by 1972 Protocol).

(Adapted from Andreas and Nadelmann, 2006, pp. 20–39)

It seems that what had been a world of piracy and 'privateering' was essentially state-sponsored and sanctioned armed robbery at sea, where 'Kings, princes, sultans, and assorted other political magnates accordingly viewed piracy as a valued source of wealth and political power, useful both for building up their own possessions and undermining the strength of competitors' (Andreas and Nadelmann, 2006, p. 22). As international society became more orderly, any benefit to be derived from stealing from one another was giving way to the greater advantage of stable commercial relations. Governments wanted and needed to monopolise the forces of violence, both within their borders and on the high seas. Diplomacy and trade were becoming increasingly important and this was reflected in the way in which certain activities were criminalised; for example, slavery, the opium trade and piracy itself all came to be prohibited (see Box 6.2).

Although certain agreements for cooperation existed (such as the searching of ships for contraband), policing of the high seas, punishing offenders, prohibiting certain activities, and so on, were still (and still are) problematic. The following sections discuss some of the attempts to overcome these difficulties.

4   Cooperation in law enforcement

At its simplest level, transnational policing is any sort of system or process that involves agents of state control cooperating across national borders. As the previous section has suggested and as Andreas and Nadelmann (2006) have demonstrated, this is not new: it has a long history. If transnational policing is a response to the needs and demands of increasingly integrated world economics (licit and illicit trade), the opportunities for criminal activities, or for those activities that governments seek to control, will also increase and continually change and develop. There are many examples of such activities, but primarily they include drug and people trafficking; the smuggling of counterfeit goods or those (such as alcohol or tobacco) on which local import duty is paid; the smuggling of works of art and illegally trapped endangered species; and international fraud, as in VAT fraud, for instance, and money laundering. At a more individual level, frauds that involve 'phishing' via the internet or postal invitations to 'get rich quick' also come within the remit of policing, individual fraud offices or local trading/consumer protection agencies. Despite the 'cross-border' or 'international' nature of activities such as these, some 'international' crimes and 'transnational' policing can be carried out without perpetrator, victim or law enforcers leaving their country of origin or jurisdiction. As Extract 6.3, from the UK Home Office, argues (rather obviously), the main goal of organised and international crime is to make money. The government claims that it is working to make the UK less attractive to 'tight-knit gangs' that work across international borders.

Extract 6.3

Organised and international crime

Organised crime reaches into communities and ruins lives by driving other crime and instilling fear.

It manifests itself most graphically in drug addiction, sexual exploitation and gun crime, but is also strongly linked to:

- immigration crime

- fraud

- money laundering

- internet-related crime

- other threats – including armed robbery, kidnap and extortion, vehicle crime, freight crime, cultural property crime, counterfeit currency and environmental crime.

Organised crime groups are essentially businesses that exist to make money. Players at the top often resort to extreme violence, intimidation and corruption to protect their businesses.

These groups operate across global frontiers in tight-knit gangs, display in-depth knowledge of law enforcement methods and exploit sophisticated technologies to conceal their activities from the authorities.

We want to send the strongest possible message that we're committed to making the UK one of the least attractive locations in the world for organised criminals to operate.

A snapshot of organised and international crime

The two most profitable and harmful enterprises controlled by organised crime groups are drugs trafficking and people smuggling.

Facts & figures

Here are some disturbing statistics illustrating the staggering economic and social impact of organised crime in this country:

- Global profits from people smuggling are estimated to be $10 billion annually.

- 280,000 problem drug users cause around half of all crime.

- Every £1 spent on heroin is estimated to generate about £4 of damage to the national economy.

- There are around 400 organised crime bosses in the UK with an amassed criminal wealth of approximately £440 million.

- So called 'dirty money' – or assets derived from crime – represents around 2% of the UK's GDP, or £18 billion – up to half of which is derived from illegal drug transactions.

- The economic and social costs of organised crime are estimated to be at least £20–£40 billion per year.

(Source: One Step Ahead: A 21st Century Strategy to Defeat Organised Crime)

Source: Home Office, undated

The link between international crime and security echoes the Westphalia system in that the UK Government is aiming to protect the country's borders. However, unlike the Westphalia system, emphasis is now given to preventing international criminal gangs from entering the country. Here, the aim appears to be to keep 'dangerous strangers' out. A problem with the statement from the Home Office given in Extract 6.3, however, is that it presents the figures quoted as 'facts': as 'disturbing statistics illustrating the staggering economic and social impact of organised crime in this country'. As Leanne Weber and Benjamin Bowling (2004, p. 195) argue, where 'increasingly free movement of capital is being accompanied by increased spending on police, prisons and migration control', 'justifications' for policing resources can lead to unnecessary and unwelcome increased surveillance of the population. This includes the 'police-like activities of immigration authorities and other agencies ... acquiring new coercive powers' (Weber and Bowling, 2004, p. 195). The increasingly policed private/public space, referred to in Section 2, is extending its reach across state boundaries. Cooperation between police and governments is now viewed as both largely unproblematic and advantageous by law enforcement agencies and governments.

Activity 6.2

You may not think you have ever been involved in an 'international crime', but can you think of any areas of your life where in fact you might have been?

Have you ever:

- found an unexplained payment on your credit card statement on returning from holiday abroad?

- received a phone or email demand for your bank details/asking for investment in a financial 'too good to be true' money exchange?

- used contractors who employ workers from non-European Union (EU) countries, possibly as illegal/cheap labour?

- bought tobacco or alcohol from a source that may not have paid customs duty?

Comment

Sometimes activities such as these are divided into supposedly 'low-level' crimes (such as individuals evading small amounts of customs duty) or, in the case of large international frauds 'medium-' or 'high-level' crimes. Small infringements of unpaid duty (such as attempting to exceed the limit at the UK border) are dealt with by the 'low police', but a terrorist threat or crimes that involve state security, often secret, are 'high' level. Definitions of 'high' and 'low' policing , developed by Jean-Paul Brodeur (1983), are sometimes used to differentiate elements of 'policing' and 'security' – the former refers to the visible, uniformed police and the latter to secret 'security' services ('high' and 'low' policing are discussed in greater depth later in Section 5). In Europe, increasing law enforcement cooperation over the past century has led to a number of formal and less formal agreements, a trend that Andreas and Nadelmann (2006) explore in terms of Brodeur's 'high' and 'low' policing.

As Section 5 will show, these definitions of 'high' and 'low' policing are inevitably blurred because of increasing knowledge of the interconnections between various forms of organised crime. Such interconnections can be seen, for example, in the funding of terrorism and in the acquisition of weapons through drug running, and in the links between both people- and drug-trafficking routes and gangs. This is further complicated by those involved in organised crime who engage in 'commodity hopping' (Hornsby and Hobbs, 2007, p. 559) when certain activities (or goods) become too dangerous or difficult to undertake (or trade in), while still evading law enforcement agencies. Furthermore, the private funds derived from illegal activities can be channelled into legitimate businesses, and 'security' can be bought using private or public funds or a mix of these.

5   Exploring transnationalism

This section explores in some depth the extent to which it is possible to begin to distinguish how 'transnational' policing and security differs from 'international' policing and security.

5.1 Distinguishing between 'international' and 'transnational'

As the previous section suggested, the use of the term 'transnational' with regard to policing usually refers to a system of policing cooperation that crosses national boundaries. Interpol is the most obvious example:

> The Interpol system provides a channel of communication between police forces, but strictly speaking it is not 'operational': the 'man from Interpol' never arrested anyone. Interpol's primary role is the exchange of messages between police forces and judicial authorities of its member countries. This is facilitated by a system of 'coloured notices': red notices are in effect international arrest warrants, blue notices are requests for information on a specific individual, green notices contain information on suspected criminals intended for circulation, yellow notices contain details of missing persons, and black notices concern the finding of unidentified bodies. Additionally, there is circulation of information about stolen goods and notifications regarding the *modus operandi* of criminals and criminal groups.
>
> (Sheptycki, 2006, p. 443)

As James Sheptycki suggests, Interpol has a wide-ranging remit, as its published aims, reproduced below, confirm.

Extract 6.4

Secure global police communications services – INTERPOL manages a global police communications system known as 1-24/7 which enables police in all of its members countries to request, submit and access vital police data instantly in a secure environment.

Operational data services and databases for police – INTERPOL manages a range of databases with information on names and photographs of known criminals, wanted persons, fingerprints, DNA profiles, stolen or lost travel documents, stolen motor vehicles, child sex abuse images and stolen works of art. INTERPOL also disseminates critical crime-related data through its system of international notices. There are seven kinds of notices, of which the most-well known is the Red Notice, an international request for the provisional arrest of an individual.

Operational police support services – INTERPOL has six priority crime areas: corruption, drugs and organized crime, financial and high-tech crime, fugitives, public safety and terrorism, and trafficking in human beings. INTERPOL also operates a 24-hour Command and

Co-ordination Centre to assist any member country faced with a crisis situation, co-ordinate the exchange of information and assume a crisis-management role during serious incidents.

Police training and development – INTERPOL provides focused police training initiatives for national police forces, and also offers on-demand advice, guidance and support in building dedicated crime-fighting components. The aim is to enhance the capacity of member countries to effectively combat serious transnational crime and terrorism. This includes sharing knowledge, skills and best practices in policy and the establishment of global standards for combating specific crimes.

INTERPOL (2009)

The difference between 'transnational' and 'international' may seem to be immaterial in the light of Interpol's wide remit, but in terms of justice and policing, regulation and control are not simply about police cooperation across borders. There are distinctions to be made between 'transnational' and 'international' security. Neil Walker (2008) suggests that although *inter*national policing involves actions and practices beyond the state, other versions (such as trans- or supranational policing) may involve wider, relatively autonomous networks and allegiances, such as the EU. As Sheptycki notes, differences between Interpol and the more recently created Europol, for instance, lie mostly in terms of political remit and control. Although it has proved difficult to make Europol accountable to any publics or electorate (despite, as Sheptycki points out, being funded from the public purse), it was set up to reflect and serve the interests of the countries of the EU (Sheptycki, 2006).

The remainder of this chapter reviews the consequences of the dissolution or blurring of what have been distinguished as internal and external security mandates, predicated as they have been on the idea of a unified nation state in the international system. This is developed in this section by examining the kinds of activities that transnational and international policing respond to, namely: organised, international and transnational crime. These responses include changing police mandates, capacities and accountabilities and how policing responds to shifting global relations and events. As an example, in the UK, the Serious Organised Crime Agency is a state-organised and state-controlled body with international and transnational mandates, as explained in Extract 6.5.

Extract 6.5

The Serious Organised Crime Agency (SOCA)

The Serious Organised Crime Agency was created in 2006 to spearhead efforts to tackle the growing problem of international crime gangs.

SOCA brings together the talents and experience of several different government agencies, and they all work together to take on drug and gun trafficking, and to focus on recovering criminal assets.

What we're doing about organised crime cartels

Legislative changes made in the last few years mean SOCA and other law enforcement agencies are now fighting organised crime more effectively.

They have the power to:

- seize the profits of criminal activities and redirect a proportion of them back into law enforcement

- compel co-operation with investigators, so that suspects and their associates have to surrender relevant documents to investigators when requested

- intercept user logs and emails of suspected criminals

- impose conditions on convicted organised criminals post-release, such as tighter restrictions on where they travel and who they associate with

- use incentives such as sentence reductions to encourage criminals to inform on their associates.

Source: Home Office, undated

In the sense of this document, which is intended for a broadly non-specialist audience, the term 'international' seems to refer to activities or cooperation between countries, police forces or officers. This seems to imply cooperation across borders at a local level around specific problems or geographical areas. For example, the building of the Channel Tunnel between England and France gave rise to a new problem of illegal immigrants entering the country as stowaways. As a result, a working agreement between UK and French police and customs control was drawn up to cover specific arrangements and practicalities, even though agreements to protect the borders of the two countries had been in place previously.

The notion of 'transnational' has connotations of passing across a large number of borders, as opposed to simply '*inter*', which suggests a smaller number of connections, perhaps between France and Germany or Britain, for example. *Trans*national policing and security suggests that more than one country may be involved, that the investigations and activities might reach over many jurisdictions and between continents. This is exemplified by reactions to the bombing of the World Trade Centre in New York on 11 September 2001. The response might have been *inter*national, in that the UK and the USA joined forces publicly as allies, but the eventual response – the so-called 'war on terror' – had global effects. It called on the cooperation of many countries, in terms of both political support and armed force. Unlike the more purely 'international' policing agreements made between the UK and France regarding the Channel Tunnel, mentioned above, the 'transnational' policing that followed 9/11 was more about cutting across shared borders in a way that suggests a global policing that is not bound by physical frontiers.

'High' policing

In some senses, 'high' policing is what is commonly thought to be the true nature of 'transnational', border-crossing policing 'since enforcing the law in the global context is dependent on the gathering and sharing of intelligence, the hallmark of high policing' (Brodeur, 2000, p. 43). There are three critical differences between 'high' and 'low' police, although both operate for the general (supposed) benefit of the state:

1 'High' police are rarely concerned with criminal prosecutions. Rather, they collect political intelligence and disrupt activities.

2 'High' police are more likely to act outside the law or 'extralegally', as in 'illegal beak-ins, letter openings, and electronic surveillance' (Andreas and Nadelmann, 2006, p. 63).

3 'High' policing investigative methods are more likely to be invasive, aggressive and manipulative (such as the use of undercover agents).

In terms of the 'high' police functions, intelligence swapping first developed between France, Britain, Germany and other countries during the nineteenth century. The role of undercover police in central Europe was largely targeted at political dissidents and refugees: 'informants recruited to spy on anarchists, social democrats, and Poles in Switzerland, Belgium, and elsewhere in Europe were shared; an active correspondence was maintained with police directors in Vienna, Paris, and other European capitals; and assistance was obtained, not always entirely willingly, from police in Denmark and Switzerland' (Andreas and Nadelmann, 2006, p. 67). More recently, in the 1960s, Interpol's Paris headquarters was designated as the centre for intelligence gathering and dissemination.

'Low' policing

'Low' policing is categorised as the 'daily' work of intercountry and interforce collaboration, often involving more traditional 'crime fighting' as opposed to preventing or detecting 'security threats' (or terrorism). Whereas 'high' police might be involved in breaking espionage rings, 'low' police might be investigating drug-trafficking organisations. One of the modern manifestations of 'low' police in Europe is the liaison officer, whom Didier Bigo (2000, p. 67) describes as a new type of specialist, responsible for managing 'the flow of information between their respective agencies' (police, customs and immigration). What might seem to be ironic, however, is that whereas the functions of the 'high' police are officially secret, these 'low' police in Europe are also generally unknown to the public within individual countries despite long-standing agreement between governments and national police organisations. In the past, the status of officers working on the 'war on drugs' (such as suppression of the trade in opiates from southern France to the USA) led to 'ambiguities', as Bigo explains:

> ... all through the 1970s there are examples of French agents working abroad and this raised questions, not only about financial arrangements, but also about the legal status of such agents. These questions were also manifest in relation to foreign agents working within France. A series of interservice agreements were made in the 1980s which helped the various services involved in this to establish the propriety of reciprocity.
>
> (Bigo, 2000, p. 75)

These comments from Bigo highlight concerns around legitimacy and accountability at the 'low' police level. In the past, the power of the state was extended by both the demands and the 'push' of capitalism and the demands and 'pull' of crime control. To some extent, this is still the case across the world, although 'borders' are now seen as mere inconveniences, temporary barriers to profit that can be overcome by powerful multinational companies. As a corollary, powerful Western states have responded by highlighting the fears and insecurities associated with globalisation in order to increase their power, blurring the boundaries between protecting the citizen and the state itself from the enemy within, on the one hand, and from 'foreign' threats and the enemy without, on the other. Discussions of high-level politics and agreements aimed at these threats often ignore the everyday interactions that take place in the policing and security worlds.

'Horizontal' and 'vertical' police–state interaction

In her review of the increasing cooperation in Europe, for example, Monica Den Boer argues that there are two forms of police–state interaction: 'horizontal' and 'vertical'. In 'horizontal' interactions, local forces that share a border, cooperate, for instance, on pursuits that require crossing into each other's territory. Den Boer states that this might involve 'befriending' neighbouring countries' police forces, in order to '"borrow" features which they consider to be resourceful in their fight against crime problems' (Den Boer, 1999, p. 59). 'Vertical' interactions, according to Den Boer, operate at a more global level and often involve discussions and negotiations not just between individual nation states but also with supranational bodies (such as the UN and the EU). In Europe, the Schengen Agreement is one example of this latter version of cooperation (See Box 6.3).

Box 6.3   The Schengen Agreement

By April 1998, thirteen of the then fifteen member states of the EU had signed up to the Schengen Agreement, which provides for the abolition of border controls and lists a series of compensatory measures for issues that warrant better security (e.g. agreements about external border controls, police cooperation, judicial cooperation, direct and automated information exchange). The UK and Ireland were the only EU member states that had not signed up to the Agreement, partly because they wanted to maintain their passport union and partly because they did not want to jeopardise their security situation. However, the Treaty of Amsterdam, which was signed on 2 October 1997, has made it possible, via a special protocol, for these two member states to 'opt into' various provisions of the Schengen Agreement, such as cross-border police competencies. Norway and Iceland have become associate members of the Schengen group, which allows the Nordic countries to maintain the Nordic Passport Union.

Source: adapted from Den Boer, 1999, p. 72

The Treaty of Amsterdam was concerned with the integration of ten new member states, which were formerly part of the Soviet bloc, and also more generally with extending the powers of Europol and absorbing the Schengen Agreement into EU law. Walker (2008, p. 129) suggests that this gave Europol new powers, such as the 'legal basis to acquire a range of new functions, including the authority to establish joint operational teams to support national investigations ... and significantly strengthened the capacity to develop common measures for harmonisation of both substantive and procedural criminal law and to facilitate co-operation between criminal justice agencies'.

Therefore, although this chapter is concerned with inter- and transnational (or 'global') policing arrangements as opposed to the more 'local' agreements between, for example, member states of the EU, Walker argues that, in effect, the policing and security of the EU is a transnational issue in that certain powers have been handed over to a supranational body or, as he describes it, a '"State-*like*" entity, even if not a full-blown state' (Walker, 2008, p. 133). On the other hand, Walker points to the EU as a place where the internal and external matters of state security are more clearly separated than in the USA. He argues that European countries lack the kind of similarities that could lead to any sort of unified 'national' identity. He includes frequently discussed differences between member states – language, history, culture, and fiscal and welfare policies – as well as 'Eurosceptic voices' and a lack of populist support for the Constitutional Treaty. Surprisingly in his view, however, there has been enthusiasm for cooperation on policing and security, even though this might be an area where 'one would expect the forces of statist resistance to supranational ambition to be strongest' (Walker, 2008, p. 133):

> In particular, German Chancellor Kohl's initial proposal for Europol in 1991 was well attuned to the political mood, an audacious statement by the increasingly dominant and most explicitly integrationist member state. It was meant, and partly succeeded, as a sign of political virility, chosen and highlighted precisely because it challenged one of the traditional areas of state hegemony. Similarly, the priority given to the Area of Freedom, Security and Justice is not just about the pursuit of a vigorous securitization approach within a particular policy sector, but again a massive statement of symbolic intent.
>
> (Walker, 2008, p. 133)

5.2 Problems for international cooperation

Considerable problems are faced by political parties and governments of member countries of organisations such as the EU, whose electorates may equate moves to increase police cooperation across states with a loss of sovereignty. Political parties may oppose the idea of what could be viewed as a global police state, even where the threat of terrorism is involved. Sometimes an initiative that begins as 'vertical' cooperation (Den Boer, 1999) between police forces, as described above, can result in inter- and then transnational agreements. Walker analyses this as being a 'professional' rather than a 'political' initiative for cooperation. In addition, high-level negotiated agreements have to be implemented at local level. For example, at border crossing points, although officers may be familiar with policy, they make individual decisions about who to stop, which flights to target for searches, and so on. In this way, the transnational and international are intimately linked and policy decisions are, in effect, made 'on the hoof' as well as at the intra-governmental or transnational level (Pratt and Thompson, 2008). Similarly, as Den Boer points out, local and eventually transnational bodies must take note of what happens on the ground, because they must be able to respond to the changing patterns of organised cross-border crime, as mentioned above, which will alter how those involved in organised crime behave and engage in 'commodity hopping' as necessary (Hornsby and Hobbs, 2007).

Figure 6.5
Despite the rhetoric of individual ministers and governments, decision making 'on the ground' at border crossings may be 'practical' and 'professional' rather than political

One of the problems for international cooperation, however, is that laws and approaches to punishment might differ. Even between bordering countries, state and governmental approaches might be in conflict. For example, it might be supposed that neighbouring countries with economic dependencies and broadly similar liberal democratic approaches (as in some areas of the EU, for instance) might have agreed policies on and approaches to law breaking and the extradition of at least some types of lawbreakers. However, there are still regular instances of international disagreements about whether perpetrators should be handed over to the country in which the alleged offence was committed. These can vary from 'serious' issues of terrorism and world security to, for example, the 'intellectual' freedom of speech (but no less 'serious') offence of the Holocaust denier Fredrick Toben (see Extract 6.6).

Activity 6.3

Read Extract 6.6 and list the potential problems that individual state prosecutors or Ministers of Justice might face in persuading their counterparts in another country to arrest and hand over a suspect.

Extract 6.6

Holocaust denier Fredrick Toben wins German extradition fight

Hannah Fletcher

The Holocaust denier, Fredrick Toben, has been released from custody after the German government gave up its legal battle to extradite him from Britain.

The controversial historian was arrested at Heathrow last month on a European arrest warrant accusing him of racism and anti-Semitism. German prosecutors were then forced to appeal to the High Court after a British Court refused to hand him over.

Kevin Lowry-Mullins, Dr Toben's solicitor, confirmed today that the appeal had been withdrawn and he had signed a consent order with the German government to end the case.

Mr Lowry-Mullins told The Times: 'Dr Toben was released from custody yesterday. He's over the moon.'

Lawyers acting for the German government argued last month that Dr Toben, the founder and director of the revisionist Adelaide Institute, should be extradited to face trial for posting claims on the institute's website that there was no mass murder of Jews by the Nazis.

But Westminster Magistrates Court district judge Daphne Wickham ruled that the warrant used to arrest the 64-year-old Australian as he travelled from America to Dubai on October 1 was 'vague and imprecise'. Dr Toben was unable to raise the

£100,000 bail however, and remained in custody awaiting Germany's appeal at the High Court.

Under Section 130 of the German criminal code, holocaust denial is illegal and offenders can face up to five years in jail, but the case caused unease in Britain where there is no such law. Attempts to extradite him were seen by many as an assault on free speech.

Mr Lowry-Mullins said: 'The offence is not made out in the UK. If Dr Toben had been extradited back to Germany for Holocaust denial, which does not exist as an offence in this country, then we would have found ourselves in a situation where hypothetically, the Iranian government could have asked for all the gay Iranian asylum seekers to be extradited back to Iran.'

Mr Lowry-Mullins said the German chief state prosecutor handling Dr Toben's case had been so confident of success at one point that he had bragged Dr Toben would be in Germany for Christmas.

But the solicitor said that he believed the German government had been shaken by comments he had made outside court after the discharge hearing.

'I said, "We will go all the way to the House of Lords with this and let the House of Lords decide". But when the draft extradition Act passed through the House of Lords in 2002, one of the questions was what would happen if someone was arrested on a European arrest warrant to be extradited to a country where Holocaust denial is an offence.

'The response was, "No, that will never happen".'

Mr Lowry-Mullins confirmed that Dr Toben was still in England waiting for his passport to be returned to him.

Dr Toben was previously convicted and jailed for nine months in Germany in 1999 after he claimed on the Adelaide Institute website that the Holocaust had been grossly exaggerated.

In a disclaimer on the present day site, Dr Toben writes that anyone who questions the 'Holocaust story/legend/myth ... will face a world-wide group of enforcers who will use any means to destroy dissenting voices.'

He adds: 'If you wish to begin to doubt the Holocaust narrative, you must be prepared for personal sacrifice, must be prepared for marriage and family break-up, loss of career, and go to prison. This is because Revisionists are, among other things, dismantling a massive multi-billion dollar industry that the Holocaust enforcers are defending.'

Source: Times Online, 20 November 2008

Comment

International extradition cases illustrate the supposed cooperation and disputes that arise between countries at governmental and judicial levels. It is clear that even in the neighbouring countries of Europe there is no 'one crime fits all' approach to law enforcement and justice. It could be argued that this is because each country has evolved its own set of laws, rules, procedures, and so on, and that some countries have good reasons for sensitivities and beliefs about particular actions or people. David Bayley (1999), for example, claims that although comparative, international research into policing is possible, many researchers argue that the difficulties of rigorous analysis in this field are too great. Laws and rules differ between countries, to say nothing of culture, which makes meaningful comparisons extremely difficult. What counts as 'crime', how crimes are processed and targeted and how crime control is resourced, make the mapping of comparisons an arduous exercise.

6 'Postmodern' policing: are the global cops coming?

The idea of a 'postmodern' police suggests something beyond the state, cutting across traditional boundaries and beyond the normal controls of legitimacy and accountability. This is because 'postmodern' policing implies something beyond the remit of 'physical' policing, moving into a virtual world of cybercrime and such offences as international currency fraud in the 'virtual launderette'. It also implies that the postmodern police will be all-seeing, all-encompassing and beyond even the international, transnational or supranational. In effect, such policing has no boundaries.

It was Sheptycki (1998), in a discussion about whether there is a possibility of a global police subculture, who asked whether the 'global cops cometh'. This is one way of questioning whether policing is being transformed by 'global' organised crime and to what extent 'local' states still control policing. Is the world moving towards a 'police with no state' as Eugene McLaughlin (2007, p. 101) asks? Similarly, to what extent is 'transnational' policing accountable and controllable? The parallels between transnational and private policing and security are troubling because of the lack of overall governance of or control over processes and procedure that they suggest. The issue of police occupational subculture is important because the concerns of legitimacy and democratic accountability are not just about international agreements at the 'high' policing level; they are also about the more local level, namely the interactions between individual officers. Furthermore, if these 'low' (and hence less visible to democratic processes and controls) forms of policing are taking place beyond national boundaries, are 'state' and 'police' being separated (McLaughlin, 2007)? This supposed 'progressive de-coupling of police and state' is summarised by Ian Loader and Neil Walker in the following way:

> While the state remains a significant player in the delivery and regulation of policing, it is no longer the only or even, arguably, the principal institutional actor involved in offering guarantees of security to citizens, but increasingly finds itself (and its agents) as one among a multiplicity of policing forms.
>
> (Loader and Walker, 2001, p. 10)

Some authors (including Loader and Walker) have questioned whether this separation is indeed taking place to the extent indicated by Sheptycki, who suggests the arrival of 'postmodern' policing. Central to their argument is the proposition that the state holds a monopoly on violence. That is, despite numerous policing providers, there are some functions that only the state can carry out, the primary one being coercive – the legitimate use of force. Secondary to this is the argument that only the state can regulate physical or violent action in the name of control.

Activity 6.4

Read Extracts 6.7 and 6.8 about the changing economics of world security and consider the wide-ranging questions they raise about the nature of policing across the world. These include:

- Is there one organisation or agency responsible for international security?

- Who controls world order?

- How can 'private' security be legitimately regulated and controlled in the way that 'public' police are?

Extract 6.7

... work on transnational policing developments is being further complicated by the post-9/11 'war on terrorism' awareness of the increasing governmental role being played by private military companies in the international security coalitions. The most obvious example to date is the strategic positioning of Private Military Corporations (PMCs) in the reconstruction of Iraq. In 2005 an estimated 100 PMCs with 30,000 personnel were operating in Iraq offering protection to government ministries, oil pipelines, building sites, power stations, hotels, etc. PMCs such as Blackwater and ISI are also lobbying the United Nations to use them for 'policing actions'.

Source: McLaughlin, 2007, p. 101

Extract 6.8

New taps? Or Iraqi security? East Europeans answer the call (cheaply)

David Batty

First came the Polish plumbers, overturning the natural order by tackling U-bends in a more reliable and affordable way than their established British rivals. Now there is another field in which east Europeans are driving well-paid Brits out of work – on the frontline in Iraq and Afghanistan.

The market in which ex-military can earn six-figure sums as private security guards overseas is drying up, with salaries in sharp decline and contracts increasingly being offered to cheaper foreign soldiers, the Guardian has learned.

The National Association of Security Professionals (Nasp), an organisation for those working in the private security industry, said

former British soldiers are being laid off by companies in Iraq who are turning to east Europeans instead. The number of Britons providing security in Iraq has fallen from a peak of about 5,000 in 2004–05 to nearer 2,000 this year.

Mark Shurben-Browne, a director of Nasp, said the market had reached saturation point, with companies receiving 10–20 CVs a day. But many firms were trying to reduce costs by hiring staff from eastern Europe, particularly Serbs and Croats.

'One company sacked half their British workforce and replaced them with cheaper guys with a special forces background from eastern Europe,' said Shurben-Browne.

'The companies are mixing the teams up, keeping two or three expat or British guys on in a team with the rest from eastern Europe.'

Shurben-Browne, who served in the 2nd battalion, the Parachute Regiment in the Falklands and as a private security guard in Iraq, said he knew of about 200 ex-British solders waiting six or seven months for a contract to go back to Iraq.

Changing conditions on the ground in Iraq have also had an impact on wages. Firstly, heavy insurgent attacks after the 2005 elections meant a lot of firms cut back because they could not send staff outside the safe zones. Now, with a reduction in enemy activity in Iraq and Iraqi security forces taking a more active role, there has been an impact on demand from private security firms. 'Jobs are hard to come by now,' Shurben-Browne said.

Andy Bearpark, director general of the British Association of Private Security Companies (BAPSC), said: 'There may be some blokes in Iraq earning £100,000 a year tax-free, but £50,000 tax-free is a much more likely figure now.'

Bearpark has heard of Fijians, Gurkhas, Ukrainians and Sierra Leoneans being employed, usually on much lower wages than British and US personnel. 'There was a US firm which was not even paying Sierra Leoneans 10% of what they paid their US staff,' he said.

While most former British soldiers only did the private security work for a fixed length of time, a few did keep returning to it, he added, usually because they had invested the money they made unwisely. 'It's not unusual for guys to go and buy shares in a Bangkok brothel and within three months they've lost it all and then they have to try to get another contract to pay off their debts. They're not people used to handling a lot of money. The average guy is earning £40,000–£45,000 in Afghanistan, which is nothing like what people were earning in Iraq,' said Bearpark.

A former corporal in the Royal Signals regiment who worked for a private security firm in Iraq, said he noticed work was dropping off when he left in January 2006. The 29-year-old, from Bournemouth, identified only as Andrew, has now trained as a building surveyor. He said: 'I only wanted to do it for a fixed amount of time. It's dangerous work. The money's great but it's not worth it if you get killed.'

Source: *The Guardian*, 17 November 2008

Comment

There are no satisfactory answers to the questions about who is responsible for international security or who controls world order, or the legitimacy or accountability of those who provide security. These extracts raise issues concerning the way in which world economics and the threat of war and insurgence in some countries lead to commercial opportunities in other countries. In a way, this mirrors the phenomenon of people trafficking. Unlike those who are trafficked, however, the people who migrate (albeit temporarily) to carry out security roles, are moving at the behest of governments or 'occupying forces' and are paid to help maintain order. But in both examples working in certain countries holds out, for some, the promise of making a good life for themselves or for the families they have left at home. They will earn sums of money that would be difficult to achieve in their own countries (Extract 6.8 cites 'six-figure sums' for security workers), to send home for carrying out difficult and dangerous work.

Of course, states are still powerful; and large, rich states remain very powerful. As the speech of incoming US President Barack Obama suggests, although safety at home is important, world security is a major issue (see Extract 6.9).

Extract 6.9

Homeland security

'We are here to do the work that ensures no other family members have to lose a loved one to a terrorist who turns a plane into a missile, a terrorist who straps a bomb around her waist and climbs aboard a bus, a terrorist who figures out how to set off a dirty bomb in one of our cities. This is why we are here: to make our country safer and make sure the nearly 3,000 who were taken from us did not die in vain; that their legacy will be a more safe and secure Nation.'

– Barack Obama, Speech in the U.S. Senate, March 6, 2007

The first responsibility of any president is to protect the American people. President Barack Obama will provide the leadership and strategies to strengthen our security at home.

Barack Obama and Joe Biden's strategy for securing the homeland against 21st century threats is focused on preventing terrorist attacks on our homeland, preparing and planning for emergencies and investing in strong response and recovery capabilities. Obama and Biden will strengthen our homeland against all hazards – including natural or accidental disasters and terrorist threats – and ensure that the federal government works with states, localities, and the private sector as a true partner in prevention, mitigation, and response.

Defeat Terrorism Worldwide

- **Find, Disrupt, and Destroy Al Qaeda:** Responsibly end the war in Iraq and focus on the right battlefield in Afghanistan. Work with other nations to strengthen their capacity to eliminate shared enemies.

- **New Capabilities to Aggressively Defeat Terrorists:** Improve the American intelligence apparatus by investing in its capacity to collect and analyze information, share information with other agencies and carry out operations to disrupt terrorist networks.

- **Prepare the Military to meet 21st Century Threats:** Ensure that our military becomes more stealthy, agile, and lethal in its ability to capture or kill terrorists. Bolster our military's ability to speak different languages, navigate different cultures, and coordinate complex missions with our civilian agencies.

■ **Win the Battle of Ideas:** Defeat al Qaeda in the battle of ideas by returning to an American foreign policy consistent with America's traditional values, and work with moderates within the Islamic world to counter al Qaeda propaganda. Establish a $2 billion Global Education Fund to work to eliminate the global education deficit and offer an alternative to extremist schools.

■ **Restore American Influence and Restore Our Values:** Stop shuttering consulates and start opening them in the tough and hopeless corners of the world. Expand our foreign service, and develop the capacity of our civilian aid workers to work alongside the military.

Source: The White House, undated

This raises further questions about the changing nature of world policing, the meaning of globalised security and 'governing through security' and, most importantly for this chapter, the interconnections between the local and the global in terms of policing and security. The remaining discussion in this section explores the contentions underlying the idea that some countries are the 'world's policemen' and that international cooperation and organisations such as the United Nations, Interpol and Europol, and the private security providers, are more disorganised than might at first be imagined. One of the issues to keep in mind is that Extracts 6.7 and 6.8 illustrate two major threads of this chapter. The first is that 'private' policing or security is not 'nation state' policing, with its tradition of legitimacy and accountability (however incomplete). The second is that policing and security is no longer confined to the nation state, as the needs of its operation are beyond the boundaries of individual countries or governments.

There are some forms of policing only the state (as opposed to private security companies) can provide, such as 'high' policing functions. These include the use of high-cost, highly technical listening and detection equipment and the policing of cyberspace. McLaughlin notes that 'the state and its policing apparatus will continue to be required to intervene in order to: close "security gaps" that threaten the broader social order; maintain an effective communications and technological security/ policing/control infrastructure; and monitor, evaluate and respond to high-level security threats and risks' (McLaughlin, 2007, p. 99). Quoting a number of commentators and academics, most of whom have been mentioned in this chapter, McLaughlin goes on to point out that the consensus seems to be that 'this requires stronger rather than weaker forms of governance and "hard" rather than "soft" state formations' (McLaughlin, 2007, p. 99).

To summarise this argument, first, although transnational policing may not be new, the system underpinning it is undergoing unprecedented transformations due to the increase in global crime and terrorist threats and increasing demands made by legitimate trade and business for the control of threats to the safety of their goods and services. This causes the connections between state and policing as they currently exist to be called into question because these demands are leading both to new forms of policing and to changes in the ways in which policing within nation states is carried out (Sheptycki, cited in McLaughlin, 2007). Second, policing 'beyond the state' has taken on new forms as a result of the break-up of state monopolies of policing and an inability or unwillingness of the public police to meet late-modern world demands for security.

In some senses, then, this is simply the 'local' being made 'global': as similar threats are being faced by many countries, various ways of responding evolve, some with the benefit of policy transfer. However, although many countries face the same threat and could benefit from cooperation and sharing of best practice (or any practice), there are barriers to this information exchange, some of which are cultural or to do with issues of language. On the other hand, private security firms, such as the companies mentioned above in relation to Iraq, seem to transverse international boundaries more easily because they have no allegiances other than to capital. Former state soldiers can work as security personnel in the same war zones in which they were previously in combat with an enemy they now 'police'; and 'bouncers' control the leisure facilities and semi-public spaces at night in most large industrialised cities across the world.

What may be seen as the breaking up of the 'state monopoly' on policing is not just an issue for international policing – it had already started with the privatisation of policing within the state. Why be concerned with the accountability of 'foreign' forces when, within the state itself, accountability has been abandoned in favour of 'the market'; that is, in favour of private providers and the world of '"pick 'n mix" policing for a postmodern age' (Reiner, quoted in Jones and Newburn, 2002, p. 130)?

7   The end of nation state policing?

To return to the question first raised in Section 2 – namely, whether the nation state no longer 'owns' policing or security – what evidence has been provided that this is indeed the case? First, Walker (2002) argues that state constitutional rules mean that public policing has internal accountability and a discipline code with complaints procedures, and may have channels of representation through which the public can make their voices heard. However, Loader argues that the fracturing of policing from the nation state makes it 'less visible' in the sense of what policing does 'in our name'. In Europe, for instance, 'these benefits and burdens have been almost entirely decoupled – the policing of transnational crime being an activity directed largely *at Others* (migrants, organized criminals, drug traffickers etc.) on behalf of *us* – Europe's citizens' (Loader, 2002, p. 298, original emphasis). Loader is arguing that 'by dramatizing selected threats and indicating what is being – or "must" be – done to repress them' (Loader, 2002, p. 298) 'law-abiding' citizens are less likely to demand legitimate accountability of police.

Second, with regard to the discussion of policing and security going beyond the nation state in terms of international agreements and local cooperation, the problem is that at both 'high' and 'low' levels, democratically accountable policing is carried out 'at a distance' in foreign countries and distant continents. There is little control because officers who work in countries distant from their home nation will have no loyalties to either the state or the people they are policing. Yet incidents are rarely (if ever) reported where, for instance, out-of-nation police officers are operating and there are crises of legitimacy. Are reports of the 'death of the state' overplayed, or is it that, as McLaughlin argues, 'the state's sovereign status will continue to have a central role to play within any pluralised network of "security governance"' (McLaughlin, 2007, p. 98, citing Loader and Walker, 2004, 2005)? McLaughlin also argues that, furthermore, 'state-constituted policing embodies a complex of interlocking "sacred" qualities – monopoly of legitimate coercion, delivery of civic governance, guarantor of equitable provision and social cohesion and symbolising not just the state but the nation' (McLaughlin, 2007, p. 98). In this way, both 'low' and 'high' policing would remain covert, and so the public might never know the difference.

8   Conclusion

This chapter has explored a wide-ranging set of arguments for and against the 'end' of policing as it has been traditionally conceived. The relationship between 'the police' and policing, and the history of police cooperation across borders and how this operates, lend weight to the argument that there is nothing new in policing; nation states have always made attempts to control their own borders (keeping either some people in or others out) and the high seas, to protect their goods and trade routes. One of the unifying characteristics of the history of nation state policing is the desire to protect the needs or demands of capital.

Added to this are the problems associated with developments in 'international', 'transnational' and 'supranational' policing. These terms may be too superficial to properly explain the functions, aims and futures of world policing. Whereas flows of people and property were once of the 'physical' realm, very often now the largest and most complicated crimes rely on virtual worlds and virtual goods. Furthermore, legislative attempts at regulation of the movement of both people and physical goods rely on international agreements and parity of definition.

The increasing focus on the privatisation of policing and security and its interaction with trans/international policing and security cannot be viewed in isolation from issues of legitimacy, corruption and accountability. The notion that we are heading towards 'postmodern' policing and the end of 'state'-led policing is problematic. One of the reasons for this, as discussed in the chapter, is that however 'global' the cops 'becometh', they will always retain a relationship, however tenuous, with the local.

References

Andreas, P. and Nadelmann, E. (2006) *Policing the Globe: Criminalization and Crime Control in International Relations*, Oxford, Oxford University Press.

Bayley, D.H. (1999) 'Policing: the world stage' in Mawby, R.I. (ed.) (2004).

Bigo, D. (2000) 'Liaison officers in Europe: new officers in the European security field' in Sheptycki, J.W.E. (ed.) (2000).

Brodeur, J.P. (1983) 'High and low policing: remarks about the policing of political activities', *Social Problems*, vol. 3, no. 5, pp. 507–20.

Brodeur, J.P. (2000) 'Transnational policing and human rights. A case study' in Sheptycki, J.W.E. (ed.) (2000).

Button, M. (2007) 'Assessing the regulation of private security across Europe', *European Journal of Criminology*, vol. 4, no. 1, pp. 109–28.

Crawford, A. (2008) 'Plural policing in the UK: policing beyond the police' in Newburn, T. (ed.) (2008).

Crawford, A. and Lister, S. (2006) 'Additional security patrols in residential areas: notes from the marketplace', *Policing and Society*, vol. 16, no. 2, pp. 164–88.

Den Boer, M.G.W. (1999) 'Internationalization: a challenge to police organizations in Europe' in Mawby, R.I. (ed.) (1999).

Den Boer, M.G.W. (2002) 'Towards an accountability regime for an emerging European policing governance', *Policing and Society*, vol. 12, no. 4, pp. 275–89.

Emsley, C. (1996) *The English Police: A Political and Social History*, Harlow, Longman.

Emsley, C. (2001) 'The origins and development of the police' in McLaughlin, E. and Muncie, J. (eds) *Controlling Crime* (2nd edn), London, Sage.

Hobbs, D., Hadfield, P., Lister, S. and Winlow, S. (2003) *Bouncers, Violence and Governance in the Night-Time Economy*, Oxford, Oxford University Press.

Home Office (undated) *Organised and International Crime* [online], www.homeoffice.gov.uk/crime-victims/reducing-crime/organised-crime/ (Accessed 3 April 2009).

Hornsby, R. and Hobbs, D. (2007) 'A zone of ambiguity: the political economy of cigarette bootlegging', *British Journal of Criminology*, vol. 47, no. 4, pp. 551–71.

Hoyle, C. (2000) *Negotiating Domestic Violence: Police, Criminal Justice and Victims*, Oxford, Oxford University Press.

INTERPOL (2009) *INTERPOL: An Overview* [online], www.interpol.int/Public/ICPO/FactSheets/GI01.pdf (Accessed 23 June 2009).

Jones, T. and Newburn, T. (2002) 'The transformation of policing? Understanding current trends in policing systems', *British Journal of Criminology*, vol. 42, no. 1, pp. 129–46.

Kempa, M., Stenning, P. and Wood, J. (2004) 'Policing communal spaces: a reconfiguration of the "mass private property" hypothesis', *British Journal of Criminology*, vol. 44, no. 4, pp. 562–81.

Loader, I. (2002) 'Governing European policing: some problems and prospects', *Policing and Society*, vol. 12, no. 4, pp. 291–305.

Loader, I. and Walker, N. (2001) 'Policing as a public good: reconstituting the connections between policing and the state', *Theoretical Criminology*, vol. 5, no. 1, pp. 9–35.

Loader, I. and Walker, N. (2004) 'State of denial? Rethinking the governance of security', *Punishment and Society*, vol. 6, no. 2, pp. 221–8.

Loader, I. and Walker, N. (2005) 'Necessary virtues: the legitimate place of the state in the production of security' in Wood, J. and Dupont, B. (eds) *Democracy, Security and the Governance of Security*, Cambridge, Cambridge University Press.

Mawby, R.I. (1999) (ed.) *Policing Across the World: Issues for the Twenty-first Century*, London, UCL Press.

McLaughlin, E. (2007) *The New Policing*, London, Sage.

Newburn, T. (ed.) 2008 *Handbook of Policing* (2nd edn), Cullompton, Willan.

Pratt, A. and Thompson, S.K. (2008) 'Chivalry, "race" and discretion at the Canadian border', *British Journal of Criminology,* vol. 48, no. 5, pp. 620–40.

Shearing, C. and Stenning, P. (1983) 'Private security implications for social control', *Social Problems,* vol. 30, no. 5, pp. 493–506.

Sheptycki, J.W.E. (1998) 'The global cops cometh: reflections on transnationalization, knowledge work and policing subculture', *British Journal of Sociology,* vol. 49, no. 1, pp. 57–74.

Sheptycki, J.W.E. (2002) 'Accountability across the policing field: towards a general cartography of accountability for post-modern policing', *Policing and Society,* vol. 12, no. 4, pp. 323–38.

Sheptycki, J.W.E. (ed.) (2000) *Issues in Transnational Policing,* London, Routledge.

Sheptycki, J.W.E. (2006) 'Transnational policing' in McLaughlin, E. and Muncie, J. (eds) *The Sage Dictionary of Criminology* (2nd edn), London, Sage.

Thames Valley Police (2009) *Crime Reduction. Improvements to How We Deal with Domestic Abuse* [online], www.thamesvalley.police.uk/crprev/crprev-domabu/crprev-domabu-whatdomabu/crprev-domabu-whatdomabu-intvp-how.htm (Accessed 23 April 2009).

Wakefield, A. (2003) *Selling Security: The Private Policing of Public Space,* Cullompton, Willan.

Walker, N. (2000) *Policing in a Changing Constitutional Order,* London, Sweet and Maxwell.

Walker, N. (2002) 'Policing and the supranational', *Policing and Society,* vol. 12, no. 4, pp. 307–21.

Walker, N. (2008) 'The pattern of transnational policing' in Newburn, T. (ed.) (2008).

Walklate, S. (2008) 'What is to be done about violence against women? Gender, violence, cosmopolitanism and the law', *British Journal of Criminology,* vol. 48, no. 1, pp. 39–54.

Weber, L. and Bowling, B. (2004) 'Policing migration: a framework for investigating the regulation of global mobility', *Policing and Society,* vol. 14, no. 3, pp. 195–212.

Westmarland, L. (2001) *Gender and Policing: Sex, Power and Police Culture,* Cullompton, Willan.

The White House (undated) *Homeland Security* [online], www.whitehouse.gov/agenda/homeland_security/ (Accessed 6 April 2009).

Williams, C.A. (2008) 'Constables for hire: the history of private "public" policing in the UK', *Policing and Society,* vol. 18, no. 2, pp. 190–205.

Chapter 7
Justice, globalisation and human rights

James Mehigan, Reece Walters and Louise Westmarland

Contents

1   Introduction

We live in a world that is increasingly connected through finance, information, technology, tourism and immigration. Such flows of economy are often presented by political and corporate leaders as the cornerstones of progress and development. Inequality, poverty and injustice are assumed to be diminished by flourishing global market economies that promote economic prosperity and social and political stability. This chapter explores how processes of 'globalisation' have impacted on notions of justice and human rights. That is, what impact has the deregulation of trade markets, the breakdown of national borders, the rapid transfer of information and the advancement of global technologies had on the protection and/or violation of human rights?

As earlier chapters have identified, it is important to examine how mechanisms of justice have evolved and how they have responded to emerging landscapes of transnational harm and crime. The emergent networks of global trade have fostered opportunities for illegal and harmful activities that cross national borders and bypass or blur mechanisms of nation-state policing, regulation and enforcement. This chapter will focus specifically on how these emerging global processes have impacted on international human rights. For some commentators, the deregulation of sovereign market economies has produced a series of crises, often referred to as 'crises of modernity'. As a result, issues such as climate change, asylum, terrorism, poverty and food shortage are influenced substantially by the excesses of globalisation. Contained within these emerging issues of global crises are important questions involving human rights. It is important to note that we live in a world where human rights may be compromised in the interests of 'national security', 'political stability' and financial prosperity. We remain curious about how political leaders and government officials often use 'human rights' as a trump card to neutralise criticism while justifying actions. To criticise someone for advocating and promoting human rights is to embark on a dangerous venture. Human rights rhetoric has become sacrosanct, but what of the protection and implementation of human rights? It is issues such as these and the ways in which human rights are frequently subject to differing interpretation and expectations by diverse governmental and non-governmental organisations (NGOs) that this chapter explores.

Within criminological discourses, human rights abuses have typically been explored with reference to miscarriages of justice. A more critical imagination focuses attention on 'crimes of the powerful', which, according to Steve Tombs and David Whyte (2003, p. 8), 'have far greater economic, physical and social costs than those associated with "conventional" criminals who continue to represent the fixation of the contemporary criminal justice systems'. As a result, critical criminologists have begun to explore human rights abuses within analyses of state and corporate crime (Cohen, 2001; Green and Ward, 2004), terrorism (Scraton, 2002), human trafficking (Lee, 2007), crimes against humanity (Maier-Katkin et al., 2009); war (Hudson and Walters, 2009) and theft of cultural heritage (Mackenzie, 2005), to name just a few.

The aims of this chapter are to explore:

- the nature and role of human rights in contemporary societies

- why studying human rights is important to an understanding of crime and justice

- the relationship between criminology and human rights discourse

- the prospects and problems associated with notions of global justice.

Section 2 explores human rights through an examination of the United Nations Universal Declaration of Human Rights. Section 3 discusses the history and origins of human rights and explores notions of state power through the enforcement of rights. Section 4 identifies the ways in which discourses on human rights continue to be integrated into the criminological landscape. Finally, Sections 5 and 6 critique the universality of human rights and question notions of global justice.

2 Exploring human rights

The 10th of December 2007 was officially declared 'Human Rights Day' as the world prepared for a year-long celebration to commemorate the sixtieth anniversary of the Universal Declaration of Human Rights. The thirty-article declaration was adopted by the General Assembly of the United Nations on 10 December 1948. Forty-eight nations were in favour of the resolution and none were against it; Saudi Arabia, South Africa and the former Soviet Union abstained. The Universal Declaration of Human Rights (UDHR) is the world's most translated document. With 360 different language editions, the United Nations' attempt to bring about a universal state of equality and freedom for humankind is the most widely disseminated multilingual publication.

To launch the commemoration of the document, the Director General of the United Nations stated that the Universal Declaration of Human Rights remained 'a common standard of achievement for all peoples and all nations. Human rights belong to everybody, and we should work together to transform into a reality the motto chosen by the United Nations for the 60th anniversary: "Dignity and justice for all of us"' (Ban, 2008).

Figure 7.1
'Dignity and justice for all': the United Nations and human rights

According to the United Nations Office of the High Commissioner for Human Rights (UNOHCHR), human rights are inherent to all human beings. That is, they are innate or natural; they are essential to our very being. Such necessities are not to be negotiated or compromised, they are entitlements. All human beings have conferred on them by international law, without discrimination, a set of liberties, freedoms and entitlements that have become known as inviolable human rights. Governments around the world must 'act in certain ways or ... refrain from certain acts, in order to promote and protect human rights and fundamental freedoms of individuals or groups' (UNOHCHR, 2008, p. 1).

Activity 7.1

Read through the thirty Articles of the Universal Declaration of Human Rights reproduced in Extract 7.1. When reading each Article, be mindful of the original purpose of the UDHR: to be available to all people, to enhance dignity and to uphold justice. It could be argued that, collectively, the Articles provide a minimum standard for humanity. If this is the case, if rights are taken away or violated, is a human being denied the very essence of their humanity? Are some Articles more important than others? If so, why?

Extract 7.1

The Universal Declaration of Human Rights

Article 1

All human beings are born free and equal in dignity and rights. They are endowed with reason and conscience and should act towards one another in a spirit of brotherhood.

Article 2

Everyone is entitled to all the rights and freedoms set forth in this Declaration, without distinction of any kind, such as race, colour, sex, language, religion, political or other opinion, national or social origin, property, birth or other status. Furthermore, no distinction shall be made on the basis of the political, jurisdictional or international status of the country or territory to which a person belongs, whether it be independent, trust, non-self-governing or under any other limitation of sovereignty.

Article 3

Everyone has the right to life, liberty and security of person.

Article 4

No one shall be held in slavery or servitude; slavery and the slave trade shall be prohibited in all their forms.

Article 5

No one shall be subjected to torture or to cruel, inhuman or degrading treatment or punishment.

Article 6

Everyone has the right to recognition everywhere as a person before the law.

Article 7

All are equal before the law and are entitled without any discrimination to equal protection of the law. All are entitled to equal protection against any discrimination in violation of this Declaration and against any incitement to such discrimination.

Article 8

Everyone has the right to an effective remedy by the competent national tribunals for acts violating the fundamental rights granted him by the constitution or by law.

Article 9

No one shall be subjected to arbitrary arrest, detention or exile.

Article 10

Everyone is entitled in full equality to a fair and public hearing by an independent and impartial tribunal, in the determination of his rights and obligations and of any criminal charge against him.

Article 11

(1) Everyone charged with a penal offence has the right to be presumed innocent until proved guilty according to law in a public trial at which he has had all the guarantees necessary for his defence.

(2) No one shall be held guilty of any penal offence on account of any act or omission which did not constitute a penal offence, under national or international law, at the time when it was committed. Nor shall a heavier penalty be imposed than the one that was applicable at the time the penal offence was committed.

Article 12

No one shall be subjected to arbitrary interference with his privacy, family, home or correspondence, nor to attacks upon his honour and reputation. Everyone has the right to the protection of the law against such interference or attacks.

Article 13

(1) Everyone has the right to freedom of movement and residence within the borders of each state.

(2) Everyone has the right to leave any country, including his own, and to return to his country.

Article 14

(1) Everyone has the right to seek and to enjoy in other countries asylum from persecution.

(2) This right may not be invoked in the case of prosecutions genuinely arising from non-political crimes or from acts contrary to the purposes and principles of the United Nations.

Article 15

(1) Everyone has the right to a nationality.

(2) No one shall be arbitrarily deprived of his nationality nor denied the right to change his nationality.

Article 16

(1) Men and women of full age, without any limitation due to race, nationality or religion, have the right to marry and to found a family. They are entitled to equal rights as to marriage, during marriage and at its dissolution.

(2) Marriage shall be entered into only with the free and full consent of the intending spouses.

(3) The family is the natural and fundamental group unit of society and is entitled to protection by society and the State.

Article 17

(1) Everyone has the right to own property alone as well as in association with others.

(2) No one shall be arbitrarily deprived of his property.

Article 18

Everyone has the right to freedom of thought, conscience and religion; this right includes freedom to change his religion or belief, and freedom, either alone or in community with others and in public or private, to manifest his religion or belief in teaching, practice, worship and observance.

Article 19

Everyone has the right to freedom of opinion and expression; this right includes freedom to hold opinions without interference and to seek, receive and impart information and ideas through any media and regardless of frontiers.

Article 20

(1) Everyone has the right to freedom of peaceful assembly and association.

(2) No one may be compelled to belong to an association.

Article 21

(1) Everyone has the right to take part in the government of his country, directly or through freely chosen representatives.

(2) Everyone has the right of equal access to public service in his country.

(3) The will of the people shall be the basis of the authority of government; this will shall be expressed in periodic and genuine elections which shall be by universal and equal suffrage and shall be held by secret vote or by equivalent free voting procedures.

Article 22

Everyone, as a member of society, has the right to social security and is entitled to realization, through national effort and international co-operation and in accordance with the organization and resources of each State, of the economic, social and cultural rights indispensable for his dignity and the free development of his personality.

Article 23

(1) Everyone has the right to work, to free choice of employment, to just and favourable conditions of work and to protection against unemployment.

(2) Everyone, without any discrimination, has the right to equal pay for equal work.

(3) Everyone who works has the right to just and favourable remuneration ensuring for himself and his family an existence worthy of human dignity, and supplemented, if necessary, by other means of social protection.

(4) Everyone has the right to form and to join trade unions for the protection of his interests.

Article 24

Everyone has the right to rest and leisure, including reasonable limitation of working hours and periodic holidays with pay.

Article 25

(1) Everyone has the right to a standard of living adequate for the health and well-being of himself and of his family, including food, clothing, housing and medical care and necessary social services, and the right to security in the event of unemployment, sickness, disability, widowhood, old age or other lack of livelihood in circumstances beyond his control.

(2) Motherhood and childhood are entitled to special care and assistance. All children, whether born in or out of wedlock, shall enjoy the same social protection.

Article 26

(1) Everyone has the right to education. Education shall be free, at least in the elementary and fundamental stages. Elementary education shall be compulsory. Technical and professional education shall be made generally available and higher education shall be equally accessible to all on the basis of merit.

(2) Education shall be directed to the full development of the human personality and to the strengthening of respect for human rights and fundamental freedoms. It shall promote understanding, tolerance and friendship among all nations, racial or religious groups, and shall further the activities of the United Nations for the maintenance of peace.

(3) Parents have a prior right to choose the kind of education that shall be given to their children.

Article 27

(1) Everyone has the right freely to participate in the cultural life of the community, to enjoy the arts and to share in scientific advancement and its benefits.

(2) Everyone has the right to the protection of the moral and material interests resulting from any scientific, literary or artistic production of which he is the author.

Article 28

Everyone is entitled to a social and international order in which the rights and freedoms set forth in this Declaration can be fully realized.

Article 29

(1) Everyone has duties to the community in which alone the free and full development of his personality is possible.

(2) In the exercise of his rights and freedoms, everyone shall be subject only to such limitations as are determined by law solely for the purpose of securing due recognition and respect for the rights and freedoms of others and of meeting the just requirements of morality, public order and the general welfare in a democratic society.

(3) These rights and freedoms may in no case be exercised contrary to the purposes and principles of the United Nations.

Article 30

Nothing in this Declaration may be interpreted as implying for any State, group or person any right to engage in any activity or to perform any act aimed at the destruction of any of the rights and freedoms set forth herein.

Source: United Nations, undated (quoted from the original declaration adopted in 1948)

Comment

The Articles are designed to be 'universal', available to all people, and as such they lay the foundations for what may be referred to as 'global justice' (discussed further in Section 6), but, as this chapter will reveal, many are often violated by governments around the world. Some commentators may argue that violations are not always intentional, but are, rather, a consequence of industrial advancement, world trade, government debt or transitions to democracy. However, the great pacifist and spiritual leader, Mahatma Ghandi, once stated that the fundamentals of human existence should never be compromised, that to do so would create different sets of rights, from which the more privileged and powerful would benefit the most (Bondurant, 1988). For Ghandi, there was no hierarchy of rights: all were equally important and must be equally available to all people regardless of 'race', class or sex. He famously argued that 'all compromise is based on give and take, but there can be no give and take on fundamentals. Any compromise on mere fundamentals is a surrender. For it is all give and no take' (Bondurant, 1988, p. 32). As you read the rest of this chapter, keep in mind the questions asked in this activity – they will underpin much of the discussion in the following sections.

It is important to explore how and why the thirty Articles of the UDHR came to be regarded as a benchmark for universal human rights. This is the focus of the next section, which addresses the question 'what do the historical origins of human rights tell us about issues of justice?'

3   Origins of human rights and issues of justice

Prior to the UDHR, governments, activists, political commentators and the general public did not refer to 'human rights' as such. What has become the common language of human rights, used and applied globally, was created by the thirty Articles listed in Extract 7.1. However, it would be incorrect to suggest that societies before the development of the UDHR did not engage in discussions about humans, their freedoms and their existence. Ancient Greek philosophers, for example, often wrote about and debated such issues in what was referred to as the 'law of nature'. Subsequent Roman scholars, such as Cicero, developed the notion of 'natural law', which articulated and codified individual liberties and 'natural rights'. Such natural rights as *civitas res publica*, which gave Romans specific protections and liberties (e.g. with regard to religion, finance, property and status) as members of a Roman commonwealth, were deemed to be essential for citizenship (Wallach, 2005).

The UDHR Articles emerged out of a long history of conflict over and debate about individual rights, responsibilities and liberties. The development of the notion of human rights has pivoted on an axis where such overarching aspirations as 'freedom', 'justice', 'dignity' and 'fulfilment' have been imbued with diverse political, social and cultural meanings. These broad terrains have often defined the landscape for human rights, yet they have been shaped by cultural and political mores that differ cross-nationally. As a result, the differences in interpretation have meant that the UDHR has not been universally accepted as the cornerstone for international standards for human rights. The implementation of the Articles has been uneven due to a lack of agreement as to whether a set of rights that are indeed 'universal' and inviolable can actually exist (this is discussed briefly at the end of this section and in greater detail in Section 5). For example, in two well-known cases, former heads of state were accused of crimes against their own country's citizens, and attempts to call them to account for their alleged misdeeds in their former roles met with variable outcomes.

Activity 7.2

Read the two case studies in Extracts 7.2 and 7.3. As you do so, consider the following questions:

- What problems are there with the state having the power to prosecute either a current or a former head of state?

- Do former political leaders who violate their authority forgo fundamental judicial rights?

It is sometimes argued that the rights of one person can limit the actions of another, but that they can also offer the chance to obtain 'justice'. When reading through the following cases, make a note of those issues that you consider to be important for upholding human rights. How do the following cases influence our understandings of what constitutes 'justice'?

Extract 7.2

Pinochet case a milestone: Chile urged to prosecute ex-dictator

Human Rights Watch said today that the arrest of Augusto Pinochet represented a permanent advance in the cause of human rights, despite the decision by British Home Secretary Jack Straw to allow him to return to Chile. The group also called on the Chilean parliament to block a proposed constitutional reform that would give permanent immunity from prosecution to all former heads of state.

'It's a terrible disappointment for Pinochet's thousands of victims that he will not face trial in Spain,' said Reed Brody, Advocacy Director of Human Rights Watch. 'But the very fact that he was arrested, and that his claim of immunity was rejected, has already changed the calculus of dictators around the world. The Pinochet case signified the beginning of the end of their impunity.'

Human Rights Watch noted that the 'Pinochet Precedent' was already taking root in other countries. It praised the decision on February 3 by a Senegalese judge to indict the former Chadian dictator Hissein Habre on torture charges. ...

The Pinochet case reaffirmed the principle that human rights atrocities are subject to 'universal jurisdiction' and can be prosecuted anywhere in the world. Two rulings by the House of Lords found that Pinochet was not immune from prosecution even though he was head of state at the time the crimes were committed.

Source: Human Rights Watch, 2000

Extract 7.3

Saddam Hussein executed in Iraq

In a last act of defiance Saddam Hussein refused to wear a hood

The former Iraqi leader, Saddam Hussein, has been hanged in northern Baghdad for crimes against humanity.

Iraqi state TV showed images of Saddam Hussein going to the gallows before dawn in a building his intelligence services once used for executions.

...

Saddam Hussein was sentenced to death by an Iraqi court on 5 November after a year-long trial over the killings of 148 Shias from the town of Dujail in the 1980s.

In a statement, Iraq's Prime Minister, Nouri Maliki, said the execution had closed a dark chapter in Iraq's history.

'Justice, in the name of the people, has carried out the death sentence against the criminal Saddam, who faced his fate like all tyrants, frightened and terrified during a hard day which he did not expect,' it read.

Source: BBC News, 2006b

Comment

These two case studies illustrate processes of justice, involving former heads of state, in which tyrannical and cruel regimes have been overthrown. It is important to assess whether or not justice was served, and whether human rights were upheld. It could be argued that human rights cannot flourish, or even exist, in contexts where justice is denied, subverted or corrupted. Is the trial of a former dictator, such as Saddam Hussein, in a society and a court system surrounded by civil unrest, corruption, widespread daily violence and political instability, the best way to administer justice? The Human Rights Watch report, *The Quality of Justice*, strongly criticised the Iraqi criminal justice system in which defendants 'cannot pursue a meaningful defence or challenge evidence against them' (Human Rights Watch, 2008b, p. 1). That said, such displays of 'justice' often provide the contexts for purported progress and new beginnings.

There have, of course, been cases throughout history when revolution has been followed by assurances of new rights and freedoms, or at least safeguards against further atrocities; for example, the *Declaration of the Rights of Man and Citizen* (1789) following the French Revolution. Other states, such as the USA, were also developing written constitutions at around this time; in England, on the other hand, 'Bentham first debunked the concept of natural rights, referring to "rights" as "nonsense", and "natural rights" as "nonsense upon stilts"' (Haas, 2008, p. 25).

Human rights are sometimes alleged to be the rights of the powerful. Some countries with former colonial power leave their former subjects with a bill of rights without having adopted similar measures themselves. This happened in the case of Hong Kong prior to the UK handing back the colony to China in 1997. Following the Tiananmen Square massacre in China in 1989, the British Government quickly put a bill of rights in place before the handover, in order to give some protection to its former subjects against the incoming government. In history, such bills of rights outlawed cruel and unusual treatment and punishments unbecoming of human dignity, such as corporal and or capital punishment in public. However, as Geoffrey Robertson (1999) has argued, none of these rights is more fundamental than the right to challenge the state, for without this, any of the other rights can be violated.

The period from the mid 1980s onwards saw a series of mixed fortunes for international human rights, according to commentators who have followed the ebb and flow of what some might regard as a 'timeless' process. As Michael Freeman suggests, the events of September 2001

Figure 7.2
Protesting for human
rights in Tiananmen
Square, China, 1989

ushered in a 'post-9/11' period. He claims that rather than being 'timeless and universal', human rights are grounded in histories of struggle:

> After the adoption of the Universal Declaration of Human Rights in 1948, the struggle for human rights took place in a world dominated by the Cold War and the consequences of decolonization. The period from the mid-1980s to 2001 witnessed a surge of human-rights optimism, as many countries made the transition from authoritarianism to democracy. There were human rights disasters in this period, such as the Rwandan genocide and the conflicts in the former Yugoslavia, but, overall, the idea of human rights moved from the margins to the centre of international politics.
>
> (Freeman, 2005, p. 37)

In the UK this culminated in 1998 both in the Government's adoption of the European Convention on Human Rights and in the UK becoming a signatory to the newly founded International Criminal Court (ICC) (discussed in Section 6). One of the reasons for the UK Government taking this action was that increasing international trade and 'globalisation' were making the protection and additional powers this provided more necessary. Some authors have argued that economic globalism has led to a push for political globalism in the sense that one country or state's actions have an effect on others, and so state sovereignty has lost its stand-alone power. The single world economy has driven the demand for interventionist rules, which can enforce 'global norms'. As Michael Haas (2008, p. 8) suggests: 'A state's sovereignty, in other words, is now secure only when a government behaves according to norms generally respected by the world community or rules encoded in declarations and treaties adopted at international conferences on a wide range of issues, including human rights'.

This assumes, of course, that states and governments can agree on the nature of 'rights' and on the means to call other states to account if they violate the concept of 'international human rights', itself a new and contentious idea with a complex set of rules.

The argument for universal human rights, with rules that are enforceable using international courts, and for states or dictators who violate human rights to be brought to justice, seems to be imperative on the grounds of preventing 'crimes against humanity'. In cases such as Rwanda, for example, where the state was complicit in genocide, it seems that the international community had to stand by and watch without being willing or able to intervene (Amnesty International, 2008).

Figure 7.3
Genocide in Rwanda

As suggested above and explored further in Section 5, there is a problem with the idea of universal human rights, however. The argument between 'fundamentalists' and 'cultural relativists', for instance, is that the West has tried to impose inappropriate and oppressive 'rights' on other cultures, which, due to economic and social conditions, are not regarded by those cultures as relevant. In some regions of Africa and the Middle East, female circumcision is used to 'protect' unmarried women from being raped and from losing their virginity and thereby their chances to marry. Where the practice of circumcision is illegal, girls are sometimes sent back to countries of origin in order that the procedure can be carried out. This is one example of what most people in the West would regard as oppressive mutilation, with dangerous physical and psychological outcomes, yet in some cultures it is seen as necessary and acceptable. The question of whether female circumcision should be banned internationally or whether it is a cultural right provides an illustration of the difficulties of defining rights and freedoms on an international scale (Haas, 2008). Similarly, the 'rights and freedoms' of terrorists are often questioned because terrorists are seen as 'outlaws' and, therefore, already guilty of 'forfeiting' their rights. For example, Robertson (2005) has argued that 'fair trials for terrorists' are impossible due to the ways in which the accused are labelled, the media interest in them and the security measures in evidence at court, as a result of which the 'jury must assume they are guilty'.

As we have identified, the term 'human rights' has come to describe a set of circumstances and a culture of respect for all humans to aspire to. From the UDHR, the international community has developed a set of standards that now dictates, to a greater or lesser degree, the way in which a state relates to its people, and in some cases between non-state actors and individuals. To invoke the term 'human rights' is to bring to an argument a sense of truth and righteousness, an overarching statement that what is being said is almost beyond reproach. But is this the case? Are there 'rights' other than those set out in the UDHR and similar instruments that might also be regarded as 'human rights'? These questions are explored in later sections. The next section goes on to identify how criminology has been, and continues to be, linked to discourses of human rights.

4 Criminology and human rights

Criminological discourses have utilised human rights to understand state power and violence. In 1970, Herman and Julia Schwendinger, influenced by the US Government failures of the Vietnam war, charted new waters by suggesting that state institutions that tolerated, perpetuated or failed to eradicate violations of human rights, such as sexism, racism or poverty, were indeed criminal institutions. Stanley Cohen (1993) furthered this analysis by suggesting that human rights embodied in international law provide the benchmark for a civilised, democratic and free society. He argued that acts such as genocide, torture and other crimes against humanity, committed by sovereign governments, were abuses of state power that should become central to criminological investigation. Criminology should, therefore, seek to examine those who would threaten or take away these essential ingredients of individuality, freedom, world peace and security. Cohen argued that what was needed were criminological analyses that explored the ways in which governments violate human rights, the techniques they use to deny or justify their actions, and the methods adopted to neutralise criticism. Such analyses examine the workings and theory of the state and propose that definitions of crime be enshrined within established human rights law. As Penny Green and Tony Ward (2004, p. 7) argue, 'Human beings have certain needs that are fundamental in the sense that without them they cannot be effective purposive agents, able to pursue their chosen goals and participate in society'. They also argue that, as a result, agents of power that deny such needs and rights must be an ongoing part of the criminological gaze.

Stephen Box (1983, p. 10) argued that the criminal laws in Western nation states were 'ideological reflections of the interests of particular powerful groups'. In the spirit of the Schwendingers (1970), mentioned above, Box asserted that what was needed was a criminological agenda that focused on the actions of state and corporate actors. Within a criminology that examines human rights abuses, the lens moves away from crimes committed by the poor and the powerless to those committed by the wealthy, powerful and privileged. The uptake of such critical criminological scholarship continues to gather momentum in books (see Kannabiran and Singh, 2008; McEvoy and Mika, 2008), journal articles (see Hudson and Walters, 2009) and academic conferences (e.g. the Australian and New Zealand Society of Criminology devoted its entire 2006 conference to the theme of 'Criminology and Human Rights').

Figure 7.4
The human rights 'black hole': Guantánamo Bay, Cuba

Activity 7.3

Consider the following examples. Are such acts worthy of criminological inquiry? If so, rank them from 1 to 6 according to which you consider most deserving (with 1 being the most deserving, 6 the least). Give a reason for your ranking. When constructing your answer, consider the argument that it may be necessary at times to violate human rights for matters of national security, trade and culture. In other words, certain occasions or circumstances require that human rights be compromised for a 'greater good'.

1   US-occupied Guantánamo Bay has been referred to as a legal and human rights 'black hole'. Since 2001, more than 900 people, including children, have been taken by US soldiers and imprisoned for up to four years without access to legal representation. These so-called 'worst of the worst' are deemed by the US administration to be potential terrorist suspects and have been subjected to 'torture-lite' interrogation. Yet there has been only one conviction (Ballen and Bergen, 2008; **Green, 2010**).

2   The Parliamentary Assembly of the Council of Europe has publicly condemned the Russian Government's human rights violations in Chechnya. Russian security forces reportedly continue to commit acts of murder, torture and arbitrary detention against Chechnyan journalists, government officials and protesters as a means of creating political and social instability (House of Commons Foreign Affairs Committee, 2006).

3   In the Saudi Kingdom all women must have a male guardian, usually a father or husband, who must grant permission for an adult woman to work, study, travel or marry. This official government policy is based on Quranic teachings. Human Rights Watch (2008a) observe that 'adult women are treated like legal minors who are entitled to little authority over their own lives and well-being. Male guardianship over adult women also contributes to their risk of confronting family violence and makes it nearly impossible for survivors of family violence to avail themselves of protection or redress mechanisms'.

4   Uzbekistan is the world's second largest producer of cotton – cotton that is used for clothing and sold in high streets in the UK, the USA and across Europe. Yet the cotton is picked using child labour. Schools are closed by the Uzbekistani Government during harvest and children work long hours, often with little or no pay. Those who cannot, or refuse, to work are punished and/or expelled from their schools (BBC Two, 2007).

5 In 1989, Exxon Oil negligently caused the world's worst-ever oil spill off the Alaskan coast, resulting in devastating ecological loss. Alaskan villages along the coastline were also decimated by the disaster. After many years, during which the oil company delayed court proceedings on numerous occasions, Exxon was eventually ordered to pay US$5.3 billion. While Exxon has instituted various clean-up initiatives, the lives of villagers remain ruined and full financial settlement has not been made with those worst affected (Greenpeace, 2004).

6 In China, thousands of prisoners are executed each year in what has been described as 'state-sponsored terror'. Once executed, the Chinese authorities often sell the prisoner's body parts to the highest bidder. Executions are frequently scheduled at the precise time that an organ recipient (often from the West) is ready for a transplant. Prior to the executions, prisoners are routinely denied their rights of appeal (BBC News, 2006a; Verkaik, 2009).

Comment

The examples given above identify the tensions that sometimes exist between rights and the cultures and economies of other nations. Should we ever permit or tolerate human rights abuses? What if the implementation of 'universal' human rights stands to erode the cultural practices of a country's long-held traditions? What if human rights violations are necessary for a country's trade and financial stability? Or for world peace and security? In other words, are all human rights violations harmful? They may be, but they may also be fiscally necessary or culturally appropriate. These are questions with which criminologists must engage when assessing the actions of other countries and cultures. Doing so raises issues about the universality of rights and the extent to which the global pervasiveness of human rights may be seen as an act of cultural imperialism (imposing one's culture on to another) rather than a process of seeking 'dignity and justice for all'.

As mentioned earlier, the 60th anniversary of the historic signing of the UDHR prompted a range of commemorative events. Some commentators have observed the hypocrisy of such festivals that serve to mask human rights abuses while purporting to celebrate humanitarian achievements, for it can be the power of the state that creates harm and undermines human rights. This point is explored further in the following newspaper extract in what the author, John Pilger, refers to as 'rapacious British power'.

Figure 7.5
Adult women in the
Saudi Kingdom are
subjected to restrictions
that treat them as legal
minors

Activity 7.4

Read Extract 7.4 and list all the reported human rights violations carried
out by the UK Government. Do the issues contained in the article
provide the basis for Box's (1983) argument that criminology should
have a major focus on the actions of those people in positions of state
and corporate power?

Extract 7.4

Kafka has a rival. Today, the Foreign Office lectures us on human rights

Such an open day beggars belief. At this PR gala you will find no stall for the victims of rapacious British power

John Pilger

Today, a surreal event will take place in London. The Foreign Office is holding an open day 'to highlight the importance of human rights in our work as part of the 60th anniversary of the Universal Declaration of Human Rights'. There will be various 'stalls' and 'panel discussions', and foreign secretary David Miliband will present a human rights prize. Is this a spoof? No. The Foreign Office wants to raise our 'human rights awareness'. Kafka and Heller have many counterfeits.

There will be no stall for the Chagos islanders, the 2,000 British citizens expelled from their Indian Ocean homeland, whom Miliband's government has fought to prevent from returning to what is now a US military base and suspected CIA torture centre. The high court has repeatedly restored this fundamental human right to the islanders, the essence of Magna Carta, describing the Foreign Office actions as 'outrageous', 'repugnant' and 'illegal'. Yet Miliband's lawyers refused to give up, and were rescued on October 22 by the political judgments of three law lords.

There will be no stall for the victims of a systemic British policy of exporting arms and military equipment to 10 of Africa's most war-bloodied and impoverished countries. In his speech today, with the good people of Amnesty and Save the Children in attendance, shamefully, what will Miliband say to the sufferers of this UK-sponsored violence? Perhaps he will make mention, as he often does, of the need for 'good governance' in faraway places, while his own regime suppresses a Serious Fraud Office investigation into BAE's £43m arms deal with the corrupt tyranny in Saudi Arabia – with which, noted Foreign Office minister Kim Howells in 2007, the British had 'shared values'.

There will be no stall for those Iraqis whose social, cultural and real lives have been smashed by an unprovoked invasion based on proven lies. Will the foreign secretary apologise for the cluster bombs the British have scattered, still blowing legs off children, and the depleted uranium and other toxic substances that have seen cancer consume swaths of southern Iraq? Will he speak about the universal human right to knowledge, and announce a diversion of a fraction of the billions bailing out the City of London to the restoration of what was one of the finest school systems in the Middle East, obliterated as a consequence of the Anglo-American invasion, along with museums and publishing houses and bookstores, and teachers and historians and anthropologists and surgeons? Will he announce the dispatch of simple painkillers and syringes to hospitals that once had almost everything and now have nothing, in a country where British governments, especially his own, took the lead in blocking humanitarian aid, including Howells' ban on vaccines to protect children from preventable diseases?

There will be no stall for the people of Gaza, of whom, says the International Red Cross, starvation threatens the majority, mostly children. In pursuing a policy of reducing one and a half million people to a Hobbesian existence, the Israelis have cut most lifelines.

David Miliband was in Jerusalem recently, within a short helicopter flight of the captive people of Gaza. He did not go, and said nothing about their human rights, preferring weasel words about a 'truce' between tormentor and victims.

There will be no stall for the trade unionists, students, journalists and human rights defenders assassinated in Colombia, a country where the government's 'security forces' are trained by the British and Americans and responsible for 90% of torture, says a new study by the British human rights group Justice for Colombia. The Foreign Office says it is 'improving the human rights record of the military and combating drug trafficking'. The study finds not a shred of evidence to support this. Colombian officers implicated in murder are welcomed to Britain for 'seminars'.

There will be no stall for history, for our memory. Stored in the great British libraries and record offices, unclassified official files tell the truth about British policy and human rights, from officially condoned atrocities in the concentration camps of colonial Kenya and the arming of the genocidal General Suharto in Indonesia, to the supply of biological weapons to Saddam Hussein in the 1980s. As we hear the moralising drone of ex-British military 'security experts' telling us what to think about current events in Mumbai, we might recall Britain's historic role as midwife to violent extremism in modern Islam, from the rise of the Muslim Brotherhood in Egypt in the 1950s through the overthrow of Iran's liberal democratic government to MI6's arming of the Afghan mujahideen, the Taliban in waiting. The aim was and remains the denial of nationalism to peoples struggling to be free, especially in the Middle East, where oil, says a secret Foreign Office document from 1947, is 'a vital prize for any power interested in world influence and domination'. Human rights are almost entirely absent from this official memory, unlike fear of being found out. The secret expulsion of the Chagos Islanders, says a 1964 Foreign Office memorandum, 'should be timed to attract the least attention and should have some logical cover [so as not to] arouse suspicions as to their purpose'.

Source: *The Guardian*, 1 December 2008

Comment

A critical scholarship that reorients the criminological focus to harmful acts of the powerful is one that challenges state-defined notions of crime and seeks new intellectual terrains in areas often omitted from government and public debate. A criminology that investigates and critiques human rights abuses is one that must engage with issues of state and corporate power. This necessitates an examination of government actions, especially those that result in avoidable harm to other nations and peoples. The famous Nobel Prize-winning playwright, poet and political activist, Harold Pinter, once stated that 'the crimes of the US throughout the world have been systematic, constant, clinical, remorseless, and fully documented but nobody talks about them' (quoted in Akbar, 2008, p. 4). A criminology for human rights allows such issues to be investigated, talked about and placed within the criminal justice landscape.

5 Equality, universality and human rights

If criminology is to continue to examine those states and corporations that violate human rights, we must ask, to what extent are human rights truly universal? In other words, are the human rights described in Extract 7.1 in Section 2 representative of all human beings? To answer this question, let us provide some reflective comments.

As mentioned earlier, the most famous international human rights instrument in history, the UDHR, creates a benchmark for the notion of universal human rights. It is broad in scope, including both rights to be free from interference and rights to develop as much as possible one's potential as a human being. It became possible to adopt the UDHR at a specific moment in history. It was a moment when almost all the countries in the world (albeit there were only fifty-one countries at the time as decolonisation had not begun in earnest) were able to agree on notions of human rights because of what the world had witnessed during the Second World War and the Holocaust. The era was a fruitful one for the development of an international consensus on what a human right should be. In the same era, a group of European countries developed the European Convention on Human Rights in 1950, which contained within it a court that developed the most substantial body of jurisprudence of any international human rights court in the world. It was a groundbreaking achievement symbolic of a Europe rebuilding itself in the aftermath of war and vowing not to allow the degradation of human dignity ever to become so widespread again on the Continent. In the same short period, other great advances in defining as criminal the conduct of states that violated the rights of individuals were made. The Convention on the Prevention and Punishment of the Crime of Genocide was adopted in 1948, making genocide a discrete crime, and in 1949 the four Geneva Conventions on the laws of war created new types of war crimes and procedures for prosecuting them, both internationally (Cassese, 2003) and nationally (Machover and Maynard, 2006). In short, the period after the Second World War was a period of development, hope and aspiration as much in the world of international law as in the world of economic development.

All of this success is, of course, laudable and we could indeed describe ourselves as lucky that such instruments were created at such an apposite time. It is arguable, however, whether they could have been created today in a climate of fear and amid the talk of a 'clash of civilisations' that stalks early twenty-first-century international relations.

The UDHR, for all its symbolic power and influence, was constructed, like all international treaties, by a group of diplomats arguing over the careful drafting of a declaration in such a way as to serve their own best interests and perceptions of how the world should work. Very few African states were represented, or indeed signed up to the UDHR, for the simple reason that there were very few African states. In 1945, there were only four independent nations in Africa:

> Egypt, nominally independent, headed by a corrupt monarch but subject to British political interference ... Ethiopia, a feudal empire newly restored to Haile Selassie after five years of Italian occupation; Liberia, a decaying republic founded on the west coast in 1847 for freed American slaves ... but in reality little more than a fiefdom of the American Firestone Company, which owned its rubber plantations; and the Union of South Africa, the richest state in Africa ... given independence in 1910 under white minority rule. The rest were the preserve of European powers, all confident about the importance of their imperial mission.
>
> (Meredith, 2005, p. 10)

The drafting of the UDHR by the countries of 1948 was a process in which African voices, and indeed the voices of other colonies, went unheard: or, at least, they were heard only through the arguments and representations of their colonial masters. When it later came to the point that African countries themselves developed a regional human rights mechanism, it was one whose name and content belie a substantial divergence of opinion about what should be the substance of human rights. In 1981, the Organization of African Unity adopted the African Charter on Human and Peoples' Rights. The Charter is a substantial departure from traditionally conceived notions of human rights. Not only does it include collective or peoples' rights (i.e. rights that attach to groups rather than to individuals), it also places a substantial emphasis on 'duties'. Individuals, groups and communities each have duties to behave in a certain way, beyond merely refraining from breaching another's rights. This approach to human rights marks a radical departure from the rights-focused approach taken by the European and Inter-American human rights regimes (Steiner and Alston, 2000). If an international human rights instrument is an aspirational statement of what a group of countries consider to be the proper way to conduct their affairs with regard to their citizens, it appears that African states have a substantially different idea about what that conduct should be.

Perhaps the best example of such politicisation of human rights lies in the dichotomy between civil and political rights (CPR) and economic, social and cultural rights (ESCR). The former is a body of rights that bolsters the Western democratic model: free speech, freedom of conscience, freedom from torture, the right to a fair trial, the right to life, and so on. The latter comprises a bigger body of rights encompassing those rights that are required to sustain life, economies and cultures. These include the rights to food, education, health, housing and work (Clapham, 2007). The distinction became a substantial sticking point in human rights discourse during the years of the Cold War. On the one hand, throughout the 1980s, the USA argued that ESCR were too easily abused by repressive regimes and should be ignored. This argument was perhaps put forth less out of concern for the repressed and more because the obligations that ESCR place on states to provide for their citizens did not square with a free-market capitalist economy. On the other hand, China and Eastern-bloc countries argued that 'when poverty and lack of adequate food are commonplace and people's basic needs are not guaranteed, priority should be given to economic development' (Steiner and Alston, 2000, p. 268). Many leaders of one-party states fear the impact that free debate and self-determination would have on the future sustainability of their (often autocratic) regimes. Each of the belligerents in the Cold War used their interpretation of what a human right should be to berate the other as a failure, and to paint itself as a success. The instruments of human rights were used as campaigning tools to rally political support and attempt to undermine opposition. The instruments were, in many cases, not really intended, by those creating them, to be entirely binding or to end in the prosecution of the most serious offenders who had committed the greatest crimes. Henry Kissinger, US Secretary of State from 1973 to 1977, who negotiated numerous international treaties on behalf of the USA, put it thus:

> As one of the negotiators of the Final Act of the Helsinki conference [an international agreement on human rights concluded in 1975], I can affirm that the administration I represented considered it primarily a diplomatic weapon to use to thwart the communists' attempts to pressure the Soviet and captive peoples. Even with respect to binding undertakings such as the genocide convention, it was never thought that they would subject past and future leaders of one nation to prosecution by the national magistrates of another state.
>
> (Kissinger, 2001, p. 88)

It seems almost as if the treaties were conceived and created, not to punish those who commit the gravest crimes, but in order to harness the political capital of their apparent moral authority in order to assist in the achievement of foreign policy goals. The distinction between the two types of rights was enshrined in two Covenants that were developed in the 1960s to flesh out the detail of what human rights should contain. The division of the so-called 'International Bill of Rights' into the International Covenant on Civil and Political Rights (ICCPR) and the International Covenant on Economic, Social and Cultural Rights (ICESCR) (UNOHCHR, 1996) has left a long shadow on the study of human rights, which still struggles to treat both categories of rights as equal. It was only at the 1993 Vienna World Conference that the notion that all rights are 'indivisible and interdependent and interrelated' was adopted, although it was first coined in 1950 (Steiner and Alston, 2000, p. 268).

There are clear links between the two categories of rights and many have argued that it is impossible for a country to develop a convincing working set of one and completely ignore the other. Perhaps the most famous argument on this was made by Amartya Sen (1999) when he pointed out that no functioning democracy has ever had a major famine. This applies to relatively poor democracies as well as those with successful economies. Famines do, however, occur in colonial territories, one-party states and military dictatorships with regrettable frequency (Sen, 1999). This example of the symbiotic relationship between different types of human rights throws into clear relief the problems of taking an à la carte approach to human rights. Yet, if the two sets of rights go hand in hand, why are ESCR so often ignored and CPR exhalted? Why do international NGOs work so hard on CPR but almost ignore the questions of ESCR?

The excuse that many countries give for focusing on CPR is that to provide economic rights, such as the right to adequate water and housing, would cost too much and hinder the political freedom of countries to decide how to prioritise their resources. However, it must be plain to see that implementing CPR involves substantial expenditure. For instance, it requires that there be a criminal justice system that devours a huge chunk of many countries' budgets. Why are so many countries so quick to spend money providing a criminal justice system but not adequate education, water or housing (International Council on Human Rights Policy, 2003)? This phenomenon is not confined just to the developing world. Consider the expenditure on prisons, police, probation, community safety and the myriad other 'security' measures in the USA, the UK and other developed countries. Who can legitimately claim their version of rights to be superior?

The big question in this regard is, 'Can it be right for the West to impose its moral compass on culturally, politically, socially and economically different states?' Is this a form of cultural imperialism or a tool of foreign policy? What is it that gives human rights the power to tell other people what to do? Is it enough just to say, 'Lots of things contained in human rights are good, therefore others should be implored to abide by them'? In a diverse world, how can human rights, which are supposed to thrive on acceptance of the differences of others, be defined as a form of universal truth? This challenge is substantial. The political capital derived from references to human rights means that the meaning of 'human rights' and its authority are severely threatened. The protection of the rights of some people has been used to justify the flagrant violation of the rights of others. One need only think of the 'war on terror', where some are tortured to protect others; or the invasion of Iraq. The phrase 'human rights' can be abused by people for their own means. The notion is politicised to the extent that it risks becoming a mere exhortation or aspiration lacking any intellectual grounding. Conor Gearty argues that:

> If human rights are to survive, it is imperative to translate the political and legal success of the idea into the philosophical arena, to construct non-nonsensical foundations for human rights, support systems that defend the idea not by the simple invocation of past glories, but in terms that ring true today, that run with rather than against the grain of contemporary assumptions about what it means to be right and wrong.
>
> (Gearty, 2006, p. 28)

It may seem that just as the successes of human rights are beginning to be realised, their philosophical foundations are being tested. Human rights as a notion is under threat. Perhaps the greatest source of this threat is what Gearty (2006) calls the 'crisis of national security': that is, the belief that we are in the midst of a 'clash of civilisations', with 'terrorist' risks to the safety of the nation that are so substantial as to justify the erosion or reconfiguration of human rights (Mythen and Walklate, 2006). It is in the response to such 'threat' that the interaction of human rights, criminal justice and criminology can be seen most clearly.

6 Global justice and human rights

Some of the earliest academic commentators on globalisation argued that it is 'the intensification of worldwide social relations which link distant localities in such a way that local happenings are shaped by events occurring miles away and vice versa' (Giddens, 1990, p. 64). As we indicated at the beginning of this chapter, flows of commerce have facilitated global networks of information, technology and trade. They have also paved the way for other flows, including security, criminal activity and justice. Such interconnected global markets have created the contexts for 'cross-border crime flows' on an unprecedented scale with demanding challenges for regulatory agencies and agents of criminal justice (Loader and Sparks, 2002; see also Chapter 6). The globalised economy, with its competitive free-market policies, has also witnessed a rise in human rights abuses. As a result, Mark Findlay (2008, p. 4) argues that globalisation can be 'an analytical tool with which to understand global governance and international criminal justice'. From this perspective, for example, compulsory, unsafe and forced child labour, notably in poor and developing countries, can be firmly situated in the context of corporate expansion within globalised markets. The economic opportunities that have prospered under deregulated free-market ideologies have also decreased living standards for the world's poorest and most vulnerable peoples while accelerating corporate fraud (Benedek et al., 2007; Minkes and Minkes, 2008). Moreover, the post-9/11 period marked by US/UK-led alliance (often referred to as the 'war on terror') has provided the catalyst for an increase internationally in states violating human rights. As Pilger revealed in Extract 7.4, the so-called moral guardians of human rights have themselves been actively involved, or implicated, in human rights abuses (see Ginger, 2005). How can justice be exercised against perpetrators of human rights abuses when the violators are representatives of the most powerful nations on Earth? Before we address this question, it is important to outline what is meant by global justice and consider its effectiveness in preventing human rights abuses.

Ruth Jamieson and Kieron McEvoy (2005, p. 505) argue that transnational or global justice extends to 'violations of human rights, humanitarian law, crimes against humanity and the related developments in international criminal and transitional justice'. From their perspective, mechanisms of transnational justice must reflect the changing nature of the modern state within various forms of governance that include non-state and corporate actors. At present, there are numerous forms of global governance that attempt to provide justice on a range of issues, from trade and the environment to peace and security. Whether they are instruments of the United Nations or the European Union or are trade regulations of the World Trade Organization, such institutions, notwithstanding their widespread criticisms, serve to provide models and mechanisms for implementing global rules. Other legal institutions have been installed by law to settle international disputes and conflicts. For example, the International Court of Justice (ICJ), or 'World Court', established in 1945, convenes in The Hague (the Netherlands) and consists of fifteen judges and both provides legal opinions and settles international disputes. The ICJ cannot be accessed by private organisations and UN agencies, and individuals cannot bring matters before this court. Moreover, its decisions are binding only when 'both parties have agreed to submit to its decision' (see ICJ, 2009). The USA, for example, withdrew from the ICJ's compulsory jurisdiction in 1986 and continues to assess its commitment to the ICJ on a case-by-case basis. The European Court of Human Rights, established in 1954, is binding on all forty-seven countries of the Council of Europe, including the twenty-seven member states of the European Union.

Figure 7.6
International Court of
Justice in The Hague

The other main formal body designated with instituting global
criminal justice is the ICC. The ICC was established by the Rome
Statute of the International Criminal Court in July 1998; 120 countries
voted to adopt the Treaty (only seven countries voted against: China,
Israel, Libya, Iraq, Yemen, Qatar and the USA). The Treaty became
international law in July 2002 after the sixtieth country ratified the
legislation. It does not have retrospective jurisdiction, hence it cannot
try crimes against humanity that pre-date July 2002. The seat of the
Court is in The Hague. There are eighteen elected judges who form the
Court's judicial panel and who sit for between three and nine years
(ICC, 2009).

Up until now, individual countries have been expected to conduct their
own trials for acts such as genocide and war crimes; as a result, many
crimes against humanity have gone unpunished. The US administration
under President George W. Bush refused to acknowledge the legitimacy
of the ICC, arguing that it may exercise its jurisdiction to conduct
politically motivated investigations and prosecutions against US military
and political officials (Global Policy Forum, 2009).

The US Government has also engaged in a world campaign of 'impunity
agreements' with signatories to the ICC. Such impunity agreements,
argued by Amnesty International to be illegal (Joansen, 2006), are
contracts that prohibit signatories from bringing actions against US
nationals before the ICC. On 3 August 2003, the US Congress signed

anti-ICC legislation, called the American Service Members' Protection Act. The four main articles of this Act included:

1   a prohibition on US cooperation with the ICC

2   an 'invasion of the Hague provision' that authorises the US President to use all means necessary and appropriate to free US personnel detained or imprisoned by the ICC

3   punishment for states that join the ICC Treaty: such as refusing military aid

4   a prohibition on US participation in peace-keeping activities unless immunity from the ICC is guaranteed for US personnel (AMICC, 2009).

Anti-ICC legislation and impunity agreements have eroded the USA's credibility internationally to bring human rights abusers to court. Moreover, the US impunity agreements are seen as a form of economic exploitation. Countries such as Kenya, Ethiopia and Brazil have all signed impunity agreements with the USA, meaning that they cannot bring charges of crimes against humanity against US military, political or government officials. These acts of US coercion, which force other countries to sign legal agreements, are driven by US economic domination. Poorer countries that are economically dependent on the USA compromise notions of justice and human rights in favour of their own economic needs.

Activity 7.5

If powerful nations that abuse human rights and commit crimes against humanity fail to recognise or adhere to the rulings of the ICC, is the ICC a toothless and pointless legal apparatus? Read the following extract and list three reasons why the ICC is important and three reasons why it should be abolished. Which of your reasons are the most persuasive?

Extract 7.5

UN attacks Israeli rights 'crimes'

Israel's policies against the Palestinians are tantamount to a 'crime against humanity', the United Nations' human rights rapporteur has said.

Richard Falk said in a statement on Tuesday that the UN must 'implement the agreed norm of a responsibility to protect a civilian population being collectively punished by policies that amount to a crime against humanity'.

The statement came on the same day that the UN Human Rights Council urged Israel to implement 99 measures to improve its rights record.

Falk said it would seem 'mandatory' that the UN's International Criminal Court investigate Israel's policies in regard to the Palestinians.

'[The court could] determine whether the Israeli civilian leaders and military commanders responsible for the Gaza siege should be indicted and prosecuted for violations of international criminal law,' he said.

The Israeli government has faced a level of criticism by 'normally cautious UN officials' not seen since the 'the heyday of South African apartheid,' Falk said.

'And still Israel maintains its Gaza siege in its full fury, allowing only barely enough food and fuel to enter to stave off mass famine and disease.'

Israel has maintained tight controls on what supplies enter the Gaza Strip, home to about 1.5 million Palestinians, since Hamas, a Palestinian group, took control of it in June 2007.

The Israeli and US governments say that Hamas is a terrorist organisation.

Rights recommendations

The Human Rights Council said in its list of 99 recommendations that Israel must completely end its blockade of Gaza, while also calling for it to release Arab detainees.

Israel's ambassador to the UN in Geneva said that 'Israel remains committed to reinforcing areas in which we are succeeding and bettering those areas that need improvement.'

Aharon Leshno Yaar said the dialogue had been 'positive and productive'.

Israel is due to report to the UN council in March on how it will address the recommendations.

Deliveries allowed

The Israel military allowed dozens of lorries carrying humanitarian aid to enter Gaza and permitted the delivery of diesel to Gaza's main power plant on Tuesday.

The Karam Abu Salam crossing allowed about 40 lorries carrying supplies into the territory, while 30 lorries with grain, wheat and bird feed passed through the Karni crossing.

The Nahal Oz fuel terminal allowed in some industrial fuel for Gaza's only power plant, as well as cooking gas for the general public and petrol for UN operations.

The Erez crossing was also open for journalists and humanitarian workers coming into Gaza.

But Ayman Mohyeldin, Al Jazeera's correspondent in the Palestinian coastal strip, said the amount of supplies allowed into Gaza was of limited quantity and would only probably last for a few days.

Source: Al Jazeera English, 2008

Comment

Clearly, there are challenges to global justice when the most powerful nations abuse the rights of others and ignore international law. Amid widespread international condemnation from human rights campaigners and political leaders, Israel began bombing the Gaza Strip in late December 2008, killing hundreds of civilians as well as a senior democratically elected Hamas official. Such actions were widely reported as illegal under international law and disproportionate to Palestinian attacks – yet such denunciation did not halt the Israeli onslaught (see Chomsky, 2009).

Defiance of international pressure and transnational justice is not uncommon. It ranges from an unwillingness to adhere to decisions of international courts to a violation of due process. For example, in January 2009, two Iraqi citizens were handed over to the Iraqi authorities by the British Foreign Office in breach of a ruling of the European Court of Justice to protect the human rights and safety of the accused. The British Government's actions were deemed to be illegal and vindictive by the accused's legal representatives (May, 2009). As Findlay (2008) argues, the principles of human rights are yet to be adequately integrated into international processes of criminal justice, thereby providing mechanisms of global justice with a 'shelf life' to be determined by organisations such as the highly politicised UN Security Council.

Instead, it may be more useful to consider the ways in which global justice might be achieved through various interconnected pathways both within and outside formal state or judicially based avenues of regulation. This might be the international transfer of ideologies rather than the establishment of institutions. For example, notions of restorative justice have moved beyond the borders in which they were initially conceived and now represent a feature of criminal justice systems in many nation states (see Chapter 3). Similar integration could occur with the rhetoric and principles of, for example, human rights or environmental protection becoming embedded in the legal regimes of nation states. Such processes and practices of justice could be adopted to address issues of global harm.

Moreover, justice may need to be pursued and achieved outside of, as well as within, legal domains. For example, citizen participation or protest in areas involving the environment, trade and migration are ways through which injustices can be identified and subsequently addressed. As a result, global justice might be imagined as a network through which various actors, such as the World Social Forum, the Anti-Globalisation Movement, Human Rights Watch, Amnesty International, Statewatch and Greenpeace, working in conjunction with UN bodies

Figure 7.7
Campaigning for human rights: the bushmen of the Kalahari are thrown off their land by diamond companies. Botswana, 2002

and sovereign authorities, seek justice for all. This is not just about the actions of such agencies, but also concerns the development of a network through which individuals themselves form alliances and pockets of localised resistance to voice concerns about inequality and exploitation. It would also provide a means by which the omitted or neglected voices, discussed earlier, could be heard through policy and campaigns frameworks that assert political, social and economic pressures on governments and international governing bodies.

Citizen participation in global justice views the world as a system or a series of interconnected overlapping networks. To redress the injustices of deforestation, for example, and promote global justice, it could be argued that citizens as consumers are best placed to influence those state and corporate practices that result in human and environmental harm, through 'product boycotts' and 'fair trade purchases' (Cochrane and Walters, 2008).

7   Conclusion

Recent years have witnessed the growth of many different types or narratives of criminology. For example, the prefixes 'green', 'cultural' and 'public' have all been used to identify a specific brand of inquiry. These words have recently been added to at least twenty other distinctive brands of criminology – from classicist and positivist to feminist and radical. Is there any advantage in furthering the quest for new criminological terrains by adopting the term 'global criminology'? The term highlights the emerging horizons that criminology must continue to embrace. It recognises the challenges that criminology must continue to address as new criminal landscapes are created and fostered by the forces of globalisation. The need for criminology to have a global reach and to address issues of transnational concern has been expressed by several authors (Morrison, 2004; Aas, 2008; Findlay, 2008).

If studies of crime and justice are to remain focused solely on acts of property crime, drugs and interpersonal violence (while clearly worthy of attention), the mass harms caused by states and corporations and the excesses of modernity will go unchecked. A global criminology must begin to wrestle with these large questions. The term provides a useful banner under which to house scholarship that addresses harmful acts committed by powerful and privileged personnel across different jurisdictions. As times approach that provide life-threatening scenarios on a transnational scale, criminological inquiry must begin to examine the causes and consequences of such scenarios. Such analyses will require investigation of issues of harm, power and violence within global networks of trade, migration and international relations. The accelerating trends of free market economies have broadened the reach and opportunities for all sorts of criminal enterprises. Criminology can respond to these issues only by expanding its horizons and equipping itself with the means to understand the harms created by the various processes and practices of what is termed 'globalisation'. A global criminology must draw on existing and established discourses within the discipline as well as embracing other areas in political and environmental science, international law, migration and development studies, and economics and monetary policy.

The expansion of world trade economies, connected and intensified through networks of information technology and the movement of workers and consumers, has marked a rapid transition in the ways in which many people live their lives. Premised on notions of financial growth and stability, globalisation has promoted, and in many instances achieved, increased wealth, consumer choice and individual mobility. Although such things may have brought benefits for some, the deregulation and spread of world trade has also incurred environmental, financial and personal impacts for others. Moreover, the excesses of globalisation have created what has been termed 'crises of modernity', as mentioned in the Introduction to this chapter, in which human rights continue to be compromised and abused.

As we have outlined above, the international framework for human rights emerged in response to specific acts in the mid twentieth century. What we are now seeing is that human rights are being compromised by globalised processes of trade that have at their centre rhetoric about collective good, mutual benefit and progress. Criminology as an evolving discipline must continually engage with issues and acts of global concern. This necessitates thinking about ways in which human rights abuses, for example, can be protected and enforced through mechanisms of global justice – and how this might be challenged. Such thinking requires criminology to be ensconced within a global enterprise. A global criminology is, therefore, one that shifts the lens of inquiry to issues of global concern: issues that transcend national borders and require international collaboration and engagement with international law and policy. For a discipline traditionally embedded within state-defined notions of domestic crime, this provides new horizons and unique challenges.

References

Aas, K.F. (2008) *Globalisation and Crime: Key Approaches to Criminology*, London, Sage.

Akbar, A. (2008) 'Radical and passionate, both on stage and in life', *The Independent*, 26 December, pp. 4–5.

Al Jazeera English (2008) *UN Attacks Israeli Rights 'Crimes'*, 13 December [online], http://english.aljazeera.net/news/middleeast/2008/12/20081210551198584.html (Accessed 30 March 2009).

AMICC (2009) *Anti-ICC Legislation* [online], www.amicc.org/usinfo/congressional.html (Accessed 20 April 2009).

Amnesty International (2008) *The State of the World's Human Rights* [online], www.amnesty.org/en/region/rwanda/report-2008 (Accessed 20 April 2009).

Australian and New Zealand Society of Criminology (2006) *Criminology and Human Rights*, 19th Annual ANZSOC Conference [online], www.anzsoc.org/conferences/2006/ (Accessed 20 April 2009).

Ballen, K. and Bergen, P. (2008) *'The Worst of the Worst', Foreign Policy*, [online] www.anzsoc.org/conferences/2006/ (Accessed 19 April 2009).

Ban, Ki-Moon (2008) 'UNESCO launching 60th anniversary of the Universal Declaration of Human Rights' [online] http://portal.unesco.org/en/ev.php-URL_ID=41393&URL_DO=DO_TOPIC&URL_SECTION=201.html (Accessed 4 June 2009).

BBC News (2006a) *Organ Sales 'Thriving' in China*, 27 September [online], http://news.bbc.co.uk/2/hi/asia-pacific/5386720.stm (Accessed 20 April 2009).

BBC News (2006b) *Saddam Hussein Executed in Iraq*, 30 December [online] http://news.bbc.co.uk/1/hi/world/middle_east/6218485.stm (Accessed 27 March 2009).

BBC Two (2007) *Newsnight*, 'Cotton', 30 October [online], www.bbc.co.uk/blogs/newsnight/2007/10/tuesday_30_october_2007.html (Accessed 20 April 2009).

Benedek, W., De Feyter, K. and Marrella, F. (eds) (2007) *Economic Globalisation and Human Rights*, Cambridge, Cambridge University Press.

Bondurant, J. (1988) *Conquest of Violence: The Ghandian Philosophy of Conflict*, Princeton, NJ, Princeton University Press.

Box, S. (1983) *Power, Crime and Mystification*, London, Tavistock.

Cassese, A. (2003) *International Criminal Law*, Oxford, Oxford University Press.

Chomsky, N. (2009) *Exterminate all the Brutes: Gaza 2009* [online], www.chomsky.info/articles/20090119.htm (Accessed 20 April 2009).

Clapham, A. (2007) *Human Rights: A Very Short Introduction*, Oxford, Oxford University Press.

Cochrane, A. and Walters, R. (2008) 'The globalisation of social justice' in Newman, J. and Yeates, N. (eds) *Social Justice: Welfare, Crime and Society*, Maidenhead, Open University Press/Milton Keynes, The Open University.

Cohen, S. (1993) 'Human rights and crimes of the state. The culture of denial', *Australian and New Zealand Journal of Criminology*, vol. 26, no. 2, pp. 97–115.

Cohen, S. (2001) *States of Denial: Knowing about Atrocities and Suffering*, Cambridge, Polity.

Findlay, M. (2008) *Governing through Globalised Crime: Futures for Internal Criminal Justice*, Cullompton, Willan.

Freeman, M. (2005) 'Order, rights and threats: terrorism and global justice' in Wilson, R.A. (ed.) (2005).

Gearty, C. (2006) *Can Human Rights Survive?*, Cambridge, Cambridge University Press.

Giddens, A. (1990) *The Consequences of Modernity*, Cambridge, Polity.

Ginger, A. (ed.) (2005) *Challenging US Human Rights Violations Since 9/11*, New York, Prometheus.

Global Policy Forum (2009) *US Opposition to the International Criminal Court* [online], www.globalpolicy.org/intljustice/icc/usindex.htm (Accessed 20 April 2009).

Green, P. (2010) 'The state, terrorism and crimes against humanity' in Muncie J., Talbot, D. and Walters, R. (eds) *Crime: Local and Global*, Cullompton, Willan/Milton Keynes, The Open University.

Green, P. and Ward, T. (2004) *State Crime: Governments, Violence and Corruption*, London, Pluto.

Greenpeace (2004) *Exxon Valdez Disaster – 15 Years of Lies* [online], www.greenpeace.org/international/news/exxon-valdez-disaster-15-year (Accessed 19 April 2009).

Haas, M. (2008) *International Human Rights: A Comprehensive Introduction*, London, Routledge.

House of Commons Foreign Affairs Committee (2006) *Human Rights Annual Report 2006* [online] www.publications.parliament.uk/pa/cm200607/cmselect/cmfaff/269/269.pdf (Accessed 20 April 2009).

Hudson, B. and Walters, R. (eds) (2009) 'Criminology and the war on terror', *Special Edition, British Journal of Criminology*, vol. 49, no. 5.

Human Rights Watch (2000) *Pinochet Case a Milestone: Chile Urged to Prosecute Ex-Dictator*, Press Release, New York, 2 March [online], https://199.173.149.140/press/2000/02/pin0302.htm (Accessed 27 March 2009).

Human Rights Watch (2008a) *Perpetual Minors: Human Rights Abuses Stemming from Male Guardianship and Sex Segregation in Saudi Arabia* [online], www.hrw.org/en/reports/2008/04/19/perpetual-minors?print (Accessed 27 March 2009).

Human Rights Watch (2008b) *The Quality of Justice: Failings of Iraq's Central Criminal Court* [online], www.hrw.org/en/reports/2008/12/14/quality-justice (Accessed 27 March 2009).

International Council on Human Rights Policy (2003) *Duties sans Frontières: Human Rights and Global Social Justice*, Versoix, International Council on Human Rights Policy.

International Court of Justice (ICJ) (2009) [online], www.icj-cij.org/homepage/index.php (Accessed 20 April 2009).

International Criminal Court (ICC) (2009) *Establishment of the Court* [online], www.icc-cpi.int/about/ataglance/establishment.html (Accessed 3 January 2009).

Jamieson, R. and McEvoy, K. (2005) 'State crime by proxy and judicial othering', *British Journal of Criminology*, vol. 45, no. 4, pp. 504–27.

Joansen, R. (2006) 'The impact of US policy toward the International Criminal Court on the prevention of genocide, war crimes, and crimes against humanity', *Human Rights Quarterly*, vol. 28, no. 2, pp. 301–31.

Kannabiran, K. and Singh, R. (eds) (2008) *Challenging the Rule(s) of Law: Colonialism, Criminology and Human Rights in India*, London, Sage.

Kissinger, H. (2001) 'The pitfalls of universal jurisdiction', *Foreign Affairs*, vol. 80, no. 4, pp. 86–96.

Lee, M. (ed.) (2007) *Human Trafficking*, Cullompton, Willan.

Loader, I. and Sparks, R. (2002) 'Contemporary landscapes of crime, order and control: governance, risk and globalisation' in Maguire, M., Morgan, R. and Reiner, R. (eds) *The Oxford Handbook of Criminology* (3rd edn), Oxford, Oxford University Press.

Machover, D. and Maynard, K. (2006) 'Prosecuting alleged Israeli war criminals in England and Wales', *Denning Law Journal*, vol. 18, pp. 95–114.

Mackenzie, S. (2005) *Going, Going, Gone: Regulating the Market in Illicit Antiquities*, Leicester, Institute of Art and Law.

Maier-Katkin, D., Mears, D.P. and Bernard, T.J. (2009) 'Towards a criminology of crimes against humanity', *Theoretical Criminology*, vol. 13, no. 2, pp. 227–55.

May, L. (2009) 'Lawyers criticise the "vindictive" transfer of Iraqi murder suspects', *The Herald*, 20 April, p. 2.

McEvoy, K. and Mika, H. (2008) *Criminology, Human Rights, and Transition from Conflict: Reconstructing Justice*, Cambridge, Cambridge University Press.

Meredith, M. (2005) *The State of Africa: A History of Fifty Years of Independence*, London, Free Press.

Minkes, J. and Minkes, L. (eds) (2008) *Corporate and White Collar Crime*, London, Sage.

Morrison, W. (2004) 'Globalisation, human rights and international criminal courts' in Muncie, J. and Wilson, D. (eds) *Student Handbook of Criminal Justice and Criminology*, London, Cavendish.

Mythen, G. and Walklate, S. (2006) 'Communicating the terrorist risk: harnessing a culture of fear?', *Crime, Media, Culture*, vol. 2, no. 2, pp. 123–42.

Robertson, G. (1999) *The Justice Game*, London, Vintage.

Robertson, G. (2005) 'Fair trials for terrorists' in Wilson, R.A. (ed.) (2005).

Schwendinger, H. and Schwendinger, J. (1970) 'Defenders of order or guardians of human rights?', *Issues in Criminology*, vol. 5, no. 2, pp. 123–57.

Scraton, P. (ed.) (2002) *Beyond September 11: An Anthology of Dissent*, London, Pluto.

Sen, A. (1999) *Development as Freedom*, Oxford, Oxford University Press.

Steiner, H. and Alston, P. (2000) *International Human Rights in Context: Law, Politics, Morals* (2nd edn), New York, Oxford University Press.

Tombs, S. and Whyte, D. (eds) (2003) *Unmasking Crimes of the Powerful: Scrutinizing States and Corporations*, New York, Peter Lang.

United Nations (undated) *The Universal Declaration of Human Rights* [online], www.un.org/Overview/rights.html (Accessed 20 April 2009).

United Nations Office of the High Commissioner for Human Rights (UNOHCHR) (1996) *The International Bill of Human Rights*, Geneva, Office of the High Commissioner for Human Rights [online], www.unhchr.ch/html/menu6/2/fs2.htm (Accessed 19 April 2009).

United Nations Office of the High Commissioner for Human Rights (UNOHCHR) (2008) *What Are Human Rights?*, Geneva, Office of the High Commissioner for Human Rights [online], www.ohchr.org/EN/Issues/Pages/WhatareHumanRights.aspx (Accessed 27 March 2009).

Verkaik, R. (2009) 'China spearheads surge in state-sponsored executions', *The Independent*, 24 March [online], www.independent.co.uk/news/world/asia/china-spearheads-surge-in-statesponsored-executions-1652595.html (Accessed 20 April 2009).

Wallach, J. (2005) 'Human rights as an ethics of power' in Wilson, R.A. (ed.) (2005).

Wilson, R.A. (ed.) (2005) *Human Rights in the 'War on Terror'*, Cambridge, Cambridge University Press.

Acknowledgements

Grateful acknowledgement is made to the following sources:

Chapter 1

Text

Extract 1.1: BBC News (2007) 'Mother's battle for daughter's justice', 25 October 2007, from BBC News at http://bbc.co.uk/news. Copyright © BBC MMVII; Extract 1.2: Courtesy of Amnesty International Australia;

Figures

Figure 1.2: Copyright © Mark Weinstein; Figure 1.3: Copyright © Jim Goldberg/Magnum Photos; Figure 1.4: Copyright © Miramax Films/ Ronald Grant Archive; Figure 1.5: Copyright © Bettmann/Corbis; Figure 1.6: Copyright © Stefan Zakin/Getty Images;

Chapter 2

Text

Extract 2.1: Travis, A. (2006) 'Victims of crime reject notion of retribution', The Guardian, 16 January 2006. Copyright © Guardian News & Media Ltd 2006; Extract 2.2: Males, M, Stahlopf, C. and Macallair, D. (2007) 'Crimes rates and youth incarceration in Texas and California compared: Public safety or public waste?' Center on Juvenile and Criminal Justice, June 2007; Extract 2.3: Western Mail (2007) 'Corporate crime is 'ignored'', Western Mail, 20 August 2007;

Tables

Table 2.2: van Kesteren, J. N., Mayhew, P. and Nieuwberta, P. (2000) 'Criminal Victimisation in Seventeen Industrialised Countries: Key-findings from the 2000 International Crime Victim Survey', Ministry of Justice, The Hague; Table 2.3: Cavadino, M. and Dignan, J. (2006) 'Penal policy and political economy', Criminology and Criminal Justice, Vol 6, Sage Publications;

Figures

Figure 2.1: Copyright © Michael Maloney/San Francisco Chronicle; Figure 2.3: Copyright © Python Pictures/EMI/The Kobal Collection; Figure 2.5: Copyright © Kevin Siers. Reprinted with kind permission of King Features;

Chapter 3

Text

Extract 3.1: Excerpted with permission from Yazzie, R. (1994) 'Life comes from it: Navajo justice', In Context, Vol 38, Spring 1994, Context Institute. Copyright © 1994, 1997 by Context Institute, www.context.org;

Figures

Figure 3.3 top: Copyright © China Photos/Getty Images; Figure 3.3 bottom: Copyright © Matt York/AP/Press Association Images; Figure 3.4: Copyright © Daniel Berehulak/Getty Images;

Chapter 4

Text

Extract 4.2: Travis, A. (2007) 'Every child should be screened for risk of turning criminal under Blair justice plan', The Guardian, 28 March 2007. Copyright © Guardian News & Media Ltd 2007;

Figures

Figure 4.1: Copyright © Hasan Sarbarkshian/AP/Press Association Images; Figure 4.2: Copyright © Clive Goddard www.CartoonStock.com; Figure 4.4: Copyright © CBS Interactive, Inc; Figure 4.5: Copyright © Gordon Herrald Associates; Figure 4.6 left: Copyright © ITV/Rex Features; Figure 4.6 right: Copyright © CBS/Jerry Bruckheimer Television/Touchstone Television/Ronald Grant Archive;

Illustrations

Page 128: Copyright © Matt Cardy/Getty Images;

Chapter 5

Text

Extract 5.1: Johnson, B. (2007) 'Surveillance systems track faces on CCTV', The Guardian, 12 October 2007. Copyright © Guardian News & Media Ltd 2007; Extract 5.2: Abbott, D. (2008) 'Where's the debate on the DNA database?', The Guardian, 30 July 2008. Copyright © Guardian News & Media Ltd 2008;

Figures

Figure 5.1: Copyright © Tamara Polajnar; Figure 5.2: Copyright © Akira Suemori/AP/Press Association Images; Figure 5.3: Copyright © Steve Bell; Figure 5.4: Copyright © Optomen Television Ltd; Figure 5.5: Copyright © Tom Sieu, by permission of Amnesty International USA; Figure 5.6: Copyright © James Lennse/Corbis;

Chapter 6

Text

Extract 6.4: Interpol (2009) Interpol: An Overivew, Fact Sheet COM/FS/2009-02/G1-01, Interpol. Copyright © Interpol; Extract 6.6: Fletcher, H. (2008) 'Holocaust denier Frederick Toben wins German extradition fight', The Times, 20 November 2008. Copyright © NI Syndication Ltd; Extract 6.8: Batty, B. (2008) 'New taps? Iraqi security? East Europeans answer the call', The Guardian, 17 November 2008. Copyright © Guardian News & Media Ltd 2008;

Tables

Table 6.1: Newburn, T (2008) Handbook of Policing, Willan Publishing;

Figures

Figure 6.1: Copyright © AFP/Getty Images; Figure 6.2: Copyright © Mark Peterson/Corbis; Figure 6.3: Mary Evans Picture Library; Figure 6.4: Copyright © Private Collection/Peter Newark Military Pictures/The Bridgeman Art Library; Figure 6.5: Copyright © Sean Dempsey/PA Archive/Press Association Images;

Chapter 7

Text

Extract 7.2: Human Rights Watch (2000) Pinochet case a Milestone. Copyright © 2000 by Human Rights Watch; Extract 7.4: Pilger, J. (2008) 'Kafka has a rival. Today, the Foreign Office lectures us on human rights', The Guardian, 1 December 2008. Copyright © Guardian News & Media Ltd 2009; Extract 7.5: Al Jazeera (2008) UN attacks Israeli rights 'crimes', http://english.aljazeera.net/news/middleeast/2008/12/200812010551198584;

Figures

Figure 7.1: Copyright © UN Photo Library; Figure 7.3: Copyright © AP/Press Association Images; Figure 7.2: Copyright © AP/Press Association

Images; Figure 7.3: Copyright © Lynsey Addario/Corbis; Figure 7.4: Copyright © Brennan Linsley/AP/Press Association Images; Figure 7.5: Copyright © STR/AP/Press Association Images; Figure 7.6: Copyright © Serge Ligtenberg/AP/Press Association Images; Figure 7.7: Copyright © Sang Tan/AP/Press Association Images.

Every effort has been made to contact copyright holders. If any have been inadvertently overlooked the publishers will be pleased to make the necessary arrangements at the first opportunity.

Index